# Pistols
# & Revolvers

FROM 1400 TO THE PRESENT DAY

COLLECTOR'S GUIDES

# Pistols
# & Revolvers

## FROM 1400 TO THE PRESENT DAY

Martin J. Dougherty

amber
BOOKS

Published by
Amber Books Ltd
74–77 White Lion Street
London
N1 9PF
United Kingdom
www.amberbooks.co.uk
Appstore: itunes.com/apps/amberbooksltd
Facebook: www.facebook.com/amberbooks
Twitter: @amberbooks

ISBN 978-1-78274-150-3

Project Editor: Sarah Uttridge
Design: Zoë Mellors
Picture Research: Terry Forshaw

Printed in China

## Picture Credits

**Amber Books:** 39; **Alamy:** 9 (Interfoto), 15 (Archive Images), 18 (Prisma Archivo), 25 (Mar Photographics), 28 (Image Asset Management), 30 (North Wind Picture Archives), 41 (Prisma Archivo), 60 (Art Archive), 62 (Image Asset Management), 64 (Interfoto), 74 (Image Asset Management), 82 (Pictorial Press), 94 (Interfoto), 114 (Art Archive), 119 (Art Archive), 167 (Pictorial Press), 174 (Zuma Press), 178 (Glenn Harper), 190 (Zuma Press), 196 (CTK), 198 (Dan Leeth), 201 bottom (Zuma Press), 210 bottom (Sunpix), 212 (Colin Utz), 217 bottom (Sunpix), 218 bottom (Mim Friday); **Art-Tech:** 20, 72/73, 128, 138, 148, 149, 155, 156, 216; **Teri Bryant:** 117 top; **Cody Images:** 23, 91 bottom, 122, 145; **Colt:** 165, 166 bottom, 213; **Corbis:** 10, 11 (Bettmann), 33 (Bettmann), 58 (Tria Giovan), 140 (Hulton), 169 (2/Cocoon/Ocean); **Detonics:** 214 top; **Mary Evans Picture Library:** 8 (Interfoto/A Koch), 16, 86, 100, 105 (Illustrated London News), 108, 112, 133 (Glasshouse Images); **Fotolia:** 135 (Keith Garvelink); **Getty Images:** 12 (Archive Photos), 48 bottom (Underwood Archives), 78 (Hulton), 125 (Picture Post); **Heckler & Koch:** 179 bottom, 185; **Kel Tec:** 214 bottom; **Library of Congress:** 13, 14, 36, 46, 55, 130 bottom; **Littlegun.be:** 79; **Bertil Olofsson/Krigsarkivet:** 103; **Photos.com:** 53 top, 68, 77 top, 90; **Public Domain:** 171; **Ronald Grant Archive:** 205; **Smith & Wesson:** 180, 202, 203 bottom; **Taurus:** 201 top, 211; **TopFoto:** 43 (HIP), 67 (World History Archive), 159, (RIA Novosti), 164 (John Topham); **U.S. Coast Guard:** 182 bottom; **U.S. Department of Defense:** 136, 172, 177, 186; **U.S. Marines:** 6; **Walther:** 173

All profiles © Art-Tech unless credited above

# Contents

# Introduction

Weapons of any kind can be defined as 'tools used to break things and hurt people', but this does not make them intrinsically good or bad. It is the purpose to which a weapon is put that matters, not its inherent capability. A weapon may serve as a badge of office and never be drawn in anger, or it can be a deterrent to aggression or used to defend the lives of innocents. It can, of course, also be used for violence and mayhem.

LEFT: New Zealander marines, rifles slung, train with their backup weapons. A handgun is not the weapon of choice for a combat situation, but it does provide the means for emergency self-defence if a situation goes bad.

Certain weapons have acquired a reputation over the years, sometimes by association with law enforcement or military personnel, sometimes due to popularity with criminals. Some weapons have been given an artificial reputation by their portrayal in video games, movies and television shows, or are considered to be somehow 'good' or 'bad' depending on their use by one side or another in a war. Not all of these associations are fair, and not all elements of a weapon's reputation are accurate. Some have become classics or notoriously iconic without really deserving it, while others have somehow evaded the recognition they rightly deserve.

To the user, whose life might depend on a weapon's ability to stop an assailant, characteristics like accuracy, controllability and wounding power are critically important, but the collector might have a wholly different set of criteria for determining which weapons are interesting and which are not. Combat capability is one factor, of course, but physical beauty, perfection of design or an interesting feature not found on similar weapons might all be equally important.

## Users and Collectors

The collector might also rate a given weapon highly due to its historical importance. The first use of a now-standard feature, innovative design or incorporation of new materials and association with historical personalities or events can all spark the interest of the collector or historian. A weapon that offers fairly lousy combat performance, is inaccurate, kicks too hard and is virtually impossible to reload quickly might still be a favourite with the collector, whereas the practical user would probably arm himself with something more effective if given the chance.

And of course some firearms are worth collecting for no better reason than the owner likes them. A cheap little plinking gun, one of thousands mass-produced over the years, might be given pride of place in a collection because the owner's daughter fired her first shots with it, or simply because of fond memories of recreational shooting with friends. Where the practical gun user has fairly strict rules, the collector's world is much more subjective and this means that there is much possibility for debate among enthusiasts about which guns are worth collecting and which are considered uninteresting.

BELOW: Hunting from horseback with black powder pistols would have been quite a challenge. The inherent inaccuracy and unreliability of the weapon, combined with the motion of the target and the firer's mount, all added up to a great many missed shots.

The author's experience is that some classic handguns are pretty awful to shoot, fiddly to reload and prone to mechanical issues that can make them utterly maddening… yet they are still wonderful devices that it is a real privilege to shoot with. By way of example, I would not want to bet my life on a Mauser C96, but I did truly enjoy target shooting with one. Just operating the mechanism, opening the action to load the magazine from a stripper clip – even fumbling with the detachable stock was a worthwhile experience. The stock can only be attached two ways, and for some reason both of them seemed to be wrong whenever I tried it… but what a wonderful piece of practical history it was.

Thus there is no single factor that makes a weapon worth collecting or not, or which determines what is interesting and what can be ignored. Today's under-rated or wildly experimental weapon may be tomorrow's classic. What is true is that every single weapon has a story and has its own unique character. It is up to the individual to decide whether those characteristics appeal or not.

**ABOVE: Flintlock pistols were often presented and sometimes carried as pairs, giving the user two shots before reloading and ensuring that in a duel situation both combatants had identical weapons.**

## Pistols and Revolvers

Handguns are not battlefield weapons. In other words, someone who was expecting combat would probably want a more potent weapon such as a rifle or submachinegun in the field. However, a handgun is easy to carry and will serve well in an emergency – any firepower is better than no firepower. Sidearms are thus primarily defensive weapons, used to deal with a sudden threat rather than being the weapon of choice when going looking for trouble. There are exceptions, of course, such as when a weapon must be concealed until used and anything larger is thus inappropriate, but for the most part a sidearm is carried in case of emergency rather than as a primary combat weapon.

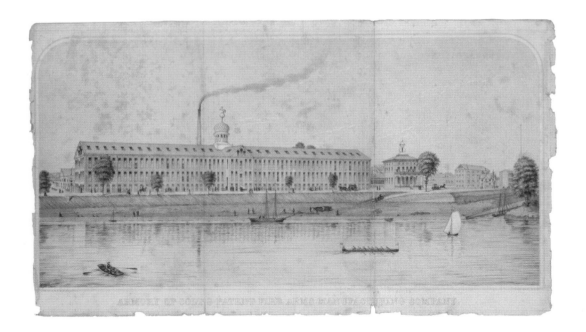

**ABOVE: Samuel Colt is often credited, incorrectly, with inventing the revolver. What he did do was to implement mass-production on an industrial scale, and to create a marketing programme to match the output of his factory.**

That said, if a weapon is needed then it should be as effective as possible. In addition to being a visual deterrent to violence, a handgun should offer a good balance of ability to hit a target – or possibly multiple targets – and the capability to 'stop' the target when hit. Stopping power is not the same thing as lethality. Any bullet can kill if it hits a vital organ, but many handgun rounds are unlikely to cause the opponent to immediately stop whatever he is intent upon doing – and that is what matters in a split-second defensive situation. Thus it could be argued that firing a round with the ability to 'stop' an opponent is the paramount requirement in a handgun intended for combat.

However, stopping power is of no real use if the bullet misses the target. In addition, some handguns are too powerful for some users – and some are too powerful for almost any user! These extremely potent guns are impressive in their own right and can be useful for hunting, but for self-defence they are not a good choice. A gun that throws itself off target because the user cannot control its recoil, or causes an involuntary flinch upon firing, is less than ideal. Some handguns will actually injure an unwary shooter.

## The Handgun in Combat

Huge cartridges also take up a lot of space in a weapon, making it bulky, heavy and reducing the amount of ammunition that can be carried in the cylinder or magazine. There is a trade-off to be made between potency of the round and the number that can be carried, which is important for several reasons. Most shooters cannot reliably hit a human-sized target with every shot under combat conditions, even at close range, so multi-shot capability is important even with a single target. There is also the possibility that a single shot will not stop a target, so shooting multiple times may be the only way to survive the encounter.

Obviously an exceedingly imprecise weapon is a liability, but accuracy – beyond a certain limit – is not critical to a combat handgun. As already noted, most handguns are acceptably accurate out to ranges far beyond those at which their users can shoot well mid-fight. A hunting weapon, or one used for competition, will need to be highly accurate over much greater distances than a weapon intended for close-range combat.

Handgun design is all about balancing these factors – ammunition capacity, accuracy, controllability and stopping power – as well as other considerations such as reliability, ease of use, comfort of carry, reloading speed, quality of sights and so forth. A good balance will create a fine weapon, but an extreme concentration on one factor might also result in a classic. Some of the most famous and influential guns are not great combat weapons, but instead personify some aspect or ideal of handgun design to the detriment of others or overall capability. As a rule, however, form follows function. Handgun design tends to be concentrated on creating either specialist weapons for hunting or to showcase a single attribute, or (more commonly) solid, general-purpose sidearms. The process began as soon as it became possible to create a firearm that could be held in just one hand.

LEFT: The imagery in this early Smith & Wesson advertisement is clear: you can bet your life on these guns. To the practical user, nothing is more important – but the collector may have entirely different criteria for what is a 'good' or 'interesting' weapon and what is not.

### Early Pistol Designs

The earliest black powder muzzleloading pistols were less than reliable, and even if they did discharge at all their accurate range was lamentably short. Indeed, some Napoleonic cavalry officers considered that if they were close enough to shoot an opponent with any degree of confidence, they were close enough to use their swords. That said, early pistols saw use from horseback, on foot and aboard ships. Many had a brass butt plate to allow the weapon to be used as a club after firing.

Attempts to increase handgun firepower ranged from the relatively simple measure of carrying a pair of pistols or using double-barrelled weapons to rather more inventive devices designed to self-reload a black powder weapon. Few examples were workable, and the black powder repeater never amounted to more than a technical curiosity. The invention of the percussion cap allowed the creation of more reliable muzzleloaders. The unreliable flintlock firing mechanism was replaced with a percussion cap struck by a hammer, but the main charge was still loaded by pouring gunpowder down the barrel and ramming a ball in on top. Although more reliable and faster, these weapons were fundamentally no different to flintlocks.

Cap-and-ball pistols offered a great leap forward in handgun firepower. Still using loose black powder as the propellant, this new technology allowed the creation of the first repeating firearms. There were two approaches to this: a 'pepperbox' pistol used multiple pre-loaded barrels rotated in turn

RIGHT: The interbar mechanism was a huge leap forward in handgun design, allowing a revolver to be safely carried with all chambers loaded. Once introduced, it became standard in virtually every model manufactured since.

Iver Johnson
Safety Automatic

Hammer, $5.00

Hammerless, $6.00

Extra length Barrels,
50c. per inch.
Pearl Stocks, $1.25 extra.

## No Fear of Accidental Discharge

if it's an

Hammer the Hammer

## IVER JOHNSON
### Safety Automatic Revolver

because the revolver hammer never touches the firing pin. This *safety principle*, found *only* in the Iver Johnson, is due to the fact that the lever which transmits the blow from the hammer to the firing pin is never in position to do so except *when the trigger is pulled all the way back*. All hardware and sporting goods dealers sell Iver Johnson Revolvers and can verify these facts if they will.

Send for our illustrated booklet "Shots," mailed free with our descriptive catalogue and learn the "how and why."

**Iver Johnson's Arms and Cycle Works, 142 River St., Fitchburg, Mass.**
NEW YORK OFFICE: 99 Chambers Street.

LEFT: This formal shooting stance was a holdover from the days of one-shot flintlocks and has been replaced with a more natural two-handed position. However, it can be very satisfying to shoot a historic handgun from a traditional stance.

into firing position, or a revolver used a rotating cylinder to align each firing chamber in turn with the barrel and firing mechanism. In both cases loading was a slow process. The firing chamber had to be filled with loose powder and then the ball or conical bullet placed atop it, with a patch to hold it in place if necessary. At the rear of the firing chamber a percussion cap was positioned to ignite the main charge when struck. The barrels or chambers were sealed with grease to prevent one cap igniting all the others in a chain-fire.

This was a lengthy business but once complete the user of a repeating handgun had far greater firepower than someone armed with a single-barrelled weapon. Misfires were more common than with modern weapons

ABOVE: **World War II resulted in an enormous need for weapons of all types. Produced in industrial quantities during the war years, these guns found their way onto the post-war market at knockdown prices.**

but far less frequent than with flintlocks, and with the advent of conical bullets and rifled barrels handgun rounds gained far greater muzzle velocity as well as being spun for stability in flight. This increased both accuracy and stopping power.

From the cap-and-ball revolver it was a small step to the all-metal unitary cartridge. The pepperbox pistol fell by the wayside of history but the far less bulky revolving-cylinder pistol remains in use to the present day. Revolver mechanics have not greatly changed since the 1830s, although some improvements have been made along the way.

The main drawbacks to using a revolving cylinder are limited ammunition capacity and bulk. A weapon that can store its ammunition in a holding device and feed rounds one by one into a single firing chamber can be slimmer and lighter than one that needs a separate chamber for each round, plus enough surrounding metal to prevent a rupture. Although earlier attempts were made to create such a weapon, it was not until the late nineteenth century that the self-loading (or semi-automatic) pistol became possible. Unitary cartridges were an essential requirement for such a weapon. By the beginning of the twentieth century, recognizably modern handguns were available. Today's revolvers and semi-automatics use the same basic principles as their counterparts of a century ago. There has been no huge revolution in handgun design in all that time, despite a few brave efforts. There has, however, been a steady evolution as new ideas and technologies have emerged.

This evolutionary process has led to some impressive 'firsts', some intriguing novelties and some highly regarded classics as well as a vast array of workaday handguns that, upon closer inspection, may turn out to be more interesting than first impressions suggested. Some of these guns are fascinating precisely because they are so ordinary – they represent a snapshot of mainstream weapon design at the time of their creation.

## Order of Appearance

In the following chapters, some small liberties have been taken regarding which section to place some weapons in. It is impossible to create hard-and-fast eras in handgun design, and in some cases a weapon seemed to be better placed in a later section than in the era in which it emerged. Thus it may be possible to find a combat revolver from 1920 found alongside its descendants in the 1935-onward chapter. There are various reasons for this, notably that the first appearance of a weapon may be less important than the era in which it was commonly used or with which it is most closely associated. In other cases it is a simple matter of narrative flow, placing coherent text above absolute breakdown by dates. Since there is so much subjectivity in what constitutes a classic or notable handgun, perhaps there is also some room for manoeuvre about what era a weapon belongs to.

BELOW: For operations in very tight spaces, handguns are sometimes the only option. These U.S. Army personnel are about to enter a tunnel complex during the Vietnam War, a situation requiring steady nerves and a reliable sidearm.

# Early Handguns

Projectile weapons offer a number of advantages to the user, not least the ability to strike at an enemy who might not be able to hit back. On the ancient battlefield, projectile weapons could be used to harass an enemy force and wear it down, or to soften it up for an attack by formations equipped with hand weapons such as sword or pike. Ideally these actions could be accomplished without exposing friendly troops to much risk, as lightly equipped missile soldiers could hopefully evade contact with units armed and armoured for hand-to-hand combat.

Thrown weapons such as javelins or rocks lacked range, requiring the men armed with these projectiles to be light on their feet if they wanted to escape retribution. Nevertheless the tactic worked – on one occasion a heavily armed force of Spartan hoplites was sent packing by lightly equipped javelin-throwing peltasts, against whom the Spartans simply could not get close enough to fight.

LEFT: By the time of the English Civil War (1642–51), black powder pistols were a viable weapon system.

## MEDIEVAL HANDGUN
**COUNTRY OF ORIGIN**
Kingdom of Hungary
**DATE**
c.1400
**CALIBRE**
18mm (.71in)
**WEIGHT**
3.6kg (7.9lb)
**OVERALL LENGTH**
1.2m (48in)
**FEED/MAGAZINE**
Single shot, muzzleloader
**RANGE**
7m (7.67yds)

**ABOVE: A musketeer carried 11 pre-measured charges of powder in clay pots and slung on a belt or strap.**

Mechanical propulsion offered greater advantages. Bows and crossbows could throw a projectile further and faster than a man's arm, giving both the accuracy to hit a moving target and the punch to penetrate armour. These types of weapons reached a high peak of efficiency, but ultimately there was only so far that a mechanical device could go. The limits of the technology had been reached by the time the first firearms appeared on the battlefield.

In time, gunpowder weapons came to dominate the arena, driving out first mechanically propelled projectiles and then relegating hand weapons to what was very much a secondary role. This did not happen overnight of course, but it was noted during the 'pike and shot' era of European warfare that everyone wanted to be a musketeer. Whether this was to be further from the enemy and thus safer from harm or to have less to carry than the armoured pikemen who protected the musketeers is not clear. Probably it was a bit of both.

However, even though the firearm had come to be a decisive battlefield weapon by the early 1600s, it was still a huge, clumsy thing that was not well suited to personal defence. That role was still the province of the sword, and it remained so for many years. Eventually, though, hand weapons were displaced into an only-in-emergency role and the handgun took its place as the primary weapon for personal defence. It was a long process, and one that did not have a very promising beginning.

## The Earliest Handguns

Gunpowder, or black powder, was known in ancient China and was at times used to create 'fire tubes' that would throw a gout of flame (and part-burned powder) out of the end when ignited. The discovery that mixing a few small stones in with the powder increased the amount of injury and dismay caused to the enemy allowed the creation of a rather crude shotgun-like weapon. This was a 'hand gun' in that it was a hand-held firearm, although not in the modern sense, and the term applies in the same context to the earliest European handguns. The earliest known use of these weapons was in 1364, and it is rather hard to see how anyone could have thought them to be a technological step forward.

At the time, the bow and the crossbow were highly effective, proven battlefield weapons. The 'handgonne', on the other hand, was a crude and unreliable device that threw its projectile less distance and with inferior accuracy than either the bow or crossbow. Consisting of a pot on a stick, which was aimed in the general direction of the target by holding the stick over one shoulder while a comrade ignited the gunpowder within the pot, this was hardly a weapon that showed great promise.

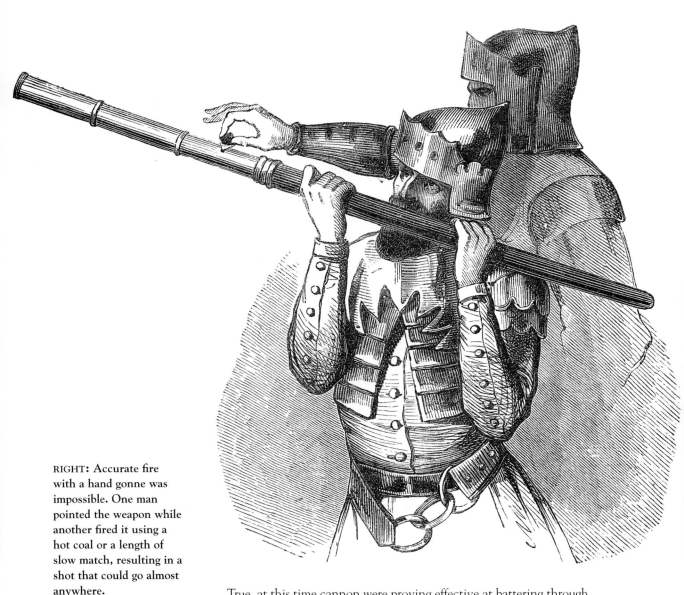

RIGHT: Accurate fire
with a hand gonne was
impossible. One man
pointed the weapon while
another fired it using a
hot coal or a length of
slow match, resulting in a
shot that could go almost
anywhere.

True, at this time cannon were proving effective at battering through
fortifications, but hand-held firearms were singularly ineffective. It is possible
that only by association with cannon did hand guns avoid being tossed aside as
a dead-end technology. They did find a place, however, and could be useful in
a siege situation where a gun muzzle could be poked through a fortress breach
or loophole that could not accommodate the arms of a bow or crossbow.

By the late fourteenth century, hand guns were in use across Europe
although they were hardly an effective weapon system. Weapons like wall-
guns, which were somewhere between personal firearms and light cannon
and used to defend fortified places, became an effective addition to the

arsenal of a castle or fortress. Despite this the impact of gunpowder on the open battlefield remained trivial. The main obstacle to the creation of an effective battlefield firearm was initiating the weapon's propellant in a reliable manner. 'Reliable' is of course a relative term but the matchlock, which appeared in the 1500s, allowed the creation of something recognizable as a workable personal weapon. The matchlock system used a length of burning slow match to ignite priming powder that would in turn initiate the main charge and fire the weapon.

Loading a matchlock weapon was a slow and complex process, and the weapon itself was of necessity a large and heavy piece of equipment. A stand was normally required to support it, and musketeers were vulnerable to attack while reloading. To counter this, they deployed on the battlefield in large formations protected by pikemen, and fired in volleys while others were reloading.

## MATCHLOCK
**COUNTRY OF ORIGIN**
Germany
**DATE**
c.1450
**CALIBRE**
10.9mm (.42in)
**WEIGHT**
4.1kg (9lb)
**OVERALL LENGTH**
1.2m (48in)
**FEED/MAGAZINE**
Single shot, muzzleloader
**RANGE**
45m (49.2yds)

## SERPENTINE MECHANISM
**COUNTRY OF ORIGIN**
Germany
**DATE**
c.1450
**CALIBRE**
10.9mm (.42in)
**WEIGHT**
4.1kg (9lb)
**OVERALL LENGTH**
1.2m (48in)
**FEED/MAGAZINE**
Single shot, muzzleloader
**RANGE**
45m (49.2yds)

RIGHT: Soon after the invention of the wheel-lock pistol (around 1500), manuals of arms began to appear that gave instruction in its correct use. Similar manuals already existed for the sword, lance and other traditional weapons.

The matchlock musket was a useful battlefield weapon for firing at masses of enemy troops, but was not in any way accurate. This was partially because the weapon was a smoothbore, with no rifling to spin the projectile, and partly because the projectile itself was a ball that might be quite irregular and in any case was significantly smaller than the barrel diameter so that it tended to rattle around on its passage towards the muzzle. Another reason for inaccuracy was the delay between the decision or command to shoot and the weapon discharging. Known as 'lock time', this delay exists with all firearms but was quite lengthy in a matchlock. Most matchlocks used an 'S'-shaped lever called a Serpentine to move the slow match from its holding position to contact with the priming powder, which hopefully would ignite quite quickly and in turn fire the main charge. A target could move quite a long way during this delay, and of course the user's aim might be disturbed.

All of this mechanical activity was acceptable in a weapon to be used en masse by troops protected by a wall of pikes, but was hardly suited to self-defence or individual combat. Matchlock pistols were produced, many for use by cavalrymen, but they were clumsy and awkward, and did not find much favour. What they did achieve was to make firearms an essential part of warfare, and thus ensure that they had a future in which to develop. There is a persistent belief that muskets blasted the armoured knight from the battlefield, but this is nothing more than a myth. In fact, advanced plate armour was quite capable of deflecting a musket ball, and those buying armour would check it had a dent to show that it had been 'proven' by shooting it. Early guns were also less accurate than bows, shot more slowly and possessed a shorter effective range. There was little chance that guns would do what bows had not already achieved.

## The Advantages of Firepower

The advent of firearms made it possible to raise an army in a short time and to disband it when no longer needed, therefore reducing costs. It took little time to train a man in the mechanical evolutions of loading and levelling a musket in the general direction of a block of troops, whereas a good archer capable of handling a bow powerful enough for the battlefield required a lifetime of practice. There were also social advantages to switching to the use of firearms. Gunpowder supplies were relatively easy to control, making any weapons retained by 'unofficial' users potentially useless. Former soldiers

might take their shooting skills back to the farm, but if they rebelled at some later date they would lack the weapons to use them whereas archers could make their own highly effective weapons.

Firearms therefore came to be the standard battlefield weapon not because they were more effective than what was already available, but because they were convenient and cost-effective. The matchlock remained in use long after it had become obsolete, largely because it permitted the acquisition of an acceptable level of firepower for a small outlay. For a military or pseudo-military force this trade-off was entirely acceptable, but for the individual user something better was required.

## Wheel-lock Pistols

The problem of creating a firearm that could be conveniently carried yet quickly readied for firing, and held ready for some time if necessary, was

**WHEEL-LOCK**
**COUNTRY OF ORIGIN**
Italy
**DATE**
c.1550
**CALIBRE**
10.9mm (.42in)
**WEIGHT**
1kg (2.25lb)
**OVERALL LENGTH**
400mm (15.75in)
**FEED/MAGAZINE**
Single shot, muzzleloader
**RANGE**
9m (9.84yds)

**ENGLISH DOGLOCK**

**COUNTRY OF ORIGIN**
England
**DATE**
c.1650
**CALIBRE**
10.9mm (.42in)
**WEIGHT**
1kg (2.25lb)
**OVERALL LENGTH**
400mm (15.75in)
**FEED/MAGAZINE**
Single shot, muzzleloader
**RANGE**
9m (9.84yds)

solved around 1509 by the invention of the wheel-lock. The soldier of that era could tell it was time to load his weapon from the approach of enemy troops within range, or more likely his commander would order him to make ready when he judged this was about to happen.

That commander would of course not shoot at the enemy with a musket of his own, but if a battle came to close quarters he might have to fight in self-defence. His sword was the only option for a long period, but the idea of having a pistol or two to discourage anyone from coming too close was certainly attractive. A wheel-lock, which could be readied just in case and held until needed, was perhaps the first gunpowder weapon really suited to the role of a sidearm.

The wheel-lock replaced the clumsy length of slow match with a spring-loaded rotating wheel that struck sparks from a striker. Once the weapon was loaded and priming powder ready in the pan, a cover protected it from damp and held it in place until moved out of the way by the action of pulling the trigger. This allowed the wheel-lock to be carried in a ready condition and operated with one hand – the other perhaps holding another pistol, the reins of a horse or a sword – when needed.

The term 'dog lock pistol' is sometimes used for certain wheel-locks, referring to the 'dog', the arm that held the spark-creating material (iron pyrite) and brought it into contact with the wheel when the weapon was to be fired. The dog could be carried in a safe position where it could not create sparks, but once moved into the ready position it would engage the spinning wheel and create a shower of sparks when the trigger was pulled. The term dog lock also sometimes applies to weapons of this type that had a catch (also known as a dog) to hold the lock safely at half-cock.

The ability to shoot one-handed was extremely useful to horsemen, and the pistol became a favourite weapon of cavalry. A manoeuvre called the Caracole was invented, in which successive lines of cavalry would ride close to the enemy, fire their pistols then retire to reload. This rather stately evolution had less shock value than charging home with swords, but it also offered far less risk to the horsemen, especially if they wore armour that was proof against musket balls.

The wheel-lock was expensive and complex to produce, and was only deployed in small numbers. Cavalry, already an expensive force to raise, were worth the expense. Many officers of infantry forces armed with matchlocks carried a wheel-lock pistol for personal defence. Private individuals also armed themselves with wheel-locks for self-protection. Some wheel-lock weapons were deliberately aimed at extremely wealthy or powerful users, and were richly decorated as prestige items that combined cutting-edge weapon technology with practicality and artistic beauty. Others were simply functional, and a few experimental designs did emerge. Attempts were made to create multi-shot pistols and other exotic devices, but these were not successful enough to enter the general marketplace.

## Flintlock Pistols

The search for more reliable and cost-effective personal weaponry resulted in the development of the snaplock, which replaced the iron pyrites striker

BELOW: **With a flintlock pistol there is a noticeable delay between the powder in the priming pan firing and the main charge igniting – assuming that it ignites at all!**

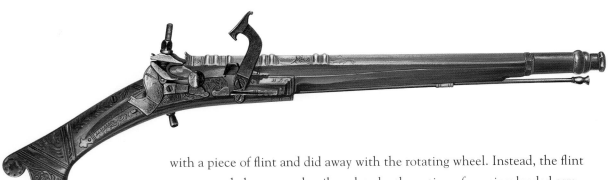

## DUTCH SNAPHANCE
**COUNTRY OF ORIGIN**
Netherlands
**DATE**
c.1650
**CALIBRE**
17mm (.675in)
**WEIGHT**
1.67kg (3.7lb)
**OVERALL LENGTH**
400mm (15.75in)
**FEED/MAGAZINE**
Single shot, muzzleloader
**RANGE**
15m (16.4yds)

with a piece of flint and did away with the rotating wheel. Instead, the flint was scraped along a steel striker plate by the action of a spring-loaded arm, creating a shower of sparks in the same manner as the earlier wheel-lock. Snaplock weapons appeared around 1540. Like similar weapons, a snaplock could be loaded and carried with the 'cock' (the lever holding the flint) in a safe position and the priming-pan cover closed. When danger threatened, the user pulled the lever back to its firing position. This action gave rise to the term 'cocking' a weapon that is still used today. Pulling the trigger removed the catch that prevented the spring-loaded cock from snapping back to its natural position, causing the flint to strike sparks and – usually – igniting the priming powder and then the main charge.

The snaplock was much cheaper to make than a wheel-lock, permitting the mass-production of pistols. However, by the 1550s a more advanced version termed the snaphance was emerging. A snaphance weapon was broadly similar to a snaplock, but incorporated a device to open the flash-pan cover as part of the action of firing. This removed one action that the user had to carry out when readying his weapon, making deployment

## POCKET PISTOL
**COUNTRY OF ORIGIN**
United States
**DATE**
1795
**CALIBRE**
12.7mm (.5in)
**WEIGHT**
0.34kg (0.75lb)
**OVERALL LENGTH**
76mm (6.6in)
**FEED/MAGAZINE**
Single shot, muzzleloader
**RANGE**
1.5m (1.64yds)

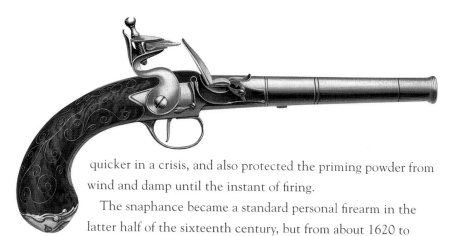

quicker in a crisis, and also protected the priming powder from wind and damp until the instant of firing.

The snaphance became a standard personal firearm in the latter half of the sixteenth century, but from about 1620 to 1630 onwards it was gradually replaced by the next evolution in lock technology – the flintlock. This continued to use the elements of the snaphance but incorporated a combined pan cover/striker plate called the frizzen. The frizzen is the hallmark of a 'true' flintlock as opposed to a snaphance or snaplock. Around the same time, a variant known as the English lock appeared. This was a transitional stage between the snaphance and the true flintlock. The relative simplicity of the flintlock and English lock mechanisms made them easy to mass-produce, and as well as countless flintlock muskets for infantry use, pistols found favour with many private and military users.

## Longevity of the Flintlock

Once a reliable flintlock pistol design appeared, it remained in existence for many years. The flintlock was not

### QUEEN ANNE PISTOL
**COUNTRY OF ORIGIN**
United Kingdom
**DATE**
c.1750
**CALIBRE**
16.5mm (.65in)
**WEIGHT**
0.79kg (1.75lb)
**OVERALL LENGTH**
235mm (9.25in)
**FEED/MAGAZINE**
Single shot, muzzleloader
**RANGE**
6m (6.5.36yds)

### IMPROVED FLINTLOCK
**COUNTRY OF ORIGIN**
United Kingdom
**DATE**
1770
**CALIBRE**
15.9mm (.62in)
**WEIGHT**
1.39kg (3b)
**OVERALL LENGTH**
540mm (21.25in)
**FEED/MAGAZINE**
Single shot, muzzleloader
**RANGE**
15m (16.4yds)

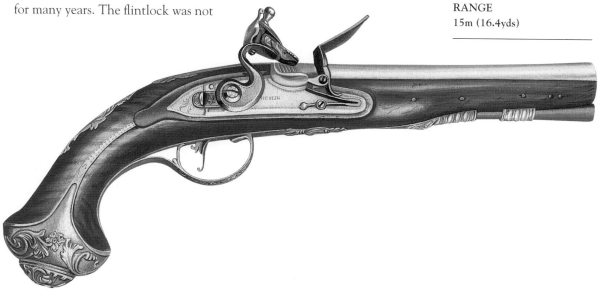

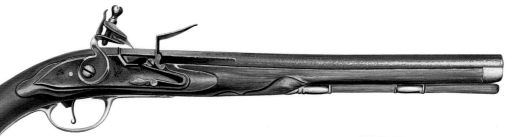

displaced by percussion-cap weapons for over two centuries, and in that time a great many designs using the principle appeared, many of them tailored to a specific application.

Small flintlock pistols that could be carried in a pocket were primarily intended for self-defence by gentlefolk. A pistol was a great deterrent – produced from a pocket and cocked it was a broad hint that further aggression might result in serious injury. Of course there was always the possibility that the weapon was not primed or even loaded, or that the user might miss, but a cocked pistol could create sufficient doubt in the mind of an aggressor that he might decide to withdraw.

A pistol was also much easier to carry than a sword, and usually quicker to deploy due to its shorter length. A robber or similar assailant might decide to take his chances against a sword, reasoning that in close combat his own fighting ability might be greater than that of his intended victim, but a pistol offered the chance of being shot down without even getting close enough to strike a blow, and that could be a profound deterrent. Indeed, the same principle still works today.

## Naval Pistols

Small pistols were also sometimes issued to military personnel such as those who carried a regimental or national colour in battle, or those that escorted him. A pistol might be a lot easier to use than a sword for someone who had to hold a flag aloft with the other hand, and offered a chance to strike at an approaching enemy horseman before he got into range to make a grab for the flag or to strike with his sabre. Some officers also armed themselves with pistols for emergency use in a battlefield crisis, but combat use of pistols was mostly the province of sailors and cavalrymen. At sea, a pistol offered the ability to strike over a short distance, such as shooting into an enemy crew as they attempted to board or resist a boarding, and was also short and handy for use on a crowded deck or in the confines of a ship's interior.

---

**LONG-BARRELLED PISTOL**
COUNTRY OF ORIGIN
United States
DATE
1805
CALIBRE
15.9mm (.62in)
WEIGHT
1.42kg (3.1lb)
OVERALL LENGTH
552mm (21.75in)
FEED/MAGAZINE
Single shot, muzzleloader
RANGE
25m (27.3yds)

---

LEFT: Pistols were only effective at extremely close quarters, such as amid the chaos of a naval boarding action. A discharged pistol was still useful as a club.

**ABOVE:** In the vast majority of pistol duels, neither duellist was hit. Some would deliberately and obviously 'fire into the air', feeling that honour was satisfied by taking part. Others, however, would aim to kill.

Naval pistols tended to be of large calibre, making them potent weapons if they hit a target – which was quite likely when firing into a massed enemy crew during a boarding action. Once discharged the weapon was anything but useless. Most had a reinforced grip covered in brass, which made the pistol a formidable club when held by the barrel. Naval ('sea service') pistols were anything but small, so a sailor armed with one was not really at much disadvantage against someone equipped with a 'proper' hand weapon.

Pistols were also commonly used by cavalry and mounted troops. Some cavalry used the sword or lance as their principal weapon, and few were not equipped with a sword of some kind, but firearms were in common use even by cavalry forces that specialized in the charge with swords. A pistol held in the left hand along with the reins offered the chance for an opportunistic

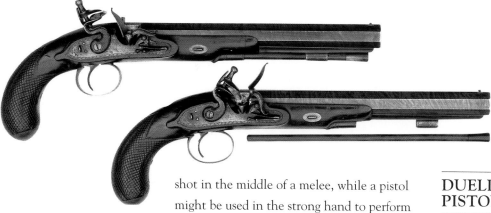

shot in the middle of a melee, while a pistol might be used in the strong hand to perform a ride-by shooting that exposed the cavalryman to little risk.

The primary firearm used by cavalry was the carbine or 'dragoon musket'. The term dragoon comes from 'dragon', which was the name given to the short muskets that equipped troops of this type. Originally dragoons were mounted infantry, although in different nations at different times the word came to have a variety of meanings. Some cavalry were trained to skirmish with the carbine rather than charging home to fight at close quarters. Even among heavy cavalry units intended to charge and smash an enemy formation it was common to equip at least some of the men in a squadron as 'flankers' with carbines. Pistols were very much a backup weapon in most cases, other than the period where the Caracole manoeuvre was in favour and pistols were considered the main fighting tools of the cavalry.

Cavalrymen were often issued long-barrelled 'horse pistols' in the hope that a long weapon would improve accuracy. The effect was almost certainly marginal, as a smoothbore fired one-handed from horseback is never going to be the most precise of weapons. Some cavalrymen carried two or even four horse pistols in buckets on the saddle, sometimes backed up by more pistols of a smaller type about their person. Horse pistols and cavalry carbines were often in the same calibre, which in theory made ammunition supply simpler. However, since powder was usually carried in pre-measured paper cartridges along with the ball, this meant that the same measure of powder was used in both weapons. A wise cavalryman tossed a little of his powder away when loading his pistols, as the full charge for a carbine was excessive in a handgun.

## Duelling Weapons

Pistols were also used for duelling, with specifically designed weapons becoming available after around 1750. Almost always purchased in matched

**DUELLING PISTOLS**
COUNTRY OF ORIGIN
France
DATE
1760
CALIBRE
15.9mm (.62in)
WEIGHT
1.39kg (3lb)
OVERALL LENGTH
540mm (21.25in)
FEED/MAGAZINE
Single shot, muzzleloader
RANGE
9m (9.84yds)

RIGHT: A discharged pistol was nothing more than an encumbrance to the user unless it could be used as a hand weapon. Various attempts to fit bayonets to pistols were made, but the concept never caught on.

pairs, the idea was to make a pistol duel as fair as possible by giving both duellists identical weapons. At the beginning of a duel there were strict regulations about the selection of weapons and the examination of both to ensure that neither had hidden rifling or other modifications that could give the user an advantage. The rules for pistol duelling varied over time and from place to place. The general principle was that the duellists would face one another at a range where a hit was not certain, and could fire any time after the command to shoot had been given. In some regions it was expected that the duellists would shoot immediately, and indeed deliberate aiming could be grounds for a murder charge whereas a point-and-shoot attempt to kill the opponent was perfectly acceptable.

This was not universal. A duellist who fired and missed was expected to stand still and wait for the opponent to take his shot without ungentlemanly and undignified attempts at dodging. Sometimes duellists would blatantly fire somewhere that their opponent was not, and this might or might not be acceptable depending on the custom. The term for this was to 'delope', and there were various reasons to delope in a duel. The duellist might prefer not to harm his opponent once honour had been satisfied by taking part in the duel. It was also a way to avoid having to shoot again. In some duelling systems, if neither participant was hit then either or both could demand to shoot again. It was, however, considered bad form to demand a second shot after the opponent deloped. Thus if a weapon misfired or the shooter simply missed, the other duellist had a choice of trying to wound or kill him, or obviously deloping in the hope that the matter would be considered settled.

Pistol duels were a dangerous business, and could be more random than an affair with swords. Indeed, this was one reason why some duellists

## BLUNDERBUSS PISTOL

**COUNTRY OF ORIGIN**
United Kingdom
**DATE**
1780
**CALIBRE**
16.5mm (.65in)
**WEIGHT**
1.3kg (2.9lb)
**OVERALL LENGTH**
444mm (17.5in)
**FEED/MAGAZINE**
Single shot, muzzleloader
**RANGE**
3m (3.28yds)

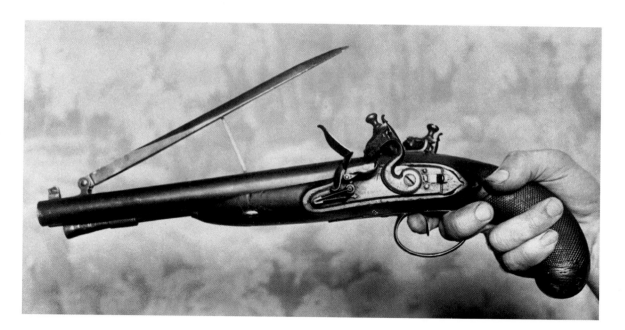

chose to fight with pistols. A sword fight would almost always be won by the superior swordsman, but a pistol duel had more opportunities for the underdog to get lucky. There was also a better chance of escaping from the affair with both honour and skin intact. A pistol bullet, it was observed, could go almost anywhere whereas a sword was virtually certain to cause a wound sooner or later.

## Unusual Designs

Various attempts were made to create flintlock pistols that gave the user more firepower or had some other advantages. Some were rather silly, such as combined sword/pistols, with a flintlock pistol mounted on the

### SCOTTISH ALL-STEEL
COUNTRY OF ORIGIN
Scotland
DATE
1800
CALIBRE
15.9mm (.62in)
WEIGHT
2.9kg (5.6lb)
OVERALL LENGTH
540mm (21.25in)
FEED/MAGAZINE
Single shot, muzzleloader
RANGE
6m (6.56yds)

## DUCK'S FOOT
**COUNTRY OF ORIGIN**
United Kingdom
**DATE**
1800
**CALIBRE**
15.9mm (.62in)
**WEIGHT**
1.2kg (2.6lb)
**OVERALL LENGTH**
254mm (5in)
**FEED/MAGAZINE**
Multi-barrel muzzleloader
**RANGE**
6m (6.56yds)

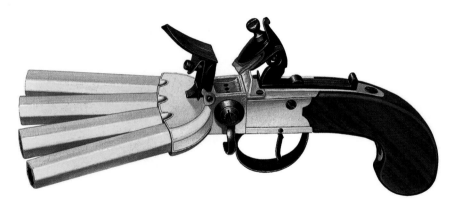

## FLINTLOCK REVOLVER
**COUNTRY OF ORIGIN**
France
**DATE**
c.1730
**CALIBRE**
12mm (.47in)
**WEIGHT**
1kg (2.2lb)
**OVERALL LENGTH**
362mm (14.25in)
**FEED/MAGAZINE**
5-round cylinder
**RANGE**
15m (16.4yds)

blade and aligned to fire along it. In theory this gave the user the best of both worlds, with the opportunity for a sneaky shot to even the odds or to surprise an opponent. In practice it created an unreliable pistol that was hard to aim, mated to an ill-balanced sword that would actually reduce the user's fighting ability.

Some designs were rather more useful. Double-barrelled pistols were used by, among others, military engineers who needed a defensive weapon that could be easily carried and used at close quarters. Some such weapons had one rifled barrel and one smoothbore. Rifling was invented at the very end of the fifteenth century but was not used much other than for some hunting weapons as it made loading much slower. A rifled barrel offered a more accurate and hard-hitting shot, while the smoothbore could be reloaded quickly or perhaps loaded with shot instead of a single ball.

Another way to speed up reloading was to use a bell-mouthed pistol. This was the same principle as a blunderbuss – the wide mouth made the weapon quick and easy to reload but also impaired accuracy in a weapon that was already less than precise. At pistol ranges it probably did not matter that much, and the gaping maw of the weapon might prove an effective deterrent.

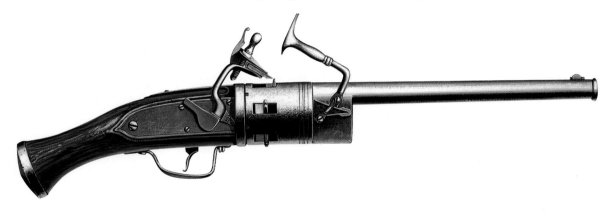

Another weapon of dissuasion was the duck's foot pistol, which used a single lock to simultaneously fire several splayed barrels. This weapon might stop the initial rush of a mob but its main use was as a deterrent. By creating the virtual certainty that at least some members of a group would be hit, the duck's foot pistol allowed a lone person to face down a group. These pistols were favoured for naval use, theoretically allowing an officer to quell a mutinous crew. If the duck's foot pistol had to be fired, then at best it would thin the mob. The chances of stopping everyone with a single blast were slim at best, as this weapon offered no repeat-fire capability. There were attempts to do that, however. The world's earliest revolvers used several pre-loaded chambers fired by a single flintlock mechanism and each moved into alignment with the barrel in turn. The principle of these weapons was no different to that of a modern revolver, but the technology was ahead of its time and did not prove effective.

A musket version of the same principle was developed but this, too, failed to deliver an effective weapon system. However, concepts that had been experimented with during the flintlock era would be revisited once more advanced technologies were available, this time with success.

### JOSEPH MANTON
COUNTRY OF ORIGIN
United Kingdom
DATE
1810
CALIBRE
12.7mm (.5in)
WEIGHT
1.13kg (2.5lb)
OVERALL LENGTH
375mm (14.75in)
FEED/MAGAZINE
Single shot, muzzleloader
RANGE
9m (9.84yds)

### KENTUCKY PISTOL
COUNTRY OF ORIGIN
United States
DATE
1805
CALIBRE
15.9mm (.62in)
WEIGHT
1.39kg (3lb)
OVERALL LENGTH
540mm (21.25in)
FEED/MAGAZINE
Single shot
RANGE
15m (16.4yds)

# Percussion-cap Pistols

**The main drawback with flintlock firearms was the priming system. The main charge could be held ready for some time, sealed into place with a ball and a wad rammed down atop it. The small amount of powder in the priming pan was far more vulnerable. It could be blown away by wind, dampened by the elements or it might simply fall out of the pan if the weapon was tipped up.**

LEFT: By the time of the American Civil War, the percussion-cap revolver had largely supplanted the sabre as the primary weapon for horsemen. The sabre was still carried as a backup, of course.

Keeping the pan covered improved reliability a lot, but even with a good priming charge in place there was no guarantee that the sparks from the flintlock would ignite the priming powder, or that the flash from this powder would pass through the touch hole and initiate the main charge. The term 'flash in the pan' has become a figure of speech for something promising that fails to deliver, but in its original context it was a potentially life-threatening disaster.

## PERCUSSION PISTOL
**COUNTRY OF ORIGIN**
United Kingdom
**DATE**
1820
**CALIBRE**
12.7mm (.5in)
**WEIGHT**
1kg (2.2lb)
**OVERALL LENGTH**
Not known
**FEED/MAGAZINE**
Single shot, muzzleloader
**RANGE**
10m (10.93yds)

## Percussion Caps

The invention of the percussion cap in the early 1800s largely solved the problem of powder failing to ignite. Rather than setting fire to loose gunpowder, the initial flash was provided by a small explosion. This was produced by the cap, which contained fulminate of mercury that would explode when struck. The striking mechanism was already extant, in the form of a spring-loaded lock that could easily be replaced by a hammer, which made flintlocks ideal candidates for conversion to percussion-cap operation.

The usual form of the percussion cap was a disc of brass or copper. This was placed on a hollow nipple that presented it to the hammer and whose shaft guided the flash into the firing chamber. Weapons were still muzzleloaders, so the first part of loading remained the same. Pouring powder, inserting the ball and ramming the wad home on top remained the same and required exactly the same steps, but the slowest part of the process – priming the pan – was replaced.

Priming the pan was not only slower than slipping a cap onto the nipple, but it was also easier to make a small mistake that would result in a misfire. Thus the percussion cap not only made the actual detonation more reliable, but it also speeded up the loading process while removing some of the possibilities for human error. However, only some possibilities were removed. Caps were small and could be hard to manipulate with cold, wet hands or amid the stress and chaos of combat. A poorly seated cap might fall off or not detonate properly, and of course it was easy to drop and lose a cap while loading. Overall, though, the percussion cap was a significant step forward.

Other ways of using percussion caps were tried, notably the concept of creating a roll of caps on a paper tape, as used in children's toys today. In

### FLINTLOCK CONVERSION

**COUNTRY OF ORIGIN**
United Kingdom
**DATE**
1825
**CALIBRE**
Not known
**WEIGHT**
1kg (2.2lb)
**OVERALL LENGTH**
323mm (12.75in)
**FEED/MAGAZINE**
Single shot, muzzleloader
**RANGE**
10m (10.93yds)

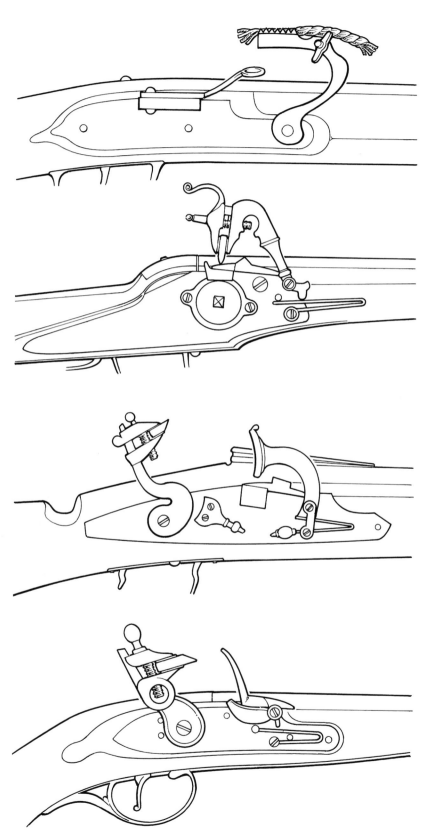

LEFT: The percussion-cap mechanism was the end product of an evolution that ran (illustrated from top to bottom) from the matchlock through wheel-lock, snaphance and finally flintlock mechanisms. The percussion-cap system replaced the flint with a hammer and the unreliable priming-pan mechanism with a percussion cap resting on a nipple.

theory a paper strip could be advanced each time the weapon was fired and would automatically present a new cap when the weapon was ready to fire. In practice these systems were unreliable and the loose percussion cap became standard.

The earliest percussion-cap weapons were essentially modified flintlocks that had become more reliable and somewhat more elegant for losing their lock and priming pan in favour of a hammer and nipple. Over time, new applications of the cap led to pre-loaded multi-shot weapons and finally the idea of incorporating the cap into a single cartridge. Early unitary cartridge weapons used a cloth, paper or cardboard cartridge containing bullet, propellant and cap, but eventually the all-metal unitary cartridge was developed. The primer in a modern cartridge is essentially a percussion cap built into the base of a cartridge, suggesting that this invention was one of the key steps along the way to modern firearms. Indeed, the percussion-cap era marked firearms' transition from marginal effectiveness to the dominant weapon system for combat and self-defence, finally relegating hand weapons such as swords to a distant second place.

### From Flintlock to Percussion

Although the percussion cap was available from 1810 or so, there was no immediate leap towards universal use. At this time the Napoleonic Wars engulfed most of Europe, with hundreds of thousands of men under arms. The standard infantry weapon of the era was a flintlock musket of mature and proven design, and these were turned out in the thousands. Flintlock pistols were produced in smaller but still enormous numbers. With industry geared to mass-production of these weapons, early experimentation produced

## JOHN MANTON PERCUSSION PISTOL

COUNTRY OF ORIGIN
United Kingdom
DATE
1828
CALIBRE
12.7mm (.5in)
WEIGHT
1kg (2.2lb)
OVERALL LENGTH
323mm (12.75in)
FEED/MAGAZINE
Single shot, muzzleloader
RANGE
10m (10.93yds)

little but novelty weapons. After the Napoleonic Wars ended, vast amounts of military equipment remained extant and was surplus to requirements. The gun market of that time was not a good place to be pushing a new technology when so many weapons were already available.

It is perhaps unsurprising that early percussion weapons tended to be small-run or individual projects, aimed at clients who could afford something a bit better than the weaponry flooding the post-war market. Militaries have to balance individual improvement against large-scale cost-effectiveness, and they tend to be slow to adopt a new technology if they already have something that gets the job done acceptably well. Thus while the militaries of Europe and elsewhere did not rush to adopt the new technology, some users bought the new percussion pistols and

ABOVE: The Napoleonic Wars occurred at the end of the flintlock period, at a time when new percussion-cap technology was emerging. Many Napoleonic-era weapons soldiered on for decades afterward in converted form.

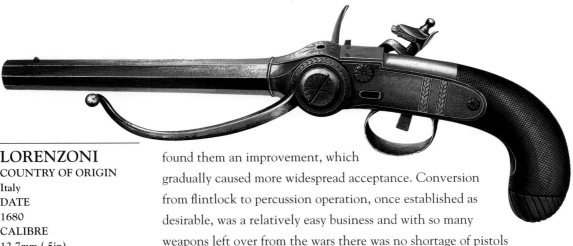

## LORENZONI

**COUNTRY OF ORIGIN**
Italy
**DATE**
1680
**CALIBRE**
12.7mm (.5in)
**WEIGHT**
1.76kg (3.9lb)
**OVERALL LENGTH**
483mm (19in)
**FEED/MAGAZINE**
7-round experimental repeater
**RANGE**
10m (10.93yds)

found them an improvement, which gradually caused more widespread acceptance. Conversion from flintlock to percussion operation, once established as desirable, was a relatively easy business and with so many weapons left over from the wars there was no shortage of pistols ready for conversion.

Any conversion will of course be less than ideal compared to a custom design, but in the case of a flintlock to percussion conversion the mechanism was so similar that many newly made percussion pistols were identical to converted weapons. This took advantage of established construction techniques and facilities. Thus in the early years of the nineteenth century, percussion-cap single-shot pistols were used alongside their flintlock predecessors and were visually very similar.

### Early Repeaters

While more reliable, a percussion-cap pistol offered no real improvement in personal firepower over a flintlock. The loading process was still sufficiently lengthy that once fired a pistol was virtually useless. One shot was better than none, but there was a definite need for a pistol that could be fired more than once without having to reload. One answer to this problem, already used with flintlocks, was a multi-barrel pistol. Various designs appeared, some with two (or even more) fixed barrels and some with barrels that could be turned into firing position in sequence. A 'turnover' pistol might have two or four barrels, separately loaded and manually rotated into line with the firing mechanism. This system had been used with a small number of top-end flintlocks but became more popular with the advent of percussion-cap ignition.

Each barrel had its own nipple, and a cap had to be placed on this just before firing. Although quicker than reloading, this was still not fast enough to allow a follow-up shot if the first attempt to stop a charging opponent failed. The alternative was to load each barrel and fit the cap well ahead

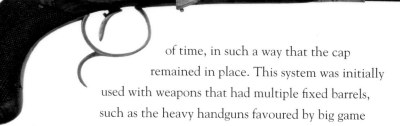

of time, in such a way that the cap remained in place. This system was initially used with weapons that had multiple fixed barrels, such as the heavy handguns favoured by big game hunters who used elephants for transport. Known as 'howdah pistols' these weapons were intended for use against a tiger or similar creature that took exception to being shot at with rifles, offering the hunter a chance to defend himself, his elephant and his crew with a weapon that could stop such a big creature but still be used from the back of an elephant under attack.

The chief danger with multi-barrel weapons was the possibility that firing one cap might ignite the others, causing a chain-fire or gang-fire. Some weapons with various firing systems did this deliberately, creating a 'volley gun', but when it happened by accident it was at best wasteful of ammunition and at worst it could be life threatening. With a fixed multi-barrel weapon, at least the firing chambers were sealed and the barrels unimpeded if a gang-fire occurred, but all the same it was something to be avoided if possible.

The usual way to reduce the chances of flashover causing a gang-fire was to seal each percussion cap in place with wax or grease. This was a fairly lengthy process, so once all barrels had been discharged there was no prospect of reloading until things had calmed down. Some users preferred to seal their caps in place and then load the barrels of their weapon, so that if a cap were accidentally detonated then at least it would not cause the weapon to discharge. The more common process was to load the barrel with powder and ball, then seal the caps in place. Once this was done, the weapon was closed up and could be carried ready to fire when needed.

Multiple fixed-barrel handguns never represented a major segment of the marketplace, and in any case only offered a slight improvement in firepower over a single-barrelled pistol. The pepperbox pistol, on the other hand, represented a significant increase in repeat shot capability.

## FORSYTH PERCUSSION PISTOL

**COUNTRY OF ORIGIN**
United Kingdom
**DATE**
c.1830
**CALIBRE**
N/A
**WEIGHT**
1 kg (2.5lb)
**OVERALL LENGTH**
323mm (12.75in)
**FEED/MAGAZINE**
Single shot, muzzleloader
**RANGE**
10m (10.93yds)

Pepperbox pistols were built using earlier lock systems, but it was the percussion cap that enabled them to come into their own. Named for their resemblance to a pepper grinder, these weapons used several barrels rotated in turn into alignment with a single firing mechanism. Early pepperbox pistols were hand operated, i.e. the barrels were rotated manually after firing, but many later models had mechanisms to rotate the barrels when the hammer was cocked.

The percussion-cap pepperbox pistol became common after 1830, and was cheap enough for purchase by large numbers of ordinary citizens rather than the rich elite. Some were very well made despite being inexpensive, while others were dangerously shoddy. An ill made pepperbox pistol might have poor alignment between barrel and firing mechanism, which at best made the weapon unreliable. Such pistols might allow hot gas to escape between firing mechanism and barrel, endangering the user and making a gang-fire more likely, and in some cases they could literally come apart under the stress of firing, inevitably to the detriment of the user.

Despite these drawbacks the pepperbox was a popular weapon and large numbers were made. The most practical examples balanced firepower against ease of carry, and had three to seven barrels. Some designs had an excessive number of barrels that made them clumsy and perhaps prone to mechanical problems. Pepperboxes were also difficult to aim at the best of times, and could be excessively front-end heavy. Fitting sights to rotating barrels was unfeasible, and in most cases the hammer was in the way of any sight line. Thus the pepperbox was best suited to desperate point-and-shoot self-defence at close range.

## PEPPERBOX REVOLVER

**COUNTRY OF ORIGIN**
United States
**DATE**
1830
**CALIBRE**
6mm (.23in)
**WEIGHT**
Not known
**OVERALL LENGTH**
210mm (8.25in)
**FEED/MAGAZINE**
1 shot per barrel
**RANGE**
5m (5.47yds)

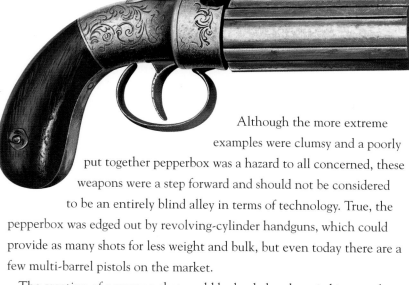

## PRACTICAL PEPPERBOX

**COUNTRY OF ORIGIN**
United States
**DATE**
1840
**CALIBRE**
10mm (.40in)
**WEIGHT**
Not known
**OVERALL LENGTH**
279mm (11in)
**FEED/MAGAZINE**
1 shot per barrel
**RANGE**
12m (13.12yds)

Although the more extreme examples were clumsy and a poorly put together pepperbox was a hazard to all concerned, these weapons were a step forward and should not be considered to be an entirely blind alley in terms of technology. True, the pepperbox was edged out by revolving-cylinder handguns, which could provide as many shots for less weight and bulk, but even today there are a few multi-barrel pistols on the market.

The creation of a weapon that could be loaded and carried in a pocket until it was needed also provoked some thought in the consideration of safety. Percussion caps would detonate if struck, so if the hammer was jarred there was a real possibility of an accidental discharge. Some pepperbox pistols were fitted with a guard to prevent the hammer from striking a cap, and it was always possible to carry the weapon with one chamber (the one under the hammer) empty.

The development of a device that rotated the barrels when the hammer was cocked, or cocked the hammer and rotated the cylinder when the trigger was pulled, benefited revolver design as well as the pepperbox pistol industry. Ultimately the revolver came to dominate the marketplace and the pepperbox gradually faded from the scene, but for many years the handgun user had a choice between the two types, each with its own merits.

## Early Revolvers

The development of the revolving-cylinder handgun owes much to Samuel Colt (1814–62), although claims that he invented the concept are perhaps overstated. According to legend (one probably started by Colt himself) the idea for a revolver cylinder came to him during his early career when he was serving as a cabin boy aboard ship. The segments of the ship's wheel suggested the idea of multiple chambers in a revolving cylinder.

This is a nice story, but revolving-cylinder weapons had been around for a while before Colt was born. As early as 1717, James Puckle demonstrated

RIGHT: Samuel Colt's firearms business benefited from association with the Texas Rangers, who demanded a high-capacity firearm that could stop a man or even a horse with a single bullet.

a revolving-cylinder weapon intended for use on ships. This was a light artillery piece, but the concept of ammunition held ready in a cylinder and rotated into alignment with the firing mechanism and barrel was included in the weapon's patent. Attempts had been made to create revolving-cylinder weapons before the percussion cap was invented, so Colt cannot be said to have done more than reinvented the wheel-gun.

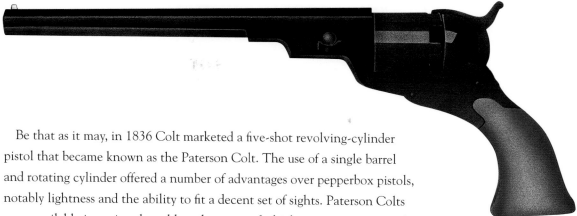

Be that as it may, in 1836 Colt marketed a five-shot revolving-cylinder pistol that became known as the Paterson Colt. The use of a single barrel and rotating cylinder offered a number of advantages over pepperbox pistols, notably lightness and the ability to fit a decent set of sights. Paterson Colts were available in various barrel lengths, some of which seem excessive. Colts with barrels of over 254mm (10in) eventually became known as 'Buntline Specials' and some examples were fitted with 355mm (14in) or even 40.6cm (16in) barrels. The accuracy benefits of a long barrel were probably offset by the difficulty in supporting such a front-end-heavy handgun. To tackle this problem a detachable stock was made available for some models, enabling the user to turn his handgun into a sort of carbine. Whether this was much of an improvement remains open to doubt.

The Paterson Colt was a single-action weapon in which the hammer was manually cocked, rotating the cylinder ready to fire. The trigger only released the hammer; the weapon could not be cocked by trigger action. It could, however, be fired without use of the trigger.

## Accidental Discharge

Carrying an early revolver with all the chambers loaded was hazardous. If the hammer were jarred then it might discharge the weapon. This might be useful in the event of a trigger malfunction – if the hammer mechanism became damaged the weapon could still be fired by striking the hammer when it was in the down position, resting on a loaded chamber. However, outside of desperate emergencies this was definitely a safety issue rather than any sort of advantage.

It was possible to carry the weapon with the hammer half-cocked, fully cocked or resting on a loaded chamber, all of which were hazardous. The only way to prevent accidental discharge was to carry the weapon with the chamber under the hammer unloaded. Cocking the weapon would ready a loaded chamber so this caused no delay but it did mean that a Paterson Colt was essentially a four-shot weapon, with one of its five chambers unloaded.

Reloading was a rather slow and cumbersome process, requiring that the

**COLT PATERSON**
**COUNTRY OF ORIGIN**
United States
**DATE**
1836
**CALIBRE**
9.1mm (.36in)
**WEIGHT**
1.93kg (4.25lb)
**OVERALL LENGTH**
355mm (14in)
**FEED/MAGAZINE**
5-shot revolver
**RANGE**
20m (21.9yds)

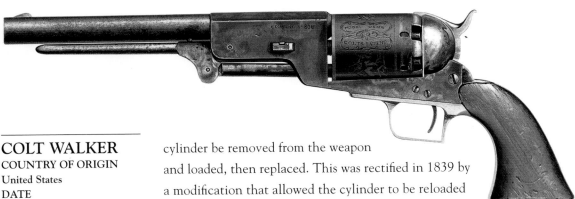

## COLT WALKER

**COUNTRY OF ORIGIN**
United States
**DATE**
1847
**CALIBRE**
11.2mm (.44in)
**WEIGHT**
2.04kg (4.5lb)
**OVERALL LENGTH**
343mm (13.5in)
**FEED/MAGAZINE**
6-shot revolver
**RANGE**
20m (21.9yds)

cylinder be removed from the weapon and loaded, then replaced. This was rectified in 1839 by a modification that allowed the cylinder to be reloaded in place. Despite these drawbacks, the Colt revolver was an effective weapon that offered greater personal firepower than had been previously available. It should be noted that its introduction came only two decades after the end of the Napoleonic Wars, which were fought almost exclusively with flintlocks. In an environment where unreliable single-shot flintlocks were still very common, a Paterson Colt was a very potent weapon indeed.

Among the primary proponents of repeating pistols were those who routinely fought from horseback, such as the Texas Rangers. These

RIGHT: The Colt Walker was developed to meet the needs of the Texas Rangers, who often fought from horseback and needed a hard-hitting, accurate repeating pistol.

individuals were influential in the development of the revolver, making their needs clear and providing an opportunity to field-test the weapons made to those specifications. There exist accounts of individuals whose lives were saved out on the American frontiers by their repeating pistols – a group of hostiles might choose to rush an individual who had just fired, knowing that it would take time to reload his weapon. The ability to shoot again… and again… in rapid succession was a huge advantage in these circumstances. The Texas Rangers in particular were pleased with the marvellous firepower of their Colt revolvers, which were often chambered for big, powerful rounds. Some models of pistol proclaimed their suitability for mounted combat by the name 'Dragoon', and weapons evolved steadily.

## Evolution of the Revolver

Colt was of course not the only manufacturer experimenting with revolvers in the first half of the nineteenth century. This was an era when personal firepower was increasingly important. Explorers were mapping South America, Africa and parts of Asia, while the American West was being opened up. Even without conflict with the native people and neighbours such as the Mexicans, the West could be a lawless place. Meanwhile the armies of Europe were increasingly involved in colonial warfare, usually against large numbers of relatively ill armed but courageous warriors.

The revolver developed rapidly once the basic concept was proven. Reloading times could be vastly reduced by carrying a spare loaded cylinder in a pocket and swapping it for an empty one when needed. This did not do away with the lengthy reloading process but it did increase the number

**COLT HARTFORD DRAGOON**
**COUNTRY OF ORIGIN**
United States
**DATE**
1847
**CALIBRE**
11.2mm (.44in)
**WEIGHT**
1.87kg (4.125lb)
**OVERALL LENGTH**
305mm (12in)
**FEED/MAGAZINE**
6-shot revolver
**RANGE**
20m (21.9yds)

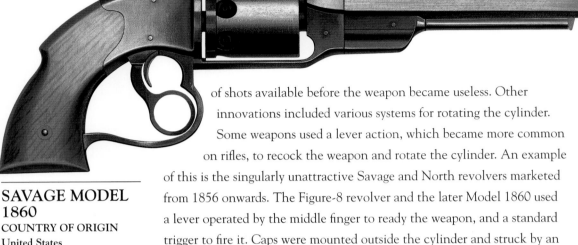

## SAVAGE MODEL 1860
**COUNTRY OF ORIGIN**
United States
**DATE**
1860
**CALIBRE**
9.1mm (.36in)
**WEIGHT**
1.6kg (3.525lb)
**OVERALL LENGTH**
330mm (13in)
**FEED/MAGAZINE**
6-shot revolver
**RANGE**
20m (21.9yds)

## BENTLEY
**COUNTRY OF ORIGIN**
United Kingdom
**DATE**
1853
**CALIBRE**
11.2mm (.44in)
**WEIGHT**
0.94kg (2.1lb)
**OVERALL LENGTH**
305mm (12in)
**FEED/MAGAZINE**
5-shot revolver
**RANGE**
12m (13.12yds)

of shots available before the weapon became useless. Other innovations included various systems for rotating the cylinder.

Some weapons used a lever action, which became more common on rifles, to recock the weapon and rotate the cylinder. An example of this is the singularly unattractive Savage and North revolvers marketed from 1856 onwards. The Figure-8 revolver and the later Model 1860 used a lever operated by the middle finger to ready the weapon, and a standard trigger to fire it. Caps were mounted outside the cylinder and struck by an angled hammer.

While less than pretty, these guns worked well enough that the U.S. military purchased thousands for use in the Civil War. Accuracy was not enhanced by all that finger activity but at close range this mattered less than the ability to shoot repeatedly. The same kind of system was used by Tranter in 1855, creating a revolver that was first cocked with the middle finger then discharged with light pressure of the forefinger. Pulling both together cocked and fired the revolver in a single movement.

Other innovations of the era were more elegant. An Englishman, Joseph Bentley, developed two new features that have since become standard on many weapons. His revolvers used trigger action to set the hammer, creating what is today normally known as a double-action pistol. Such a handgun could be carried with the hammer down and brought rapidly into action

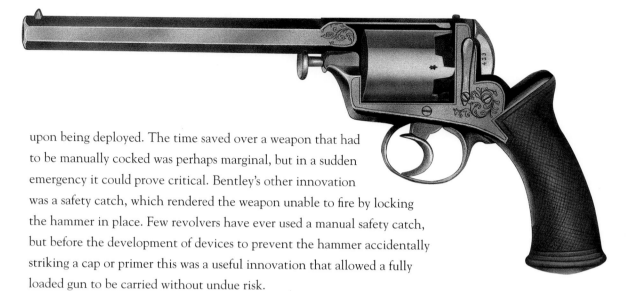

upon being deployed. The time saved over a weapon that had
to be manually cocked was perhaps marginal, but in a sudden
emergency it could prove critical. Bentley's other innovation
was a safety catch, which rendered the weapon unable to fire by locking
the hammer in place. Few revolvers have ever used a manual safety catch,
but before the development of devices to prevent the hammer accidentally
striking a cap or primer this was a useful innovation that allowed a fully
loaded gun to be carried without undue risk.

Other manufacturers produced their own innovations. The British
Adams revolver, which appeared in 1851, was marketed as 'self-cocking' as
its hammer was set and then dropped by a single trigger pull. The Adams
revolver distinctively had no hammer spur for cocking as it needed none.
This might reduce the chance of snagging as the weapon was drawn but
it did mean that the weapon could not be cocked for a light trigger pull
and thus greater accuracy. This possibly deficiency was remedied by the
Beaumont-Adams in 1862. This weapon could be cocked manually or by
trigger action. In the former case, the set hammer required little trigger
pressure to drop and was thus unlikely to be disturbed from its aim point by
trigger pull. When necessary, however, the pistol could be quickly fired by
pulling the trigger hard.

It might seem that the invention of double-action pistols, which could
be fired repeatedly without manually cocking the hammer, was a leap
forward that would quickly made obsolete the single-action handgun.
However, this was not the case. While some users liked their double-action
pistols, most did not. The U.S. military adopted the Starr Double Action
in 1858, but found it to be too complicated. A single-action variant was
requested and from 1863 onwards it was delivered in large numbers to
military clients.

There was also much experimentation with calibre. It had long been
understood that a bigger, heavier bullet causes more damage to the target
and higher velocity improves both hitting power and accuracy. However, the

## ADAMS SELF-COCKING REVOLVER
**COUNTRY OF ORIGIN**
United Kingdom
**DATE**
1851
**CALIBRE**
11.4mm (.49in)
**WEIGHT**
1.27kg (2.8lb)
**OVERALL LENGTH**
330mm (13in)
**FEED/MAGAZINE**
6-shot revolver
**RANGE**
12m (13.12yds)

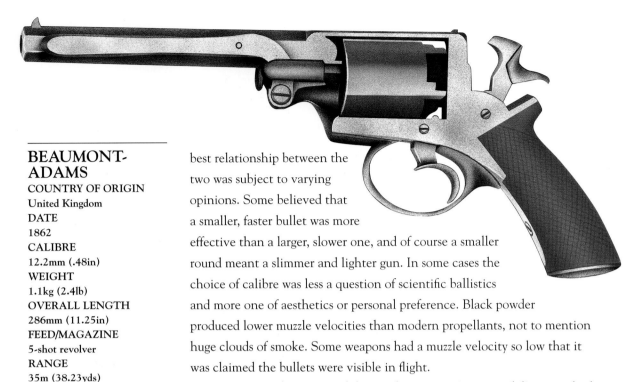

## BEAUMONT-ADAMS

**COUNTRY OF ORIGIN**
United Kingdom
**DATE**
1862
**CALIBRE**
12.2mm (.48in)
**WEIGHT**
1.1kg (2.4lb)
**OVERALL LENGTH**
286mm (11.25in)
**FEED/MAGAZINE**
5-shot revolver
**RANGE**
35m (38.23yds)

## STARR SINGLE ACTION

**COUNTRY OF ORIGIN**
United States
**DATE**
1863
**CALIBRE**
11.2mm (.44in)
**WEIGHT**
1.36kg (3lb)
**OVERALL LENGTH**
343mm (13.5in)
**FEED/MAGAZINE**
6-shot revolver
**RANGE**
20m (21.88yds)

best relationship between the two was subject to varying opinions. Some believed that a smaller, faster bullet was more effective than a larger, slower one, and of course a smaller round meant a slimmer and lighter gun. In some cases the choice of calibre was less a question of scientific ballistics and more one of aesthetics or personal preference. Black powder produced lower muzzle velocities than modern propellants, not to mention huge clouds of smoke. Some weapons had a muzzle velocity so low that it was claimed the bullets were visible in flight.

One concept that emerged during this era was 'navy model' guns, which tended to have a fairly small calibre such as .36, and 'army model' versions of the same weapon that might be chambered for .44 or .45. In fact, this was nothing more than a marketing ploy – both versions were typically just as popular with the army and the navy, with no institutional preference. However, this has led to the persistent perception that naval pistols were generally of small calibre for some ill defined reason.

One of the great driving forces of this marketing campaign was Samuel Colt, whose genius as a gun designer was at least matched by his showmanship and ability to sell his guns and the underlying concepts all

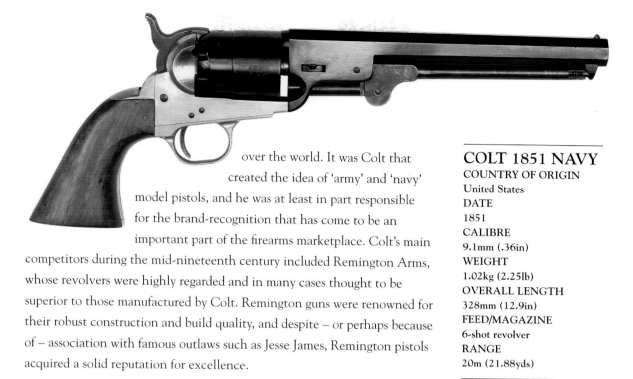

over the world. It was Colt that created the idea of 'army' and 'navy' model pistols, and he was at least in part responsible for the brand-recognition that has come to be an important part of the firearms marketplace. Colt's main competitors during the mid-nineteenth century included Remington Arms, whose revolvers were highly regarded and in many cases thought to be superior to those manufactured by Colt. Remington guns were renowned for their robust construction and build quality, and despite – or perhaps because of – association with famous outlaws such as Jesse James, Remington pistols acquired a solid reputation for excellence.

## Bold Experiments

During the mid-nineteenth century Europe was plunged into the Crimean War, the last in which European troops were primarily armed with muzzleloading firearms. Not long after the war ended in 1856, North America suffered its Civil War. Both of these conflicts saw significant development of firearms technology. Often this development was incremental, with new versions of proven designs appearing during the course of the war. Not all of the progress was in terms of weapon design; techniques for reducing costs or increasing the speed of mass-production

### COLT 1851 NAVY
COUNTRY OF ORIGIN
United States
DATE
1851
CALIBRE
9.1mm (.36in)
WEIGHT
1.02kg (2.25lb)
OVERALL LENGTH
328mm (12.9in)
FEED/MAGAZINE
6-shot revolver
RANGE
20m (21.88yds)

### REMINGTON NEW MODEL ARMY 1863
COUNTRY OF ORIGIN
United States
DATE
1863
CALIBRE
11.2mm (.44in)
WEIGHT
1.1kg (2.4lb)
OVERALL LENGTH
349mm (123.75in)
FEED/MAGAZINE
6-shot revolver
RANGE
12m (13.12yds)

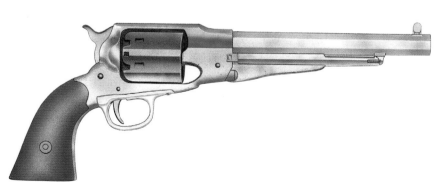

## LE MAT

**COUNTRY OF ORIGIN**
France
**DATE**
1858
**CALIBRE**
7.62mm (.3in)
**WEIGHT**
1.64kg (3.625lb)
**OVERALL LENGTH**
337mm (13.25in)
**FEED/MAGAZINE**
9-shot revolver plus single
shot, shotgun
**RANGE**
15m (16.4yds)

## COLT M1860 ARMY

**COUNTRY OF ORIGIN**
United States
**DATE**
1862
**CALIBRE**
11.2mm (.44in)
**WEIGHT**
1.25kg (2.75lb)
**OVERALL LENGTH**
349mm (13.75in)
**FEED/MAGAZINE**
6-shot revolver
**RANGE**
12m (13.12yds)

were implemented to cope with the huge demand for weapons that these conflicts created.

There were also numerous attempts at innovation. Not all of these experiments were successful. The Le Mat revolver, a smoothbore that combined a nine-shot revolver with a single-shot shotgun, was in theory a potent weapon for a cavalryman, giving him a significant firepower advantage. Adjusting the hammer allowed the user to fire the shotgun when this seemed most opportune. However, the Le Mat was not well made and was supplied in small numbers. A few users liked them but the weapon never achieved any real market penetration or widespread approval and faded quickly away.

Another less-than-successful experiment was Colt's revolving rifle project, which attempted to scale up a revolver into a carbine or rifle. The Model 1855 became the U.S. military's first repeating rifle, and in theory offered a number of advantages. It shared ammunition with the revolvers used by cavalry troopers, and used the same components as well. However, there was always the possibility of a chain-fire that would cause all remaining rounds in the cylinder to discharge at one. With a revolver, this could burst the cylinder but the user might escape serious injury; with a rifle the user's left arm would be alongside and in front of the cylinder and was sure to be harmed.

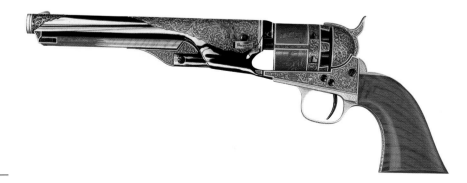

**LEFT: Photographs from the American Civil War often feature military personnel proudly posing with their weapons, and Colt revolvers feature prominently among them.**

Although effective in action, the revolving rifle was too much of a liability if something went wrong and it quickly disappeared after the war. The concept of arming personnel with a pistol and a longarm in the same calibre also fell by the wayside, although it has been revived in the modern era with the FN P90 Personal Defence Weapon and Five-Seven pistol.

It is notable that while the sword was the primary weapon of European cavalry in the Crimean War, firearms came to dominate cavalry actions of the American Civil War half a decade later. Cavalry – particularly on the Union side – frequently dismounted to fight on foot rather than in the traditional sweeping sabre charge. This was partially due to the firepower now available to infantry, which made a charge far more costly than against flintlocks, and partly due to the generally lower standard of horsemanship of the northern recruits.

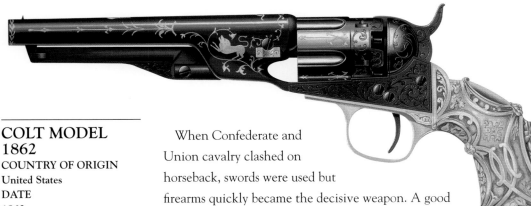

## COLT MODEL 1862

**COUNTRY OF ORIGIN**
United States
**DATE**
1862
**CALIBRE**
11.2mm (.44in)
**WEIGHT**
1.25kg (2.75lb)
**OVERALL LENGTH**
349mm (13.75in)
**FEED/MAGAZINE**
6-shot revolver
**RANGE**
12m (13.12yds)

When Confederate and Union cavalry clashed on horseback, swords were used but firearms quickly became the decisive weapon. A good revolver – or perhaps more than one – allowed several opportunistic shots during a cavalry skirmish, and where flintlock pistols proved generally inferior to swords for mounted combat, the reverse was true for more modern weapons. The Union cavalry in particular adopted the revolver as its primary weapon, and small raiding parties benefited from the very significant increase in personal firepower to be obtained from a collection of revolvers. Sabres, if carried at all, were often slung from the saddle for mounted use only, but the revolver was worn on the belt as a personal weapon – indicating that it had displaced the sword as the sidearm of choice.

By the outbreak of the American Civil War the first all-in-one cartridge weapons were becoming available, but they did not see action in sufficient numbers to be decisive. Indeed, some units were issued with flintlocks for lack of anything better. The Civil War was largely fought with muzzleloading percussion weapons, and many of these guns went West afterwards. Today's Westerns usually portray the cartridge firearms that became prevalent later, but the West was opened up largely with cap-and-ball weapons.

### Projectiles and Rifling

The concept of rifling was known from 1500 onwards, and was used in some hunting weapons from that time. A set of spiral grooves cut into the inside of a weapon barrel would spin a bullet and make it far more stable in flight – but only if the bullet made contact with the grooves.

Most early firearms were smoothbores with an unrifled barrel, firing a more or less spherical projectile that was sufficiently smaller than the weapon's bore to pass along it unhindered. To prevent the ball from simply rolling out of the barrel, a paper wad or greased patch was rammed in on top of it,

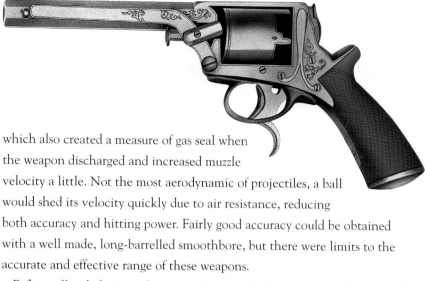

which also created a measure of gas seal when
the weapon discharged and increased muzzle
velocity a little. Not the most aerodynamic of projectiles, a ball
would shed its velocity quickly due to air resistance, reducing
both accuracy and hitting power. Fairly good accuracy could be obtained
with a well made, long-barrelled smoothbore, but there were limits to the
accurate and effective range of these weapons.

Rifling offered obvious advantages, but required a more precisely cast ball
that gripped the rifling as it proceeded down the barrel. This meant it had
to be almost exactly the same size as the weapon's bore, and was thus much
harder to ram home. Where a smoothbore projectile could often be dropped
down the barrel, a rifled weapon required the ball to be pushed down, and
this was made more difficult by fouling once the weapon had been fired a few
times and powder residue coated the inside of the barrel.

## Ballistic Developments

For massed infantry on the battlefield, the ability to fire many shots might
outweigh precision and range, making smoothbores a viable option long
after rifled weapons were widely available. For the handgun user whose
two or three shots absolutely had to count, making the most of each round
fired made a lot of sense – especially if the weapon took a long time to load

### TRANTER REVOLVER
COUNTRY OF ORIGIN
United Kingdom
DATE
1855
CALIBRE
11.2mm (.44in)
WEIGHT
.88kg (1.9lb)
OVERALL LENGTH
165mm (6.5in)
FEED/MAGAZINE
5-shot revolver
RANGE
12m (13.12yds)

### LANCASTER 1882
COUNTRY OF ORIGIN
United Kingdom
DATE
1882
CALIBRE
9.6mm (.38in)
WEIGHT
1.13kg (2.5lb)
OVERALL LENGTH
279mm (11in)
FEED/MAGAZINE
4-barrel, single shot per barrel
RANGE
15m (16.4yds)

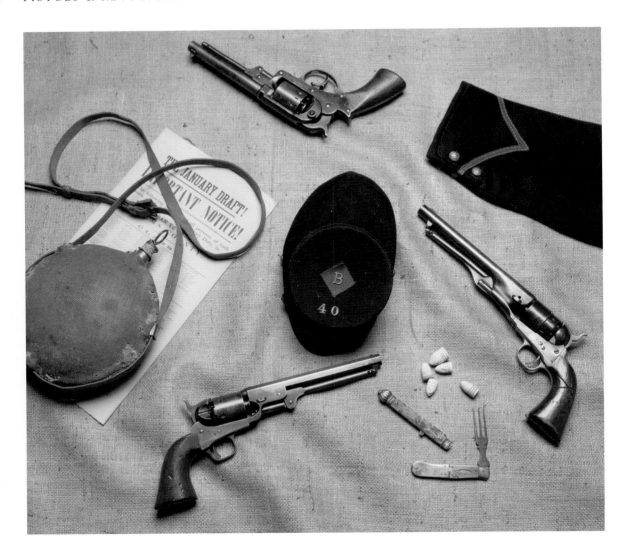

ABOVE: Artefacts from the American Civil War are highly collectible. Some guns from the era are still in shootable condition, but any new acquisition should be thoroughly checked out by a qualified gunsmith before use.

whether rifled or not. Early rifled handguns used a round projectile, but the invention of the conical bullet offered a significant step forward. Conical bullets are of course not perfectly cone shaped, and the term refers to pretty much any bullet that is not a ball; most have a rounded cone shape which is far more aerodynamic than a sphere as long as the bullet travels pointed end first.

Conical bullets were invented in the 1820s but did not find favour until the Minié bullet was introduced in 1847. Within a decade conical bullets were in military use and have remained so ever since. The Minié bullet was cone shaped and slightly smaller than the diameter of the weapon's bore, allowing it to be muzzleloaded. When the weapon was fired, expanding gas filled a hollow at the base of the bullet, causing it to expand slightly and grip

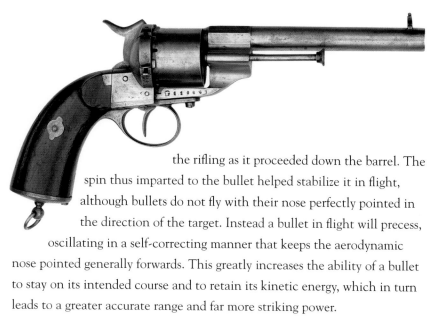

**LEFAUCHEUX**
COUNTRY OF ORIGIN
France
DATE
1861
CALIBRE
9mm (.35in)
WEIGHT
0.56kg (1.2lb)
OVERALL LENGTH
213mm (8.4in)
FEED/MAGAZINE
6-shot revolver
RANGE
12m (13.12yds)

the rifling as it proceeded down the barrel. The spin thus imparted to the bullet helped stabilize it in flight, although bullets do not fly with their nose perfectly pointed in the direction of the target. Instead a bullet in flight will precess, oscillating in a self-correcting manner that keeps the aerodynamic nose pointed generally forwards. This greatly increases the ability of a bullet to stay on its intended course and to retain its kinetic energy, which in turn leads to a greater accurate range and far more striking power.

Rifled handguns quickly displaced smoothbores. Although the barrel was somewhat harder to manufacture and bullets were more expensive, the advantages of a rifled sidearm greatly outweighed any disadvantages. Loading took just as long as with a smoothbore cap-and-ball pistol, but each shot was potentially more effective. For the frontiersman, cavalry soldier or military officer – indeed anyone who needed a pistol for self-defence – there were clear advantages to be had from a rifled weapon.

By the middle of the nineteenth century, rifled guns firing conical bullets were becoming standard. Only one element of the modern firearm was still missing – the unitary cartridge. Experiments with paper, cloth and metal cartridges were ongoing and a few guns were available that used them, but it was not until after the end of the American Civil War that these guns became prevalent. Once they did, the modern era of firearms development could begin.

**WEBLEY
LONGSPUR**
COUNTRY OF ORIGIN
United Kingdom
DATE
1853
CALIBRE
11.2mm (.44in)
WEIGHT
1.05kg (2.3lb)
OVERALL LENGTH
317mm (12.5in)
FEED/MAGAZINE
5-shot revolver
RANGE
202m (220.9yds)

# Early Cartridge Pistols

The term 'cartridge' had been in use long before the creation of the modern metal all-in-one cartridge. Originally it referred to a paper container holding a ball and a pre-measured amount of gunpowder. A little of this had to be saved for priming the pan when pouring the main charge into the muzzle, but the provis ion of a pre-measured charge offered the black-powder shooter certain advantages. It was of course possible to pour a charge directly from a powder horn and guesstimate the amount needed, but this had certain drawbacks. Among those was the possibility that a rogue spark might turn a powder horn into a hand-held bomb. To avoid this, a measure was generally used. A spark could still ignite the powder in the measure but this would be much less serious than an exploding powder horn.

LEFT: In April 1900, a small British detachment under Captain Towse beat off a determined assault by Boer riflemen. The incident was unusual in a war characterized mainly by long-range rifle marksmanship.

## KUFAHL NEEDLE-FIRE REVOLVER

COUNTRY OF ORIGIN
Germany
DATE
1870
CALIBRE
7.36mm (.29in)
WEIGHT
.62kg (1.375lb)
OVERALL LENGTH
244mm (9.6in)
FEED/MAGAZINE
6-shot revolver
RANGE
15m (16.4yds)

A pre-packaged cartridge saved the time required to use a measure while still offering its other advantages: safety and a known charge. Getting the amount of gunpowder in the weapon right was important. Too much could make the weapon uncontrollable or injurious to fire, and could perhaps even burst an overstressed barrel. Too little would produce a weak shot that was even less accurate than usual, travelled less distance and inflicted only slight injury. That assumed that the weapon discharged properly. A very weak charge might not even push the round out of the muzzle, and it was not always possible to tell that this had happened in the middle of combat. This was more of a problem for the infantry soldier than the pistol user, as the latter knew that his weapon would be useless after one shot whereas a soldier would expect to fire repeatedly in the course of an engagement.

The unfired ball and whatever remained of the charge might be rammed back down the barrel and another ball and charge loaded on top. In all likelihood this would make the weapon unfireable, but occasionally the whole charge might ignite on a subsequent attempt. It could still happen on a misfire with cartridges, but at least the user knew that he had put enough powder in the barrel to clear it.

BELOW: This diagram shows how a muzzle loading revolver was converted to a breechloader. This was accomplished by the removal of the rear of the cylinder and the percussion cap nipples, and the insertion of the circular plate in fig. 2 which contained the striker and extractor.

# THE COLT BREECH-LOADING REVOLVER.

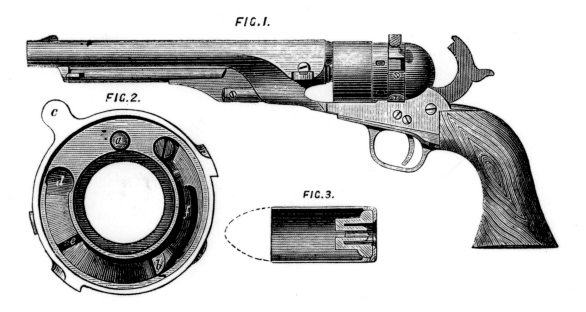

FIG.1.

FIG.2.

FIG.3.

## Needle-fire Detonation

The cartridge, with its pre-measured powder and ball held ready, was thus an advantageous technology, but its numerous drawbacks led to a desire for something less cumbersome. The first all-in-one cartridges appeared in the early 1800s, invented by the Swiss Jean Samuel Pauly and the French Francoise Prelat. These cartridges were of paper, but with a copper base that held fulminate of mercury – the same compound used in percussion caps. The body of the cartridge was still of paper, with a gunpowder charge and bullet resting on the cap/base. This was struck with a needle, giving this kind of weapon the name 'needle-fire'.

The new cartridge was viewed with some suspicion by prospective users, since a sharp knock on the base could detonate the cartridge at any time. Given how unstable early caps could be, this wariness was probably well founded. Despite this, the needle-fire cartridge was gradually improved, with an 1812 patent following the original 1808 one. Needle-fire weapons had to be loaded from the breech, as it was not feasible to ram a unitary cartridge down the barrel into a firing position. This resulted in a number of breech loading weapons, many of which used a break-open action.

The needle-fire concept was developed during the eighteenth century, with variants including a cloth cartridge with the percussion cap in front of the powder charge, between the bullet and the powder. This was initiated by a needle stabbing through the cloth and powder. The same configuration, albeit with a paper cartridge, was used by the 'needle rifle' developed by the German gunsmith Johann Dreyse. Although not a handgun, the Dreyse 'needle ignition rifle' or simply 'needle gun' is of interest because it graphically demonstrated the superiority of cartridge firearms over muzzleloaders. In the Prussian–Austrian War of 1866, Prussian troops armed with Dreyse rifles were able to shoot further and faster than their Austrian opponents, who had to stand up to reload their muzzleloaders while the Prussians could take cover in an altogether more modern manner.

In the meantime, the Frenchman Casimir Lefaucheux patented the first pinfire cartridge, an alternative to needle-fire based but on similar principles. Pinfire weapons used an all-in-one cartridge with an embedded percussion cap that was ignited by a small pin protruding from the cartridge. When struck by the weapon's hammer, this pin in turn set off the cap. Pinfire required a somewhat different hammer action to needle-

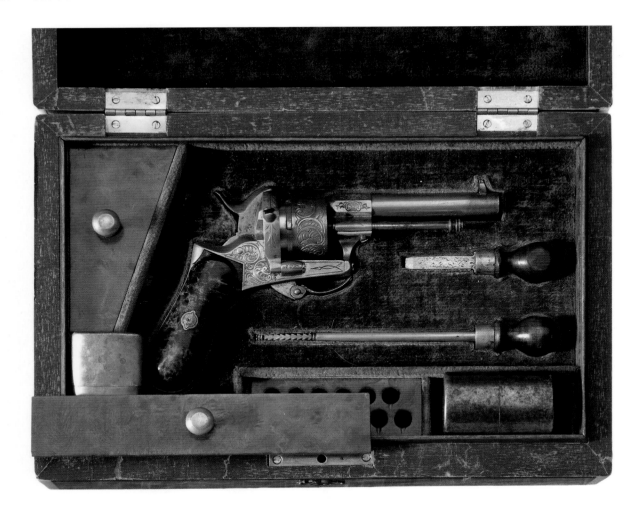

ABOVE: **Although it may look primitive by today's standards, a good quality pinfire revolver was a state-of-the-art weapon in its day, worthy of a presentation box containing tools and accessories.**

fire. A pinfire weapon had to be struck from the side, whereas a needle-fire weapon required the needle to be driven directly forward by the hammer. This was a simple mechanical problem to solve, but did create handguns with distinctively different hammer arcs. A needle-fire gun (and later centre-fire weapons) could have a hammer that did not move outside the line of barrel and top strap. On a pinfire weapon a more pronounced arc was required.

As both pinfire and needle-fire weapons became prevalent, handgun design had to change. Loading a unitary cartridge, especially one with a protruding pin or rod, however small, necessitated a weapon that could be opened and loaded through the breech. This led to numerous break-open designs, in which the barrel and cylinder were hinged to swing away from the grip and firing mechanism, usually in a downward direction. An alternative was to use a loading gate at the rear of the cylinder.

## Modern Cartridges

Pinfire and needle-fire weapons became common during the mid-nineteenth century, but alternatives were already appearing. The first rimfire cartridge was more of a novelty than anything else – the percussion cap formed a rim upon which a very light ball rested directly. With no propellant powder, this was a short-range target-shooting cartridge for recreational use only.

By 1857, a workable rimfire cartridge was available. This used a rim of priming material around the base of the cartridge, where it could be struck by the weapon's firing pin. Once the technology was proven, it was applied to various cartridge sizes for use in rifles as well as handguns. For larger weapons, centre-fire proved more effective but the rimfire cartridge has survived to this day. The most notable rimfire cartridge is .22in Long Rifle, which was and still is used in immense numbers. A recent revival in rimfire shooting has produced new calibres, but these are almost without exception small and light.

The idea of building the percussion cap into a cartridge was explored by gunsmiths around the world, eventually resulting in what is now known as a primer. This is essentially a percussion cap designed to simultaneously ignite as much of the main propellant as possible. Resting at the centre of the rear face of the cartridge, the primer is initiated by a sharp blow of the weapon's firing pin. Effective primers were patented in both Britain and the USA, by different inventors, in 1866. Designs differed but the principle was much the same. One consequence of the move to centre-fire ammunition was the adoption of brass cartridges, which are more robust than the previous copper ones and less likely to distort when the primer was forced into position. Centre-fire ammunition proved most useful in more potent calibres, and has displaced rimfire in all but the smallest-calibre weapons. Most modern firearms use this system, which has been in use for a century and a half.

## Smokeless Powder

It is arguable that modern firearms began with the invention of a unitary metal cartridge that was robust enough to survive rough handling – including being moved around by mechanical devices. Lever-action and bolt-action weapons, and later semi-automatic and fully automatic systems, required a cartridge that would not distort or come apart under the stress of being loaded or ejected. There was, however, one last requirement for the modern handgun to appear – a propellant more efficient than black powder.

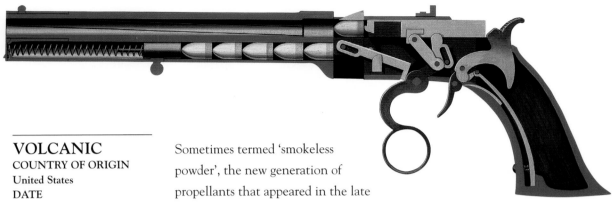

## VOLCANIC

**COUNTRY OF ORIGIN**
United States
**DATE**
1855
**CALIBRE**
11.2mm (.44in)
**WEIGHT**
0.8kg (1.75lb)
**OVERALL LENGTH**
279mm (11in)
**FEED/MAGAZINE**
6-round internal magazine
**RANGE**
15m (16.4yds)

**RIGHT: These promotional images of the Smith & Wesson factory in Springfield, Massachusetts, show a hive of industrial activity producing huge numbers of handguns for the domestic and export market.**

Sometimes termed 'smokeless powder', the new generation of propellants that appeared in the late nineteenth century were not entirely smokeless and did not take the form of powder, but the term stuck. In some areas other names were used, mainly relating to specific propellants or brand names such as cordite.

Black powder burns relatively slowly, creating a pushing effect that accelerates the round down the barrel. Modern propellant explodes far more quickly, with the effect that the new generation of handguns kick suddenly rather than pushing back at the user. Modern propellants also have less solid residue to foul a barrel or to create clouds of smoke. The latter not only made it harder to locate a shooter but also eliminated much of the smoke that would envelop a battlefield. For the individual user, new propellants resulted in a weapon that could shoot faster and with greater accuracy, hit harder and could be rapidly reloaded. Increased chamber pressures also had implications for weapon design.

More potent propellants meant that a weapon was subject to greater stress when a round was fired. Weak areas that previously had not been significant were now potentially hazardous to the user, so weapons had to become more robust. Joins and seams were potential failure points, while the firing chamber in particular required more metal around it to prevent a rupture. The other great change wrought by modern propellants was the ability to make use of recoil or gas pressure. Self-reloading weapons, typically using a bolt or slide, were made possible by the new generation of ammunition, and this in turn made it worthwhile to carry ammunition in a detachable or fixed magazine. Metal cartridges were robust enough to survive being fed into the breech by a spring-loaded mechanism as the weapon's action was opened by recoil or gas pressure tapped off from the barrel.

Thus the machinegun, the semi-automatic rifle, the assault rifle and of course the semi-automatic pistol were all made possible. Their evolution was a long process, however.

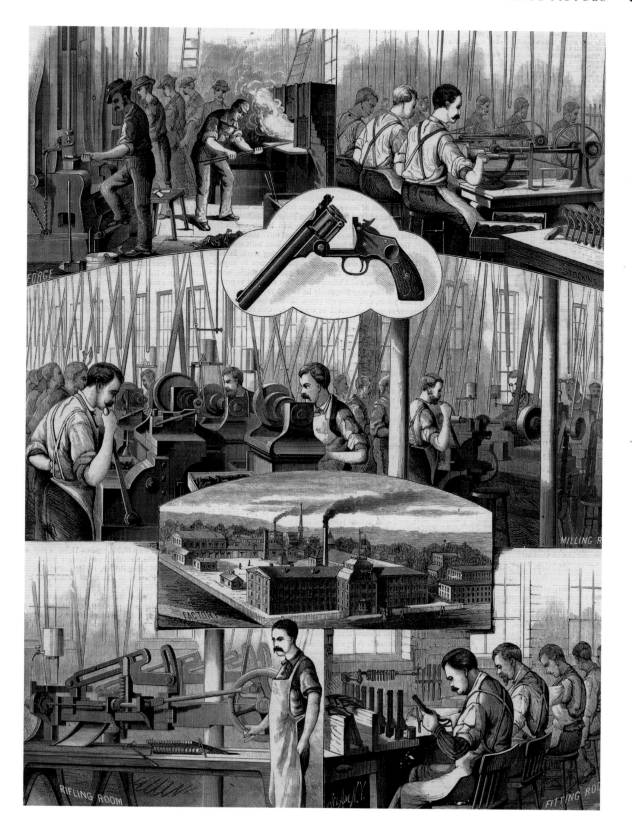

## Early Smith & Wesson Pistols

The first handguns making use of all-in-one cartridges became available in the mid-1800s. Among them was the Volcanic pistol, an innovative design created by Horace Smith and Daniel Wesson. This was a mechanical repeater, using a finger-operated lever-action system to chamber rounds from a tubular internal magazine under the barrel. At the time of its introduction, the Volcanic pistol offered a significant firepower advantage over many of the available weapons, not least because its internal magazine could be reloaded much more quickly than a cap-and-ball revolver's cylinder. Despite this, the Volcanic pistol concept did not catch on and the weapon remains a curiosity. Internal-magazine handguns have since been produced, and other lever-action pistol designs were marketed, but the Volcanic's designers soon moved on to other projects.

Smith and Wesson formed a company to produce their handguns, which was initially named for the partners. A name change to 'Volcanic Repeating Arms Company' tied the company's fortunes to the new handgun and its rifle version. Smith and Wesson left the firm, which then went through various troubles to emerge as a leading manufacturer of lever-action rifles under the name of Winchester Repeating Arms. The Volcanic pistol was thus something of a dead end as a handgun, but it paved the way for iconic rifles such as the Henry and the many incarnations of Winchester.

Meanwhile, the inventors of the Volcanic pistol formed a new business entity, the Smith & Wesson Revolver Company, and in 1857 marketed the Smith & Wesson Model 1. A simple seven-shot revolver with a guardless stud trigger, the Model 1 used a unitary cartridge developed specially for it. This was named .22 Short, a .22 rimfire cartridge that showed the way for later rimfire ammunition. For reloading, the Model 1 used a tip-up system,

### SMITH & WESSON MODEL 1
**COUNTRY OF ORIGIN**
United States
**DATE**
1857
**CALIBRE**
5.6mm (.22in)
**WEIGHT**
.33kg (.72lb)
**OVERALL LENGTH**
178mm (7in)
**FEED/MAGAZINE**
7-shot revolver
**RANGE**
10m (10.93yds)

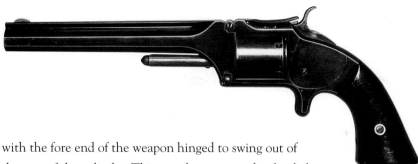

**SMITH & WESSON NO 2**
COUNTRY OF ORIGIN
United States
DATE
1866
CALIBRE
8.12mm (.32in)
WEIGHT
.33kg (.72lb)
OVERALL LENGTH
178mm (7in)
FEED/MAGAZINE
7-shot revolver
RANGE
10m (10.93yds)

with the fore end of the weapon hinged to swing out of
the way of the cylinder. This was then removed, reloaded
and replaced. While not the most efficient of systems, this was still a quick
weapon to reload by the standards of the 1850s, and it was successful in the
marketplace. Having sold over 11,000 of their revolvers, Smith & Wesson
marketed an improved version named Model 1 Second Issue in 1860 and
sold a 100,000 of them. A third Issue version, with some modifications, went
on sale from 1868 until 1882 and over 130,000 were sold.

The Model 1 was small and easy to carry but lacked effective range and
stopping power. It was very successful in the marketplace, but for military use
a larger calibre seemed desirable. In 1861 Smith & Wesson produced the .32
calibre No 2 revolver, better known as the Smith & Wesson Old Army. This
revolver is perhaps best known for its association with 'Wild Bill' Hickok,
and was widely used by military personnel during the Civil War. The
No 2 revolver was not formally adopted by either side in the war, but was
purchased privately by many individuals and some units. It was an enlarged
version of the Model 1, and in 1865 it was joined in the marketplace by the
'Model 1½' which was also chambered for .32 rimfire but was built on the
Model 1 frame.

Despite being very underpowered, even by the standards of the day,
these revolvers sold in huge numbers and established the Smith & Wesson
Company as a heavyweight contender in the pistol marketplace. Their next
offering, the 1870 Smith & Wesson No 3 revolver, had a far more modern

**SMITH & WESSON NO 3**
COUNTRY OF ORIGIN
United States
DATE
1870
CALIBRE
9.65mm (.38in)
WEIGHT
1.02kg (2.25lb)
OVERALL LENGTH
317mm (12.5in)
FEED/MAGAZINE
6-shot revolver
RANGE
20m (21.92yds)

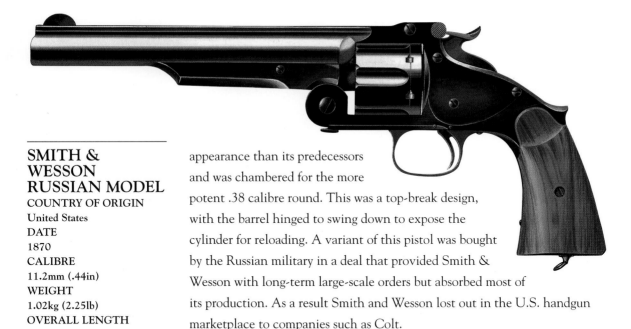

## SMITH & WESSON RUSSIAN MODEL

**COUNTRY OF ORIGIN**
United States
**DATE**
1870
**CALIBRE**
11.2mm (.44in)
**WEIGHT**
1.02kg (2.25lb)
**OVERALL LENGTH**
317mm (12.5in)
**FEED/MAGAZINE**
6-shot revolver
**RANGE**
20m (21.92yds)

appearance than its predecessors and was chambered for the more potent .38 calibre round. This was a top-break design, with the barrel hinged to swing down to expose the cylinder for reloading. A variant of this pistol was bought by the Russian military in a deal that provided Smith & Wesson with long-term large-scale orders but absorbed most of its production. As a result Smith and Wesson lost out in the U.S. handgun marketplace to companies such as Colt.

### A New Generation of Handguns

By the end of the American Civil War, cartridge firearms were becoming increasingly prevalent. The immense cost of re-equipping a large army with updated weapons meant that infantry rifles lagged behind the weapons being purchased for personal defence or to equip small forces. The cap-and-ball revolver, along with needle-fire and pinfire versions, was gradually edged out in favour of more user-friendly sidearms. Chief among these was the Colt Single Action Army, otherwise known as the M1873 or Peacemaker. Rather than a hinged barrel, the Peacemaker was loaded through a gate at the rear of the cylinder. Placing the hammer at half-cock allowed the cylinder to spin freely, enabling the user to align each chamber in turn with the loading gate. The ejector rod, located below the barrel, was then used to push out the spent cartridge and a new one was inserted through the gate.

A weapon could of course go off at half-cock, and the Colt was usually carried with one chamber empty as, like other guns of its time, it had no mechanism to prevent a knocked hammer from discharging the round it struck. One advantage of the loading-gate system was the ability to slip a single round into the gun in an emergency. An experienced user could then align the loaded chamber correctly, cock the hammer to place it in firing position and get off a quick shot.

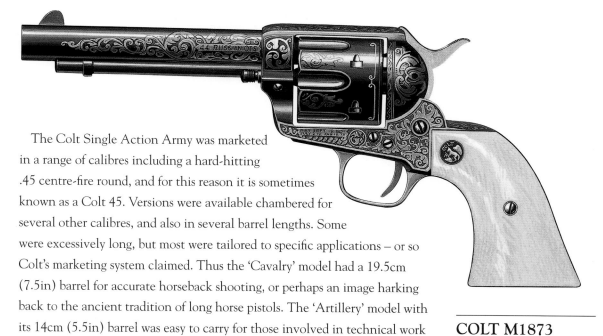

The Colt Single Action Army was marketed in a range of calibres including a hard-hitting .45 centre-fire round, and for this reason it is sometimes known as a Colt 45. Versions were available chambered for several other calibres, and also in several barrel lengths. Some were excessively long, but most were tailored to specific applications – or so Colt's marketing system claimed. Thus the 'Cavalry' model had a 19.5cm (7.5in) barrel for accurate horseback shooting, or perhaps an image harking back to the ancient tradition of long horse pistols. The 'Artillery' model with its 14cm (5.5in) barrel was easy to carry for those involved in technical work but who might need a handgun that could be deployed in a hurry. The even shorter 'Storekeeper' or 'Sheriff' models were marketed at those that might want a concealable and quickly deployed pistol.

The Single Action Army was highly successful in its role as a military sidearm, sufficiently so that even after its ostensible replacement in the late nineteenth century it remained in semi-official use during the American–Spanish War of 1898. This was not least due to disappointment with the stopping power of smaller-calibre weapons brought in to replace the ageing Colts, and it seems likely that lasting affection for the potent .45 Single Action Army was a driving factor in the adoption of the M1911 semi-automatic – which was also chambered for .45. In 1878, Colt marketed a double-action revolver based on the Single Action Army by way of an earlier interim design. This was essentially the same weapon, but with the addition of a connecting link from the trigger to the hammer, which allowed cocking of the hammer by trigger action. The force required to do this was significantly greater than that required to cause the hammer to drop, making double-action shooting less accurate but quicker in an emergency point-and-shoot situation.

The double-action pistol did not immediately displace the single-action version, possibly due to misgivings about the reliability of the mechanism. Over time, however, the double-action revolver became the standard

## COLT M1873 SINGLE ACTION ARMY
**COUNTRY OF ORIGIN**
United States
**DATE**
1873
**CALIBRE**
11.2mm (.44in)
**WEIGHT**
1.08kg (2.4lb)
**OVERALL LENGTH**
330mm (13in)
**FEED/MAGAZINE**
6-shot revolver
**RANGE**
20m (21.92yds)

military, law enforcement and personal sidearm of choice. Offering the best of both worlds – fast shooting when necessary and the chance to thumb-cock the weapon for an accurately aimed shot – once these weapons proved their reliability there was really little reason to stick with single-action-only except for the most powerful of weapons. Much later, in the mid-to late twentieth century, double-action-only weapons became more popular. Set up with a hammer that cannot be thumb-cocked, these weapons help protect the user against a certain kind of lawsuit. The (rather convoluted) logic goes

that in the case of a justified shooting, the shooter cannot be found guilty of murder or inflicting harm… but if the prosecution can show that the shooting was accidental then the shooter can be charged.

The ploy in this case is to claim that the shooter had cocked his weapon, creating a 'hair-trigger situation' and then accidentally and needlessly shot the victim without intending to, i.e. negligently shooting someone he would be justified in deliberately firing upon. One defence against this, paradoxically perhaps, is to use a weapon that cannot be cocked in this

**BELOW:** The Franco-
Prussian War was one of
the first major conflicts in
which cartridge firearms
played a major role.
Cavalry simply could not
close with rifle-armed
infantry fast enough to
avoid being shot to pieces.

manner. Having thus proven that there was no 'hair-trigger situation' and the shooting was totally deliberate, then providing a deliberate shooting was justified, the shooter is protected from legal action. This is a rather sad situation, but there has been real concern about it at times – sufficiently so that double-action-only revolvers with no external hammer proved a popular home-defence purchase. Firearms design thus does not only follow technological and tactical influences, it is also driven by social factors.

## Worldwide Revolvers

The latter part of the nineteenth century was characterized by exploration, colonialism and expansion into territories claimed by local groups who were usually – but not always – less well armed than the new arrivals. The so-called 'gunfighter era' of the American West existed for a fairly short time – 50 years at most – and although the movie industry has made it seem that it was nothing but an endless exchange of bullets, the reality was somewhat different.

Fast-draw gunfights out in the street at noon, and shootouts of the OK Corral sort, were in fact exceedingly rare. Range wars and disputes between landowners or cattle ranchers, and fights between native people and settlers, were also less common than popular conception might suggest. However, there was a real need for personal firearms to defend life and property in a fairly wild and lawless time and region. The repeating firearm meant that an individual lawman or rancher was not powerless against a group, and may have contributed to reducing the level of violence.

At the same time as the West was being won, Europe was in a state of upheaval. The nation of Italy was forming – not without conflict – and the Ottoman Empire was in decline. A series of European wars in the 1860s led up to the Franco–Prussian War of 1870–71. This era was significant as a transition period between the 'old style' of warfare and the new. Breech loading firearms, primitive machinegun-like weapons and the use of railways for troop and supply movement were changing the face of warfare.

Traditional cavalry forces were by this time obsolete, unable to get into range with sword or lance before being shot to pieces. Traditions die hard,

**REMINGTON M1875**
**COUNTRY OF ORIGIN**
United States
**DATE**
1875
**CALIBRE**
11.2mm (.44in)
**WEIGHT**
1.2kg (2.6lb)
**OVERALL LENGTH**
330mm (13in)
**FEED/MAGAZINE**
6-shot revolver
**RANGE**
8m (8.75yds)

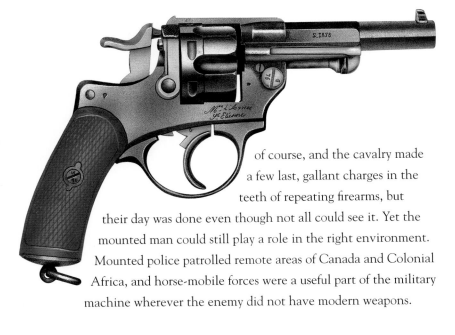

## CHAMELOT-DELVIGNE 1874

COUNTRY OF ORIGIN
Belgium
DATE
1874
CALIBRE
10.4mm (.4in)
WEIGHT
1.13kg (2.5lb)
OVERALL LENGTH
284mm (11.18in)
FEED/MAGAZINE
6-shot revolver
RANGE:
6m (6.56yds)

of course, and the cavalry made a few last, gallant charges in the teeth of repeating firearms, but their day was done even though not all could see it. Yet the mounted man could still play a role in the right environment. Mounted police patrolled remote areas of Canada and Colonial Africa, and horse-mobile forces were a useful part of the military machine wherever the enemy did not have modern weapons.

### Empire Builders

This was the age of colonial empires, in which small garrisons or modest response forces had to battle much larger armies. In some parts of the world a few mounted patrols or an armoured cruiser somewhere offshore were the only forces available, and they had to deal with whatever happened with little prospect of backup. Never had personal firepower mattered so much as to the horsemen of those patrols, the ratings of a naval landing party or the members of an expedition seeking treasure or knowledge. Those that could provided themselves with the best weapons available. Many military personnel purchased the latest or most fashionable revolver to back up or

## BODEO REVOLVER

COUNTRY OF ORIGIN
Italy
DATE
1889
CALIBRE
10.35mm (.4in)
WEIGHT
.91kg (2lb)
OVERALL LENGTH
235mm (9.25in)
FEED/MAGAZINE
6-shot revolver
RANGE
20m (21.87yds)

replace their service weapon. The gun market flourished, and produced some very interesting designs. Some of these perhaps deserved more recognition than they received; others were flawed from the outset.

Long a competitor of Colt, Remington fielded a .44 calibre single-action six-shot revolver designated M1875 in that year. An aesthetically pleasing and powerful weapon, the M1875 was intended to compete for U.S. military contracts but achieved few sales even though a .45 variant was available as a direct competitor to Colt's M1873. Some overseas sales were made, notably to Egypt and Mexico, but large-scale military contracts did not appear.

Two years earlier, the Belgian Chamelot-Delvigne revolver entered the European marketplace. The 1873 and 1874 models were taken into French service, making the French military one of the first to adopt repeating firearms of any sort. The Chamelot-Delvigne was a double-action revolver, built very tough and well suited to the rigours of military service in most ways. However, its 11mm (.43in) cartridge was underpowered and its trigger pull very heavy. Despite this the Chamelot-Delvigne remained a popular

## REMINGTON DERRINGER
COUNTRY OF ORIGIN
United States
DATE
1850
CALIBRE
10.4mm (.4in)
WEIGHT
.34kg (.75lb)
OVERALL LENGTH
121mm (14.76in)
FEED/MAGAZINE
1 shot per barrel
RANGE
3m (3.28yds)

## NAGANT M1895
COUNTRY OF ORIGIN
Russia
DATE
1895
CALIBRE
7.62mm (.3in)
WEIGHT
.79kg (1.75lb)
OVERALL LENGTH
229mm (9in)
FEED/MAGAZINE
7-shot revolver
RANGE
20m (21.87yds)

civilian and police weapon in Europe, and many came out of reserve in World War I. Its design influenced a number of other weapons, including the Italian-designed Bodeo Model 1889. This heavy-framed revolver was used by Italian and Spanish forces, with one variant having an unguarded folding trigger. The Bodeo revolver, with or without trigger guard, has a quintessentially 'late-nineteenth-century military pistol' look about it that is echoed in many similar weapons of the era.

Another Belgian design was created by Leon and Emile Nagant for Russian service. Their M1895 revolver was built around a custom cartridge, which was not uncommon at the time. It incorporated a device to push the cylinder forward when the hammer was cocked, creating a gas-tight seal between the barrel and chamber. Most revolvers have a small gap here, allowing some gas to escape and making it impossible to use a suppressor. This innovation did not achieve widespread popularity and was not included on Nagant revolvers

BELOW: Although it was clear by the time of the Austro-Prussian War (1866) that firearms offered the user a decisive advantage, the cavalry of most nations tried to find justification to cling to their traditional weapons.

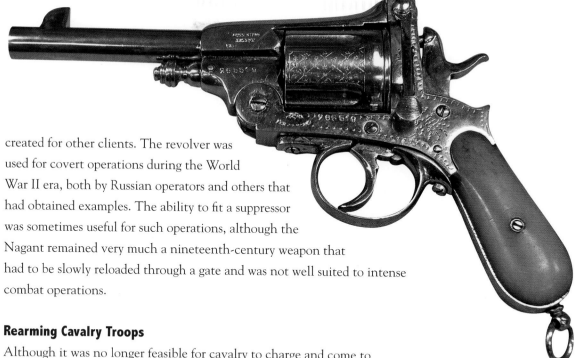

created for other clients. The revolver was
used for covert operations during the World
War II era, both by Russian operators and others that
had obtained examples. The ability to fit a suppressor
was sometimes useful for such operations, although the
Nagant remained very much a nineteenth-century weapon that
had to be slowly reloaded through a gate and was not well suited to intense
combat operations.

## Rearming Cavalry Troops

Although it was no longer feasible for cavalry to charge and come to
handstrokes, many nations retained large forces of cavalry as a traditional
status symbol, and attempts were made to render them as capable as possible.
Conversion to a sort of carbine-armed mounted infantry offered the best
chance of survival for cavalrymen personally and for the arm in general, but
this was not very prestigious and the move was resisted in all nations. On
the other hand the provision of a good revolver was considered an excellent
idea, bringing cavalry somewhat closer to the modern era.

In Austro-Hungary, the firm Gasser produced a revolver intended for
cavalry use, which was adopted by other arms and private users as well.
It was built around an 11mm (.43in) cartridge that had originally been
developed for carbines, and incorporated an automatic ejection system. This
took the form of a 'star plate' at the rear of the cylinder that was pushed
outwards when the revolver's barrel was tipped down. Done gently, this
ejects the cartridges slightly out of the weapon, allowing them to be picked
out for replacement or to make the weapon safe. If the barrel is jerked down
more vigorously, all rounds in the gun are dramatically scattered out of the
weapon, leaving it clear for reloading. The author has shot with a weapon of
this type and firmly believes that the world needs more top-break revolvers.
A modern side-swinging cylinder design may produce a stronger frame but
the top-break action is far more pleasing to use!

## GASSER MONTENEGRIN

**COUNTRY OF ORIGIN**
Austro-Hungary
**DATE**
1870
**CALIBRE**
11.2mm (.44in)
**WEIGHT**
1.3kg (2.9lb)
**OVERALL LENGTH**
185mm (7.28in)
**FEED/MAGAZINE**
5-shot revolver
**RANGE**
20m (21.87yds)

## GASSER REVOLVER
**COUNTRY OF ORIGIN**
Austro-Hungary
**DATE**
1898
**CALIBRE**
8mm (.31in)
**WEIGHT**
.85kg (1.81lb)
**OVERALL LENGTH**
225mm (8.86in)
**FEED/MAGAZINE**
8-shot revolver
**RANGE**
20m (21.87yds)

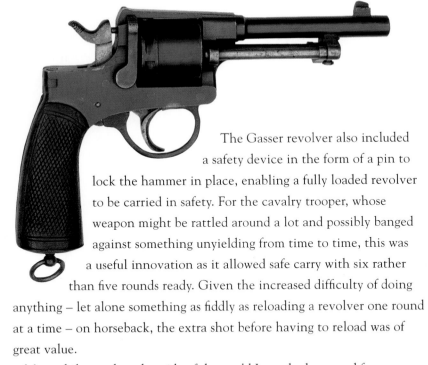

The Gasser revolver also included a safety device in the form of a pin to lock the hammer in place, enabling a fully loaded revolver to be carried in safety. For the cavalry trooper, whose weapon might be rattled around a lot and possibly banged against something unyielding from time to time, this was a useful innovation as it allowed safe carry with six rather than five rounds ready. Given the increased difficulty of doing anything – let alone something as fiddly as reloading a revolver one round at a time – on horseback, the extra shot before having to reload was of great value.

Meanwhile, on the other side of the world Japan had emerged from centuries of isolation. This had included a general rejection of firearms in favour of swords, and as Japan industrialized and began to seek a place on the world stage, modern weapons became a priority. Among these was a sidearm for military officers. The resulting weapon was named Meiji Type 26, referring to the 26th year after the restoration of Imperial rule to Japan under the Meiji Emperor. Many Japanese firearms used this naming/dating system.

## MEIJI TYPE 26
**COUNTRY OF ORIGIN**
Japan
**DATE**
1893
**CALIBRE**
9mm (.35in)
**WEIGHT**
.91kg (2lb)
**OVERALL LENGTH**
235mm (2.25in)
**FEED/MAGAZINE**
6-shot revolver
**RANGE**
20m (21.87yds)

The Type 26 looks similar to many contemporary handguns in terms of general lines, and indeed it seems visually more modern than many. However, it was not a particularly effective weapon. Its double-action-only mechanism suffered from an extremely heavy trigger pull, making any kind of accuracy difficult. The 9mm (.35in) cartridge it fired was also underpowered and less than effective in action. Despite this, the Type 26 was a lot better than what it replaced, being the first cartridge handgun available to Japanese forces, and it saw action well into the twentieth century even though it was officially replaced by equally disappointing semi-automatics.

## Webley Revolvers

The quintessential top-break revolver of the era was produced by the British firm Webley and became known as simply the Webley Revolver, although it was not the firm's first effort. The Webley-Pryse five-shot revolver, chambered for a large .476 cartridge, was well regarded by military and civilian users during the colonial period of the 1870s.

An army officer or explorer might find himself faced with one or more warriors armed with hand weapons. These warriors were almost without exception fiercely brave and usually in top physical condition. Unafraid of firearms or any other weapon, the only way to stop, say, a Zulu warrior was to hurt him badly enough so that he could no longer fight. A lesser wound, even one that might later prove fatal, was not always enough.

**WEBLEY PRYSE**
**COUNTRY OF ORIGIN**
United Kingdom
**DATE**
1876
**CALIBRE**
12mm (.476in)
**WEIGHT**
.7kg (1.5lb)
**OVERALL LENGTH**
215mm (8.5in)
**FEED/MAGAZINE**
5-shot revolver
**RANGE**
20m (21.87yds)

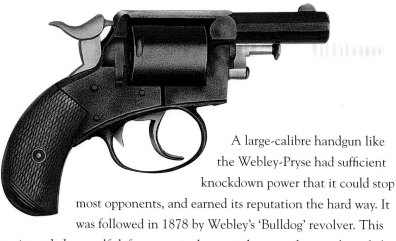

A large-calibre handgun like the Webley-Pryse had sufficient knockdown power that it could stop most opponents, and earned its reputation the hard way. It was followed in 1878 by Webley's 'Bulldog' revolver. This was intended as a self-defence gun to be carried in a pocket until needed. It could be brought into action quickly with a double-action shot, and was initially chambered for various hard-hitting large-calibre rounds. Smaller calibre versions later appeared, not least because shooting a .442 round out of a small revolver could be unpleasant.

The Bulldog was not the first double-action Webley – that was the RIC (Royal Irish Constabulary) model adopted in 1868. The Webley RIC was normally chambered for .442, although some examples were made available in other calibres. The RIC was not exclusively used by the Irish police – a pair were reputedly carried by George Armstrong Custer at the battle of Little Bighorn. Since the RIC was a gate loading revolver in the same general calibre as the Colt M1873 Single Action Army, and offered double-action shooting in addition, it may have been seen by some as a good alternative to the army's new standard pistol.

The definitive Webley appeared in 1887, and proceeded through several models to the Mk VI that was introduced in 1915. Examples remained in service with British forces well after World War II, with some reputedly still in reserve into the 1970s. By this time the Webley's official replacement, the Enfield No.2 Revolver, had also been supplanted by semi-automatic pistols. The Enfield No.2 is sometimes confused with the much earlier Enfield Mk 1 and Mk 2, which served with the British Army from 1880. Chambered in .476, these revolvers did not live up to expectations. Notably, they wore out quickly and their interesting but complex ejection system – intended to release spent ammunition and retain live rounds – proved problematic in the field. The Webley was brought in as a replacement and proved altogether more satisfactory.

## WEBLEY BULLDOG
**COUNTRY OF ORIGIN**
United Kingdom
**DATE**
1878
**CALIBRE**
8.1mm (.32in)
**WEIGHT**
.31kg (.7lb)
**OVERALL LENGTH**
140mm (5.5in)
**FEED/MAGAZINE**
5-shot revolver
**RANGE**
15m (16.4yds)

LEFT: The painting 'Saving The Queen's Colours' presents a dramatized and somewhat inaccurate version of an incident just after the battle of Isandlhwana in 1879. Typically for military paintings of the era, swords and pistols are given equal prominence.

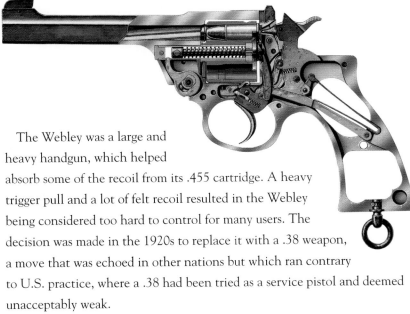

## ENFIELD MKI
**COUNTRY OF ORIGIN**
United Kingdom
**DATE**
1920
**CALIBRE**
9.6mm (.38in)
**WEIGHT**
.82kg (1.8lb)
**OVERALL LENGTH**
254mm (10in)
**FEED/MAGAZINE**
6-shot revolver
**RANGE**
20m (21.87yds)

The Webley was a large and heavy handgun, which helped absorb some of the recoil from its .455 cartridge. A heavy trigger pull and a lot of felt recoil resulted in the Webley being considered too hard to control for many users. The decision was made in the 1920s to replace it with a .38 weapon, a move that was echoed in other nations but which ran contrary to U.S. practice, where a .38 had been tried as a service pistol and deemed unacceptably weak.

The Webley, especially the Mk VI, became a symbol of the British armed forces in the first half of the twentieth century, serving from the Boer War right through both world wars and in some cases well afterward. The decision to move to the lighter .38 revolver prompted Webley to put forward their Mk IV Service Revolver, chambered for .38/200in ammunition. This was essentially the same calibre as was being manufactured by Smith & Wesson at the time, but optimized for military use. Continuing the trend towards lighter handguns, .38/200in was replaced by the .38in Mk 2 round, which fired a lighter bullet.

## WEBLEY MK1
**COUNTRY OF ORIGIN**
United Kingdom
**DATE**
1912
**CALIBRE**
11.55mm (.455in)
**WEIGHT**
.68kg (1.5lb)
**OVERALL LENGTH**
216mm (8.5in)
**FEED/MAGAZINE**
6-round magazine
**RANGE**
20m (21.87yds)

The Webley .38 was not a total success, and the British Government instead adopted an Enfield design that was visually similar. However, with Enfield unable to produce enough weapons for wartime use, Webley .38s were taken into British Army service for World War II.

## Advancing Technology

At the end of the nineteenth century, smokeless propellants were still a relatively new technology. It was understood that the same quantity of the new propellants produced a greater chamber pressure and therefore threw a projectile harder and faster, but not all of the possibilities inherent in this were grasped at once. In some cases, taking advantage of the new technology was not feasible. Many handguns were converted or had evolved from cap-and-ball designs and could not withstand the increased chamber pressures of the smokeless propellants. This remains a problem today – antique guns often cannot handle modern ammunition.

As experimentation continued and understanding increased, a new generation of ammunition, and guns to fire it, began to emerge. Smith & Wesson pioneered several new cartridges along with guns to fire them. Among these was the 1896-vintage .32 Ejector Model, also known as .32 First Model. This weapon shot the .32 Long cartridge created by Smith & Wesson. This longer cartridge could contain more propellant, producing a greater muzzle velocity with the same projectile and increasing the potency of a small-calibre handgun. The .32 Ejector Model had another important feature in the use of a swing-out cylinder.

## Side-swinging Cylinder Designs

Smith & Wesson had favoured top-break revolvers for some years, but now introduced a cylinder that was hinged to the side. Rather than unlocking the front end of the gun and pulling it down, the user operated a catch to unlatch the cylinder and pushed it out to the side on a pivot. The ejector rod, positioned below the barrel, was then used to eject spent cartridges. Early weapons of this type, with unshrouded ejector rods, look flimsy to modern eyes but the system worked well enough to be adopted on other handguns including the 1899 Hand Ejector model. This was designed to fire .38 Long Colt, but was adapted to use the new, heavier, .38 Special round developed by Smith & Wesson. The 1899 Hand Ejector became known as the Military and Police model after a large-scale order by the U.S. Government.

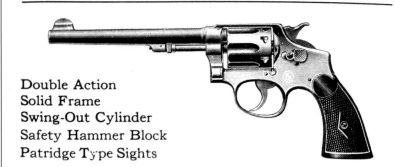

# Military and Police
## SQUARE BUTT
### NEW PATENT SAFETY HAMMER BLOCK

Double Action
Solid Frame
Swing-Out Cylinder
Safety Hammer Block
Patridge Type Sights

## Description

| | |
|---|---|
| Calibre | .38 |
| Lengths of Barrel | 4, 5, and 6 inches |
| Lengths over all | 4 inch Bbl., 9⅛ inches; 5 inch Bbl., 10⅛ inches; 6 inch Bbl., 11⅛ inches |
| Finish | Nickel Plated or Blued |
| Stock | Walnut, Checked |
| Weight | 4 inch Bbl., 29¼ ounces; 5 inch Bbl., 30 ounces; 6 inch Bbl., 31 ounces |
| Ammunition | .38 Smith & Wesson Special Cartridge |
| Penetration | Eight and one-half ⅞ inch Pine Boards |
| Number of Shots | Six |

This arm can be furnished with Target Sights in the 6 inch length, Blued Finish only, at an additional cost.

**Nickel Plated Finish Same Price as Blued Finish**

RIGHT: The Smith & Wesson Model 10, also known as the 'Military and Police' model, was one of the most popular revolvers of all time. An advanced design at its introduction, the Model 10 remained competitive against much later designs.

The decision to move to the more potent .38 Special round was prompted by concerns over a lack of stopping power demonstrated by handguns chambered for .38 Long Colt. U.S. troops serving in the Philippines found that their .38s would not stop a tribesman intent on attacking them with a machete, and wanted something more effective. Although the .38 Special round performed better it was not enough to convince the U.S. military to stick with it, and eventually a move back to .45 occurred.

In the meantime, the .38 Hand Ejector achieved massive popularity with the civilian and law enforcement market, becoming known as the Model 10. Its cartridge was considered perfectly adequate by many police departments,

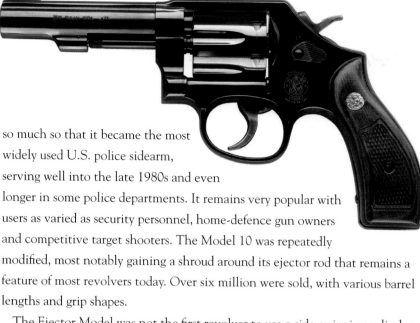

so much so that it became the most widely used U.S. police sidearm, serving well into the late 1980s and even longer in some police departments. It remains very popular with users as varied as security personnel, home-defence gun owners and competitive target shooters. The Model 10 was repeatedly modified, most notably gaining a shroud around its ejector rod that remains a feature of most revolvers today. Over six million were sold, with various barrel lengths and grip shapes.

The Ejector Model was not the first revolver to use a side-swinging cylinder. This was the Colt M1889, which was developed for the U.S. military. It was not a great commercial success but did achieve reasonable sales in the military, naval and civilian markets. The main drawback with the pistol was its cylinder, which could come out of alignment. Since a perfect line-up between barrel and cylinder is essential, this was a serious flaw.

Other manufacturers produced side-swinging cylinder revolvers, not all of them particularly successful. The French Modele 1892 was adopted for service with the military and law enforcement agencies, and became

## SMITH &WESSON MODEL 10
**COUNTRY OF ORIGIN**
Austro-Hungary
**DATE**
1899
**CALIBRE**
9.65mm (.38in)
**WEIGHT**
1 kg (2.2lb)
**OVERALL LENGTH**
236mm (9.3in)
**FEED/MAGAZINE**
6-shot revolver
**RANGE**
20m (21.87yds)

## MODELE 1892
**COUNTRY OF ORIGIN**
France
**DATE**
1892
**CALIBRE**
8mm (.314in)
**WEIGHT**
.94kg (2.1lb)
**OVERALL LENGTH**
240mm (9.44in)
**FEED/MAGAZINE**
6-shot revolver
**RANGE**
20m (21.87yds)

associated with gun designer Nicholas Lebel despite no real evidence that he had anything to do with its development. The 'Lebel Revolver' was a workmanlike handgun but fired a weak 8mm (.314in) cartridge. Despite this it remained in service with French police until the mid-twentieth century.

### Experimental Concepts

Other manufacturers were experimenting with new concepts as well. The Iver Johnson company incorporated a transfer-bar safety mechanism on their otherwise fairly conventional top-break revolvers. The firm had a brief flirtation with side-swinging cylinders before going back to a more traditional loading method, but retained the safety device. Iver Johnson pistols were, rather confusingly to modern readers, marketed as 'safety automatics'. They were in no way an automatic or semi-automatic pistol in the modern sense; the term referred to the automatic ejection of spent cases when the barrel was tipped down. The 'safety' part of the name implies that these revolvers had a manual safety catch, but in fact that is not the case. Instead, they incorporated a device that moved an interbar (or transfer bar) between hammer and firing pin when the hammer was cocked. With the interbar present, force from the hammer was transmitted to the firing pin and the weapon would discharge. Without it, no matter how hard the hammer was bashed it would spend its force on empty air.

The interbar safety device meant that a revolver could be carried with all chambers loaded and the hammer down, and it has become a standard feature of revolver design. Despite this, there is a persistent myth that a revolver can only be carried safely with one chamber empty. This is perhaps

## IVER JOHNSON
**COUNTRY OF ORIGIN**
United States
**DATE**
1894
**CALIBRE**
8.1mm (.32in)
**WEIGHT**
.59kg (1.3lb)
**OVERALL LENGTH**
197mm (7.75in)
**FEED/MAGAZINE**
6-shot revolver
**RANGE**
20m (21.87yds)

## IVER JOHNSON 2
**COUNTRY OF ORIGIN**
United States
**DATE**
1896
**CALIBRE**
8.1mm (.32in)
**WEIGHT**
.59kg (1.3lb)
**OVERALL LENGTH**
197mm (7.75in)
**FEED/MAGAZINE**
6-shot revolver
**RANGE**
20m (21.87yds)

partially due to a practice among some law enforcement and security personnel of carrying the weapon with the next chamber that would be rotated under the hammer empty. The first chamber to be fired is not the one under the hammer; it is the next one along. If the officer were to be disarmed and his own gun turned on him, the assailant's first shot would fail and give him a chance to do something desperate. Knowing this might be the edge needed to survive a particularly bad situation. It is unclear exactly how prevalent this practice ever was, but the concept has been floating around long enough that it may have been confused with the earlier means of safe carry.

The reality of the matter is that modern revolvers (i.e. most constructed after 1900) and even many replicas of classic pre-1900 guns have an interbar and are safe to carry with a round under the hammer. Even so, many Cowboy Action Shooting competitions stipulate that sixguns be loaded with only five rounds to preserve historical authenticity.

Some of the guns to emerge in the last years of the nineteenth century were driven by the peculiar social climate at the time. It is notable that the Iver Johnson company produced bicycles as well as guns. Cycling underwent an explosion of popularity in the late 1800s, and in some cases this created a rather specialist market for firearms. Apparently, late-nineteenth-century cyclists were plagued by dogs that would chase and bite them as they pedalled by. The obvious answer was to shoot the dogs as they approached, but lethal force was not necessarily warranted. The French gunsmith

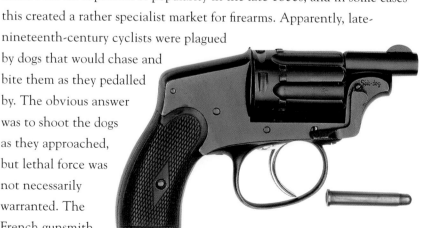

## GALAND VELO DOG
**COUNTRY OF ORIGIN**
France
**DATE**
1894
**CALIBRE**
5.75mm (.22in)
**WEIGHT**
Not known
**OVERALL LENGTH**
Not known
**FEED/MAGAZINE**
6-shot revolver
**RANGE**
15m (16.4yds)

Charles Françoise Galand marketed a small revolver that could be handily carried by a cyclist and deployed when ill intentioned canines presented themselves. The 'Velo Dog' revolver could be loaded with a non-lethal 'dust' round that would hopefully discourage the animal before any biting could occur.

## Personal Protection

Other manufacturers were quick to exploit this new marketplace, producing a range of Velo-Dog revolvers. Standard features were small size and very low calibre, with no external hammer to snag on the beleaguered cyclist's clothing as he drew the weapon. Other variants on the theme include specialist pistols intended for use against snakes, and these are still manufactured. The cyclist's anti-dog gun, however, was an artefact of its time and has faded from the scene. Another artefact of the era was the 'Apache' pistol. Readers of nineteenth-century self-defence manuals might be puzzled to find references to being set upon by Apaches while on the streets of Paris, but this term applied to certain street gangs of the era who were given the name due to its perceived savage-warrior connotations.

The device combined a pepperbox pistol, a knuckleduster and a small knife. Apache pistols could serve as hand weapons and also deliver a sneaky shot in the middle of a fight. In practice, they were flimsy, clumsy and less effective than any of their component parts might have been on their own.

Only slightly less practical than the Apache pistol was another ingenious adaptation of firearms technology. Apparently, along with dogs that liked to eat cyclists and street gangs armed with excessively complex pistol/knife/knuckleduster weapons, the gentleman-about-town also risked being garrotted by nefarious persons, for reasons unknown. One sure defence against garrotting – so the marketing materials claimed – was a belt that held a pistol cartridge aimed directly backward in a plate that rode at the small of the user's back. When the garrotting attack occurred,

## APACHE PISTOL
**COUNTRY OF ORIGIN**
France
**DATE**
1869
**CALIBRE**
7mm (.275in)
**WEIGHT**
.62kg (.8lb)
**OVERALL LENGTH**
200mm (7.8in)
**FEED/MAGAZINE**
Detachable cylinder/Pepperbox
**RANGE:**
3m (3.28yds)

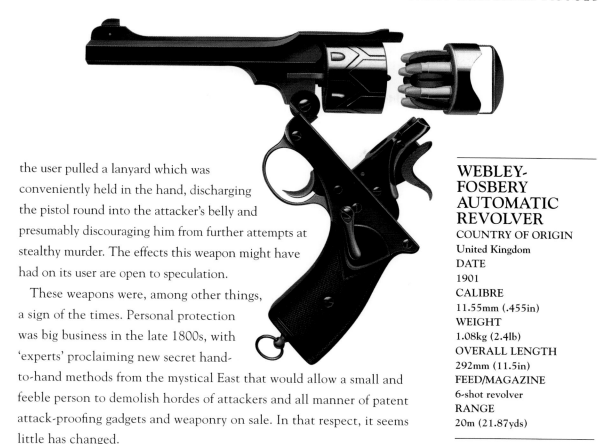

the user pulled a lanyard which was conveniently held in the hand, discharging the pistol round into the attacker's belly and presumably discouraging him from further attempts at stealthy murder. The effects this weapon might have had on its user are open to speculation.

These weapons were, among other things, a sign of the times. Personal protection was big business in the late 1800s, with 'experts' proclaiming new secret hand-to-hand methods from the mystical East that would allow a small and feeble person to demolish hordes of attackers and all manner of patent attack-proofing gadgets and weaponry on sale. In that respect, it seems little has changed.

Less fanciful were attempts to advance revolver technology by using recoil to revolve the cylinder. The 1901 Webley-Fosbery Automatic Revolver was

## WEBLEY-FOSBERY AUTOMATIC REVOLVER

**COUNTRY OF ORIGIN**
United Kingdom
**DATE**
1901
**CALIBRE**
11.55mm (.455in)
**WEIGHT**
1.08kg (2.4lb)
**OVERALL LENGTH**
292mm (11.5in)
**FEED/MAGAZINE**
6-shot revolver
**RANGE**
20m (21.87yds)

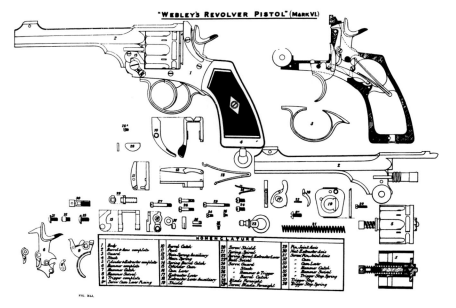

LEFT: For all their simplicity of use, revolvers are complex mechanisms. The lockwork required to revolve the cylinder must be machined with great precision and properly assembled to avoid malfunctions.

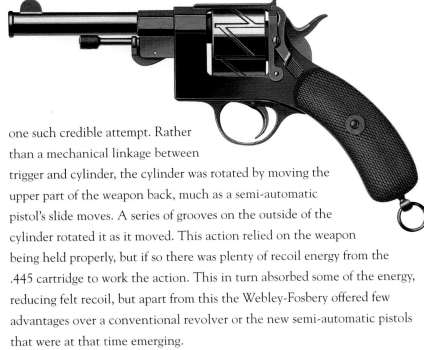

## MAUSER ZIG-ZAG
**COUNTRY OF ORIGIN**
Germany
**DATE**
1878
**CALIBRE**
10.9mm (.42in)
**WEIGHT**
1.19kg (2.63lb)
**OVERALL LENGTH**
298mm (11.75in)
**FEED/MAGAZINE**
Six-shot revolver
**RANGE**
20m (21.87yds)

one such credible attempt. Rather than a mechanical linkage between trigger and cylinder, the cylinder was rotated by moving the upper part of the weapon back, much as a semi-automatic pistol's slide moves. A series of grooves on the outside of the cylinder rotated it as it moved. This action relied on the weapon being held properly, but if so there was plenty of recoil energy from the .445 cartridge to work the action. This in turn absorbed some of the energy, reducing felt recoil, but apart from this the Webley-Fosbery offered few advantages over a conventional revolver or the new semi-automatic pistols that were at that time emerging.

The Webley-Fosbery, unusually for a revolver, had a manual safety catch, but in most other ways functioned like a Webley top-break revolver. It had few advantages over one and was in addition mechanically complex. Although privately bought by some military personnel, the Webley-Fosbery did not achieve any real success. Six-shot versions chambered for .455 and an eight-shot variant in .38 remained on offer for several years, largely because the company made more of them than could be sold.

The idea for the Webley-Fosbery's unusual mechanism may have been inspired by the earlier Mauser Zig-Zag, a solid-frame revolver loaded through

## LAUMANN 1892
**COUNTRY OF ORIGIN**
Germany
**DATE**
1892
**CALIBRE**
7.8mm (.307in)
**WEIGHT**
1.13kg (2.5lb)
**OVERALL LENGTH**
254mm (10in)
**FEED/MAGAZINE**
5-round internal magazine
**RANGE**
30m (32.80yds)

a gate. Rather than the more usual pawl and ratchet system, the Zig-Zag used a stud on the mainspring carrier, engaging with the zig-zag grooves on the cylinder that gained the weapon its name to push the cylinder around. The revolver was introduced in 1878, although a new version, this time with a tip-up action for loading, was introduced in 1886; however, the weapon did not catch on. Like the later Webley-Fosbery, the innovative design offered neither the user nor the manufacturer sufficient additional benefits to be successful in the marketplace, and the concept has faded away.

## Early Self-loading Pistols

The late nineteenth century was a time of great experimentation in which almost anything seemed possible. It was also an era when most new devices were mechanical or had large mechanical parts, enabling a certain amount of amateurish tinkering without huge development budgets. In this environment numerous new ideas were set forth, some of them quite unpromising. It is hard to imagine anyone considering that a crude steam-powered quadricycle was a technology worth pursuing, and likewise some of the prototype weapons that emerged in those years should have served only to show what could not (or perhaps should not) be done.

**SCHONBERGER**
COUNTRY OF ORIGIN
Germany
DATE
1892
CALIBRE
8mm (.314in)
WEIGHT
Not known
OVERALL LENGTH
Not known
FEED/MAGAZINE
5-round internal magazine
RANGE
30m (32.80yds)

**WEBLEY & SCOTT MKVI**
COUNTRY OF ORIGIN
United Kingdom
DATE
1915
CALIBRE
11.55mm (.455in)
WEIGHT
1.1kg (2.425lb)
OVERALL LENGTH
297mm (11in)
FEED/MAGAZINE
6-shot revolver
RANGE
20m (21.87yds)

RIGHT: **This carrying case contains a Borchardt C93 pistol, its delicate mechanism further protected from the elements and damage by a cover, plus tools and accessories.**

The first ancestors of the modern semi-automatic pistol that emerged in the 1890s were not particularly effective and certainly offered no real advantage over a good revolver. Clunky and overcomplex, many designs had no more firepower than a revolver and most malfunctioned far less often. The very first was patented in 1892 by Joseph Laumann. Chambered for a weak 7.8mm (.307in) round, the Laumann pistol was recoil-operated and self reloading from its five-round magazine. This was located in front of the trigger assembly, creating a gun that was longer than a revolver and held less ammunition – just five underpowered rounds. The Laumann pistol did, however, demonstrate that a workable recoil operated pistol was possible.

It was followed by a somewhat similar but more commercially successful design manufactured by Steyr – the Schonberger pistol. This used a reciprocating bolt inside a fixed frame rather than the slide more familiar today, and carried its ammunition in an internal magazine loaded through an open action from a stripper clip. Loading an internal magazine in this manner is fairly rapid with some practice. Rounds are prepared on a slightly curved strip that grips the rim at their base. With the pistol's action open, the clip is seated on the weapon's guide and the top round is pushed firmly down with the thumb. It is important to push the rounds right into the magazine, far enough that the top round comes back up a little when

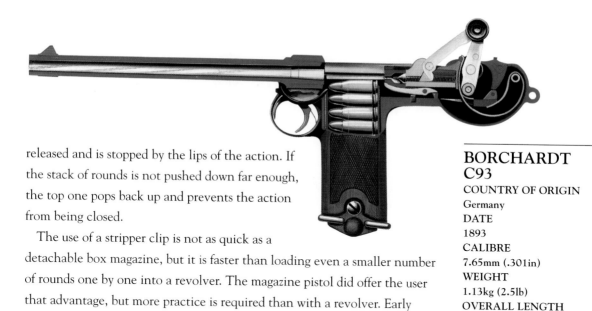

released and is stopped by the lips of the action. If the stack of rounds is not pushed down far enough, the top one pops back up and prevents the action from being closed.

The use of a stripper clip is not as quick as a detachable box magazine, but it is faster than loading even a smaller number of rounds one by one into a revolver. The magazine pistol did offer the user that advantage, but more practice is required than with a revolver. Early semi-automatics were also complex to use – possibly too complex for many potential purchasers.

## Pistol Innovations

Nevertheless the experiments continued. In 1893, Borchardt marketed a pistol based on the toggle-locking system used in the contemporary Maxim machinegun. This required a lot of mechanical activity to take place outside the weapon, and made it both bulky and vulnerable to dust and dirt. The Borchardt pistol did incorporate one important new feature – rather than the magazine being in front of the trigger assembly, and fixed, it was a detachable box loaded through the handgrip. This offered two key advantages. One was

## BORCHARDT
### C93
**COUNTRY OF ORIGIN**
Germany
**DATE**
1893
**CALIBRE**
7.65mm (.301in)
**WEIGHT**
1.13kg (2.5lb)
**OVERALL LENGTH**
355mm (14in)
**FEED/MAGAZINE**
8-round magazine
**RANGE**
30m (32.80yds)

## MARS PISTOL
**COUNTRY OF ORIGIN**
United Kingdom
**DATE**
1898
**CALIBRE**
.360 Mars (also referred to as 9mm Mars) or 8.5mm or .45 Long or .45 Short
**WEIGHT**
1.36kg (3lb)
**OVERALL LENGTH**
320mm (12.25in)
**FEED/MAGAZINE**
8 or 10-round magazine
**RANGE**
20m (21.9yds)

## BERGMANN 1896

**COUNTRY OF ORIGIN**
Germany
**DATE**
1896
**CALIBRE**
7.63mm (.3in)
**WEIGHT**
1.13kg (2.5lb)
**OVERALL LENGTH**
254mm (10in)
**FEED/MAGAZINE**
5-round internal magazine
**RANGE**
30m (32.80yds)

the ability to carry several pre-loaded magazines, and the other was ease of reloading. Unless severely impaired in some way, most people can find one hand with the other even under grave stress. With the gun in one hand and a magazine in the other, reloading was little more than a process of bringing the two together; this system has of course become standard.

Another grip-loading semi-automatic handgun was the Mars pistol designed by Hugh Gabbet-Fairfax and manufactured by Webley and Scott. In production – albeit in tiny numbers – from 1898, the Mars pistol used a rotating bolt long-recoil action and self-reloaded itself. Not that it mattered – according to the officer in charge of evaluating the Mars for British naval issue, nobody who fired it ever wanted to repeat the experience. The Mars pistol was available with a variety of chamberings, all for overpowered cartridges that produced excessive recoil and an enormous muzzle flash. The mechanical activity going on inside the weapon as it recoiled might have been disconcerting, but the user was probably distracted by the hot spent case being ejected directly to the rear – and into the face. Coupled with heavy trigger pull, excessive weight and a strange system whereby the bolt

## BERGMANN SIMPLEX

**COUNTRY OF ORIGIN**
Germany
**DATE**
1897
**CALIBRE**
8mm (.314in)
**WEIGHT**
.59kg (1.3lb)
**OVERALL LENGTH**
190mm (7.5in)
**FEED/MAGAZINE**
6- or 8-round magazine
**RANGE**
30m (32.80yds)

was held to the rear until the trigger was released, then ran forward to chamber a new round, this ensured that the Mars, or 'Webley-Mars', pistol was not a success despite being at the time the world's most powerful handgun.

### Bergmann Handguns

Another pistol with a similar name was developed by Theodor Bergmann, one of a series of Bergmann handguns. The Bergmann Mars was recoil operated and had its magazine in front of the trigger assembly. It used a 9x23mm (.35x.90in) cartridge and was sufficiently effective that the Spanish military ordered a significant quantity, designating the associated cartridge the 9mm Largo. The Bergmann Mars was not Bergmann's first handgun – that was designed for him by Hugo Schmeisser, who would later find fame in the field of light automatic weapons. The Bergmann 1896 pistol was typical of the experimental weapons of the time – it had some promising features but also a few flaws. Among these was an ejection system that bounced the spent round off the next round in the magazine. This feature was dropped on the 1897 Bergmann Simplex model and subsequent designs.

Bergmann pistols were adopted for military service, notably in Denmark, and were marketed under the name Bayard or Bergmann-Bayard. New versions and variants appeared over time, despite an interruption in production during World War I, and Bergmann pistols remained in Danish military service until after World War II. The U.S. Army, by then firmly wedded to the idea of a .45 as its service pistol, trialled the Bergman-Bayard in that calibre but decided against adoption. Nevertheless, in the early twentieth century the Bergmann-Bayard was in service with several militaries and was privately purchased by officers of other countries.

The Steyr factory, which built the Schonberger pistol, also manufactured the Mannlicher self-loading pistol. This design used a delayed-blowback principle, whereby the action was driven rearward by recoil forces but slowed and delayed by a spring-and-cam system. Originally chambered for 8mm

### BERGMANN-BAYARD M 1910
**COUNTRY OF ORIGIN**
Germany
**DATE**
1910
**CALIBRE**
9mm (.35in)
**WEIGHT**
1.01kg (2.2lb)
**OVERALL LENGTH**
251mm (9.9in)
**FEED/MAGAZINE**
6-round magazine
**RANGE**
30m (32.80yds)

## MANNLICHER M1901/1903

**COUNTRY OF ORIGIN**
Austria
**DATE**
1901
**CALIBRE**
7.63mm (.3in)
**WEIGHT**
.94kg (2.15lb)
**OVERALL LENGTH**
239mm (9.4in)
**FEED/MAGAZINE**
8-round magazine
**RANGE**
30m (32.80yds)

(.31in) ammunition, the Mannlicher pistol was rechambered at the turn of the century to use 7.63mm (.3in) ammunition. Its eight-round magazine was reloaded using a stripper clip and could be unloaded by the use of a lever that removed the retaining lips.

The Mannlicher 1901 was preceded by an earlier design that used a blow-forward principle. Rather than the now-familiar concept of recoil pushing the action backwards, the Mannlicher M1894 used a rigid breech. The barrel assembly was 'blown forward' to open the action for reloading. This system has very rarely been used since. The Mannlicher pistols, and some of Bergmann's designs, are visually very similar to the C96 handgun produced by Mauser. This is perhaps the definitive early semi-automatic pistol, using a magazine in front of the trigger assembly that can hold six, 10 or 20 rounds depending on the configuration. Early C96 handguns had a fixed, integral magazine but later models used a detachable box, giving the user the option of reloading via a stripper clip or changing the magazine.

The C96 was chambered for 7.63mm (.3in) ammunition, which remained very popular among European firearms designers, but later in its career was also available in 9mm (.35in). Variously referred to as a 'broomhandle' or 'kuhfusspistole' (cow's foot pistol, named because of the shape of its grip), the Mauser was taken into service with the German armed forces and was a popular purchase elsewhere in the world. Future British Prime Minister Winston Churchill carried a Mauser during his military service, and found it effective in action. Although suffering from the same complexity and occasional 'fiddliness' of early semi-automatics, the Mauser C96 and its later variants was an effective combat weapon. Able to hold 10 rounds and to reload them faster than a revolver user could replace six in the cylinder, the Mauser was not only one of the iconic weapons of the nineteenth-twentieth-century transition period, it was also one of the most influential.

In an effort to widen the appeal of their handgun, Mauser made available a detachable stock that – supposedly – slots easily together with the pistol's

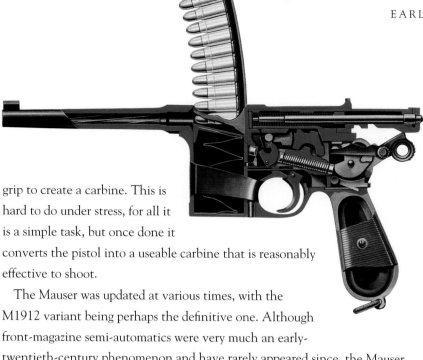

grip to create a carbine. This is
hard to do under stress, for all it
is a simple task, but once done it
converts the pistol into a useable carbine that is reasonably
effective to shoot.

The Mauser was updated at various times, with the
M1912 variant being perhaps the definitive one. Although
front-magazine semi-automatics were very much an early-
twentieth-century phenomenon and have rarely appeared since, the Mauser
was sufficiently effective to remain in German service – albeit long after
being officially replaced – until the end of World War II and was copied by
manufacturers worldwide. Numerous examples saw action in the Chinese
Civil War as late as 1947.

A 50-year combat career is remarkable for any weapon, and those that
achieve it tend to become classics. The Mauser 'Broomhandle' is one of those.
However, the era of the front-magazine semi-automatic pistol was a short
one. Loading through the grip proved far more efficient and ergonomically
effective, and most post-1900 semi-automatics followed this practice.

## MAUSER C96
**COUNTRY OF ORIGIN**
Germany
**DATE**
1896
**CALIBRE**
7.63mm (.3in)
**WEIGHT**
1.045kg (2.3lb)
**OVERALL LENGTH**
295mm (11.6in)
**FEED/MAGAZINE**
6- or 10-round internal
magazine
**RANGE**
30m (32.80yds)

## MAUSER 1912
**COUNTRY OF ORIGIN**
Germany
**DATE**
1912
**CALIBRE**
7.63mm (.3in)
**WEIGHT**
1.25kg (2.75lb)
**OVERALL LENGTH**
295mm (11.6in)
**FEED/MAGAZINE**
6- or 10-round magazine
**RANGE**
30m (32.80yds)

# The Great War Era

In the years leading up to World War I, political agitation was rife. Bolshevism was a powerful force in the politics of many countries, and in many cases politically motivated groups crossed the line into criminal operations, using robbery and extortion to fund their other activities. Some groups had a specific agenda, such as independence for a region or a government change in their home nation. Others were more general, opposing the establishment in whatever way they could in the hope of bringing about social change across the continent. Some, apparently, seemed to want anarchy for its own sake.

LEFT: During the early weeks of World War I, the mobility of cavalry forces enabled them to play an important part. Once the Western Front settled down into trench warfare, cavalry could contribute little.

## PARABELLUM '08 (LUGER)

COUNTRY OF ORIGIN
Germany
DATE
1908
CALIBRE
9mm (.35in) Parabellum
WEIGHT
.96kg (2.125lb)
OVERALL LENGTH
222mm (8.8in)
FEED/MAGAZINE
8-round magazine
RANGE
30m (32.8yds)

Many of these groups had access to modern firearms, including the new generation of self-loading pistols coming out of Europe. Perhaps the first time the general public became aware of the capabilities of these weapons was an incident in the winter of 1910/11 that became known as the Sidney Street Siege, or the battle of Stepney in London's East End. In December 1910 a gang of European robbers fired on unarmed police officers who tried to prevent a robbery, killing or wounding several of them. A manhunt led to a house in Sidney Street, where some members of the gang became cornered.

The London police, although present in large numbers, were armed with small 'Bulldog' revolvers while the robbers had a variety of semi-automatic pistols including Dreyse and Mauser weapons. Unable to approach the house due to the robbers' heavy firepower, the police received backup from rifle-armed troops. The robbers were surrounded and trapped in the house, which eventually caught fire and killed them. The incident sharply demonstrated the firepower advantages of semi-automatic weapons and may have prompted interest in them from police departments worldwide. However, occasional ill timed malfunctions delayed the move from tried-and-tested revolver technology to the new weapons in many areas.

One political group – the Serbian Black Hand – provided the spark that ignited the Great War by assassinating Archduke Franz Ferdinand of Austro-Hungary. War would likely have come sooner or later anyway, but this was the trigger incident. Once events were in motion, the web of alliances that dominated European politics ensured that the whole continent was quickly dragged into the conflict.

The militaries of the early twentieth century were a product of recent experiences, and were armed accordingly. Long-range marksmanship with rifles was the hallmark of a skilled infantry force, and had proven effective against both 'tribal' enemies and more modern forces that attempted to manoeuvre in the open. Despite this, the general expectation was for a war of manoeuvre with field battles forcing the enemy into retreat and ultimately surrender.

### Europe at War

The opening weeks of the Great War in fact unfolded much as expected, with the British and French armies driven into retreat. Defensive actions were fought in hasty positions that did not have time to ossify into the great trench systems of the later war, and mobile counterattacks were launched in nineteenth-century style. In some theatres, notably the Eastern Front,

the war retained this nineteenth-century character, with mobile forces of riflemen fighting for positions but not turning them into fortresses. Even cavalry were sometimes able to operate in their traditional style, charging with sabre and revolver. The war in the East remained fluid, but on the Western Front it bogged down into trench warfare.

This was largely due to the massive increase in personal firepower possessed by infantrymen. Even leaving aside the influence of machineguns, the bolt-action, internal-magazine-fed rifles that equipped most armies allowed

ABOVE: **One of the basic rules of modern warfare is – dig in. Life in the trenches was miserable but there was no alternative on a battlefield swept by artillery, rifle and machinegun fire.**

an infantry soldier to shoot quickly and accurately out to long ranges. That was a deadly combination. Infantry (or cavalry) could only cross ground as quickly as they ever could, but greater range meant that casualties were suffered at longer distances to the target, while greater accuracy meant that more shots hit their target – and of course it was possible to fire more times before the enemy got close. The effect of this was to make an infantry advance, particularly one made in traditional close order – much more costly. Attackers who had to stand up to move were at a huge disadvantage against men who could take cover or entrench themselves. Dispersing into skirmish order and advancing from cover to cover helped a lot – and contrary to popular myth this tactic was widely used during the Great War – but all the same the advantage was firmly on the side of the defender.

The ability to move reinforcements into a threatened area by rail meant that the defender could almost always plug a gap in the line before the attacker could exploit it, and further contributed to the prevalence of static, defensive warfare on the Western Front. Despite various attempts to break the deadlock, after the first months the war was characterized by more or less static trench lines. The rise of trench warfare was largely due to the capabilities of bolt-action rifles, which were ironically not the most effective weapon in a trench assault. Rifles were excellent weapons for inflicting casualties on an attack as the enemy advanced, but once they reached the trench line a long rifle was cumbersome and unwieldy. Shorter and handier weapons, ideally ones that could fire repeatedly without having to take a hand off the trigger to work a bolt, were better suited to trench fighting.

Thus the pump-action shotgun, the revolver and the new semi-automatic pistol were the weapons of choice for close assault work, along with the submachine gun that appeared towards the war's end. A revolver was useless in the open field, but in a trench fight a series of rapid shots might alter the course of the action. To be effective in this environment, a weapon had to be rugged and reliable, and highly resistant to dirt. In cold, damp and muddy conditions a complex pistol might become inoperable at just the wrong time, so the Great War was to some extent a proving ground for weapons and a crucible in which concepts were tested.

After the war there was continued upheaval. Revolution and civil war in Russia, street fighting in Germany between politically motivated groups and agitation in other countries ensured that peace did not suddenly break out just because the war was over. Pistols were the preferred means of removing political rivals in post-war Germany, with numerous short-range assassinations of people who might otherwise have helped shape the world differently.

The enaction of Prohibition in the United States resulted in a different kind of urban warfare between groups of well armed bootleggers and government agents. The rifle was out of place here – it was shotguns, submachine guns and of course pistols that decided these encounters. Throughout this turbulent era, firearms design moved constantly forward. All the required components for the modern handgun were now in place, but some years of experimentation and experience were required before the first generation of 'modern' revolvers and semi-automatics finally made their appearance.

## Towards the Modern Semi-Automatic Pistol

In the years preceding the Great War, several nations experimented with semi-automatic weapons. Semi-automatic rifles did not enter military service for decades, but the field of handguns moved rapidly forward.

The German Army adopted the Pistole Parabellum 1908 – better known as the Luger after Georg Luger, its creator – for service. The new service pistol was paired with a new 9x19mm (.35x.7in) round, and the combination of the two proved sufficiently effective that 9x19mm ammunition became the most widely used handgun round in the world. It is still very much the industry standard for combat handguns, and the benchmark against which the performance of a new round is measured.

LEFT: The Parabellum '08 was an excellent weapon but needed to be well looked after if it were to remain functional in the filthy conditions of the Western Front.

This new round became known as 9mm Parabellum or 9mm Luger, and offered a respectable c19.54ompromise between recoil, physical dimensions and ballistic performance. More of the relatively slim 9mm rounds could be stacked in a magazine of the same dimensions than a larger cartridge, although the debate about whether a few extra rounds or increased hitting power is more important has gone on ever since.

The pistol itself used an external jointed arm rather than the slide that has become more familiar. Its mechanism was developed from the earlier Borchardt pistol, but packed into a smaller space. The fact that this system fell out of use very quickly suggests that it was less effective than the slide used by most other semi-automatics. There were no more designs to use this mechanism although the P'08 itself had a long career. The P'08 mechanism was prone to fouling with dirt, something that was not in short supply on the trench battlefields of the Western Front. On the other hand the pistol was very 'pointable', i.e. its grip lined up the muzzle in an instinctive manner, making it fast and deadly in close-range point-and-shoot combat. Despite a tendency to clog up in muddy conditions, the P'08 was reliable if well cared for and gave good service through both world wars. It was intended to be replaced in 1938 by a Walther design but the need for large numbers of guns during World War II meant that the Luger continued in front-line service long after its ostensible retirement date.

Overall, the Luger was a very successful weapon; if it had not been, then perhaps the standard handgun chambering might have been something other than 9x19mm (.35x.7in). The P'08 was used as the basis for a number of experiments and variants. Alternate barrel lengths and chamberings were used; a 7.65mm variant was supplied to some clients, and a .45 version was offered for consideration by the U.S. military. It proved workable but was not accepted. Various services preferred different barrel lengths, and the P'08 was available in several configurations. The most extreme of these was the 'artillery carbine' variant, which was created for the use of artillerymen and other troops who needed something smaller than a rifle but might still have to engage the enemy in self-defence.

The Artillery Carbine model had an excessively long barrel and could be turned into a longarm by the addition of a detachable stock. The resulting weapon had a greater effective range than a typical pistol, theoretically enough to let artillery crews defend themselves from attack without encumbering them in their duties. It is unclear how effective these weapons actually were,

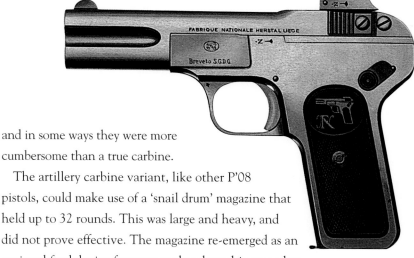

and in some ways they were more cumbersome than a true carbine.

The artillery carbine variant, like other P'08 pistols, could make use of a 'snail drum' magazine that held up to 32 rounds. This was large and heavy, and did not prove effective. The magazine re-emerged as an optional feed device for some early submachineguns but did not see much (if any) action in the Great War. An attempt was made to convert the P'08 into what today would be termed an assault pistol, i.e. a fully automatic handgun. The pistol's short-recoil system produced an excessive rate of fire, ensuring that the weapon was virtually uncontrollable. Muzzle climb quickly forced it off target, and the eight-round magazine was empty before the user had any chance to correct. The experiment was not a success, and attempts to use a drum magazine to increase firepower were not successful enough to merit further experimentation.

Thus the P'08 continued to do what it was originally designed to do – serve as a sidearm and close-combat weapon. It was well-regarded, not to mention interesting enough in its own right, that many were taken as souvenirs of the world wars and some returned to service as 'unofficial' sidearms in later conflicts. Examples still turn up in combat from time to time, although today copies of the P'08 are mainly bought as recreational guns, combining a fine and instinctive performance with a novel appearance and a bit of history.

### John Browning

One of the most influential of firearms designers, John Moses Browning, put together his first semi-automatic pistol in 1896–97, and after some development work it went into production with the Belgian company FN Herstal. Production pistols were designated Model 1900 or Browning No.1 and were chambered for .32 (7.62x17mm) ammunition. Browning's pistol introduced the concept of a recoil spring/firing pin spring above the barrel

**BROWNING MODEL 1900**
**COUNTRY OF ORIGIN**
Belgium
**DATE**
1900
**CALIBRE**
7.65mm (.301in)
**WEIGHT**
.62kg (1.375lb)
**OVERALL LENGTH**
163mm (6.4in)
**FEED/MAGAZINE**
7-round magazine
**RANGE**
30m (32.8yds)

RIGHT: John Moses Browning was one of the most influential weapon designers of all time. In addition to classic semi-automatic pistols he also developed some of the earliest machineguns, automatic rifles and semi-automatic shotguns.

but differed from later designs in that the ejector port was in the frame rather than the slide. With a simple, reliable blowback design the Model 1900 was produced in great numbers, with several hundred thousand sold.

Browning's next handgun was the Model 1903, otherwise known as Browning No.2. Chambered for .32 or 9x20mm (.35x.78in), the M1903 was manufactured in the USA by Colt and in Europe by FN Herstal. It featured

## BROWNING 1903
COUNTRY OF ORIGIN
Belgium/United States
DATE
1903
CALIBRE
9x20mm or 7.65mm (.32in or .301in)
WEIGHT
.9kg (2.1lb)
OVERALL LENGTH
205mm (8in)
FEED/MAGAZINE
7- or 8-round magazine
RANGE
50m (54.7yds)

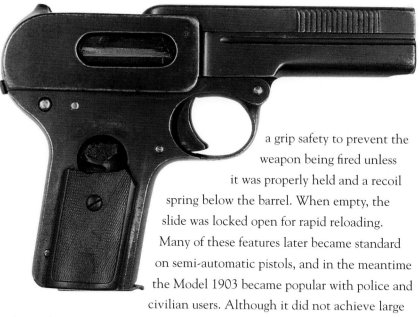

a grip safety to prevent the weapon being fired unless it was properly held and a recoil spring below the barrel. When empty, the slide was locked open for rapid reloading. Many of these features later became standard on semi-automatic pistols, and in the meantime the Model 1903 became popular with police and civilian users. Although it did not achieve large sales to the military sector, the 1903 model was highly influential in the design of military handguns.

## The Dreyse Pistol

One of the weapons that were influenced by Browning's early work was the Dreyse M1907, whose design has been attributed to Louis Schmeisser. The Dreyse pistol was chambered for the Browning .32 (7.65mm) cartridge and shared many features with Browning's weapons. There were, however, some differences. Unusually, the Dreyse pistol did not have a full-length slide. The slide only extended three-quarters of the way along the top of the weapon, so chambering a round required gripping the front part of the slide rather than the more usual rear grip. The slide and breechblock moved together inside the rear of the weapon, with the barrel located below the slide rather than inside it.

The Dreyse pistol was issued to German officers and police personnel for some years, and officially remained in police service into the 1930s when it was replaced by other handguns. In practice, with the requirement to produce large numbers of handguns during re-armament, many remained in service and large numbers were broken out of storage as World War II turned against Germany, being used to arm members of the Volksturm militia. The pistol was also used by some Austrian officers, but many were armed with the Roth-Steyr 1907. Built around a unique 8mm (.314in) round, the

**DREYSE M1907**
COUNTRY OF ORIGIN
Germany
DATE
1903
CALIBRE
7.65mm (.32in)
WEIGHT
.71kg (1.6lb)
OVERALL LENGTH
160mm (6.3in)
FEED/MAGAZINE
7-round magazine
RANGE
50m (54.7yds)

## ROTH-STEYR 1907

**COUNTRY OF ORIGIN**
Austro-Hungary
**DATE**
1907
**CALIBRE**
8mm (.314in)
**WEIGHT**
1.03kg (2.25lb)
**OVERALL LENGTH**
233mm (9in)
**FEED/MAGAZINE**
10-round magazine
**RANGE**
30m (32.8yds)

Roth-Steyr was loaded using a stripper clip into the fixed internal magazine. Although not the most advanced pistol in the world at the time, the Roth-Steyr does have the distinction of being the first semi-automatic handgun to be adopted by a military force.

The 10-round capacity of the Roth-Steyr offered good firepower, the Austro-Hungarian cavalry, but it was soon considered to be outdated. It was developed into a weapon designated Steyr M1911, with a new version introduced in 1912. Like its predecessor, this weapon was loaded through the action into a fixed magazine, this time holding only eight rounds. The gun was originally chambered for a 9x23mm (.35x.9in) round, but after 1939 many examples were converted to shoot 9x19mm (.35x.74in) Luger ammunition and taken into German service. In the meantime, the pistol enjoyed some overseas success and was used as the basis of a World War I-vintage light automatic weapon.

By extending the eight-round internal magazine of a Steyr M1912 to hold 16 rounds and offering a detachable shoulder stock/holster, Austrian designers hoped to create a weapon ideal for trench fighting. In practice the

## STEYR M1911

**COUNTRY OF ORIGIN**
Austro-Hungary
**DATE**
1911
**CALIBRE**
9mm Steyr or 9mm
Parabellum (.35in)
**WEIGHT**
1.02kg (2.25lb)
**OVERALL LENGTH**
216mm (8.5in)
**FEED/MAGAZINE**
8-round magazine
**RANGE**
30m (32.8yds)

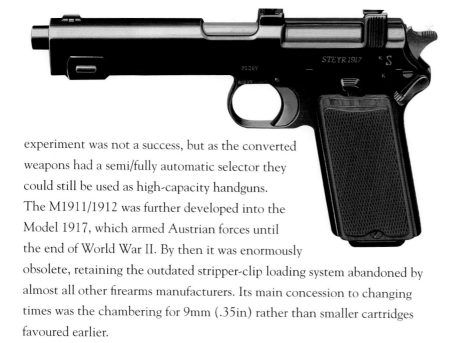

experiment was not a success, but as the converted weapons had a semi/fully automatic selector they could still be used as high-capacity handguns. The M1911/1912 was further developed into the Model 1917, which armed Austrian forces until the end of World War II. By then it was enormously obsolete, retaining the outdated stripper-clip loading system abandoned by almost all other firearms manufacturers. Its main concession to changing times was the chambering for 9mm (.35in) rather than smaller cartridges favoured earlier.

## Mauser Pistols

Unable to meet the demands of the Great War for sidearms for officers and weapons for cavalrymen, Austria turned to the German firm Mauser. Thousands of Mauser pistols, chambered for 7.65mm (.3in) ammunition, were delivered to the Austrian military. These weapons were no different to those in use with the German armed forces. Meanwhile, Germany was also having trouble providing all the handguns needed for the war, and also ordered thousands of Mausers to serve until sufficient P'08s were available. Many of these Mauser pistols were converted to fire 9x19mm (.35x.74in)

**STEYR MODEL 1917**
**COUNTRY OF ORIGIN**
Austro-Hungary
**DATE**
1917
**CALIBRE**
9mm (.35in)
**WEIGHT**
.99kg (2.18lb)
**OVERALL LENGTH**
216mm (8.5in)
**FEED/MAGAZINE**
8-round magazine
**RANGE**
30m (32.8yds)

**MAUSER M1912**
**COUNTRY OF ORIGIN**
Germany
**DATE**
1912
**CALIBRE**
7.63mm (.3in)
**WEIGHT**
1.25kg (2.75lb)
**OVERALL LENGTH**
295mm (11.6in)
**FEED/MAGAZINE**
6-, 10- or 20-round magazine
**RANGE**
30m (32.8yds)

RIGHT: At close quarters in a trench assault, a fast-firing pistol with good stopping power was a more effective weapon than a long, unwieldy rifle. In addition to being carried by officers, handguns were sometimes used by assault troops and trench raiding parties.

ammunition, and were supposed to be marked with a prominent '9' on the grip to indicate their calibre. The marking was not always done when the conversion was made, however, so some unmarked models may be chambered for 9mm rather than the expected 7.65mm.

To cover the deficiency in handguns, the German military also contracted Langenhan to provide a semi-automatic pistol. This fairly modern-looking weapon entered service in 1914, chambered for 7.65mm (.301in). With an eight-round detachable magazine, the Langenhan seemed like a good military pistol but did not stand up well to hard use. The breechblock on a worn Langenhan semi-automatic could detach itself from the weapon and be

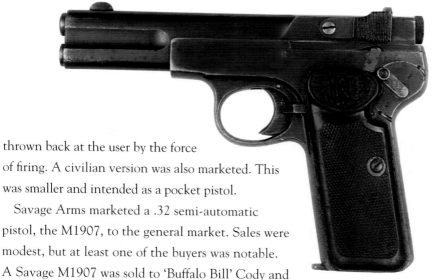

thrown back at the user by the force of firing. A civilian version was also marketed. This was smaller and intended as a pocket pistol.

Savage Arms marketed a .32 semi-automatic pistol, the M1907, to the general market. Sales were modest, but at least one of the buyers was notable. A Savage M1907 was sold to 'Buffalo Bill' Cody and remains one of the few guns he owned that is in a private collection rather than a museum. The standard Savage 1907 was modestly successful in the pocket-pistol marketplace but did not attract military interest.

With the U.S. Army looking for a new handgun, one chambered for .45, Savage produced a few hundred M1907s to take part in trials. Despite having been rechambered for a much larger round, the Savage still carried 10 rounds in its magazine and was modified with a grip safety to meet military requirements. The .45 Savage lost out to the competing Colt design on the grounds of reliability, and was not taken into U.S. military service although the French Army ordered significant numbers. It was also

## LANGENHAN
**COUNTRY OF ORIGIN**
Germany
**DATE**
1914
**CALIBRE**
7.65mm (.301in)
**WEIGHT**
.77kg (1.7lb)
**OVERALL LENGTH**
165mm (6.5in)
**FEED/MAGAZINE**
8-round magazine
**RANGE**
30m (32.8yds)

## SAVAGE M1907
**COUNTRY OF ORIGIN**
United States
**DATE**
1907
**CALIBRE**
8.1mm (.32in)
**WEIGHT**
.57kg (1.25lb)
**OVERALL LENGTH**
165mm (6.5in)
**FEED/MAGAZINE**
10-round magazine
**RANGE**
30m (32.8yds)

## SAVAGE 1915

**COUNTRY OF ORIGIN**
United States
**DATE**
1907
**CALIBRE**
8.1mm (.32in)
**WEIGHT**
.57kg (1.25lb)
**OVERALL LENGTH**
165mm (6.5in)
**FEED/MAGAZINE**
10-round magazine
**RANGE**
30m (32.8yds)

more expensive than the Colt, not least due
to its delayed-blowback recoil system. This used
a small barrel rotation during recoil to unlock
the barrel and allow it to move rearwards. The
intention was to prevent the ejection port from
opening until the bullet was out of the muzzle,
although in practice this did not work as well as the designers intended.

An updated version of the 1907 model was fielded in 1915. This pistol
was called 'hammerless' as it had no external hammer, although in fact
neither did the 1907 – what appears to be a hammer on a Savage 1907 is a
cocking lever. The 1915 model featured a slide lock, holding the slide open
when the magazine was empty to facilitate quicker reloading. After some

RIGHT: The shooting of
Archduke Franz Ferdinand
by Gavrilo Princip provided
the flashpoint for the Great
War, although the conflict
was probably inevitable
sooner or later due to the
politics of the day.

cosmetic changes, the 1915 model was remarketed as the 1917, available in .32 and in .380 with a slightly longer barrel.

### Magazine Safety

Browning's Model 1910, also known as the FN Model 1910, featured a magazine safety in addition to the manual and grip safeties. One of the commonest causes of accidents with firearms is the assumption that the weapon is safe when the magazine is removed. However, if a round remains in the chamber then the gun is very much live and hazardous to handle as if empty. A magazine safety offers a mechanical backup to good handling procedures by preventing the weapon from firing even if a mistake is made. The Model 1910 was produced in .32 and .380 (9mm Browning Short) and proved very popular with military, law enforcement and civilian users. The most famous of the latter was Gavrilo Princip, who used his pistol to assassinate Archduke Franz Ferdinand and thereby triggered the Great War. Despite this unwelcome connection, the Browning 1910 had a long career, during which a modified version designated Model 1922 was introduced for European military users.

Model 1910 and 1922 Brownings imported from Europe to the USA were usually sold as the 'Browning 380'and enjoyed a long career in production. The Model 1910 also influenced the visually similar Walther PPK and Makarov pistols, developed in Germany and Russia respectively, and the Remington 51. The latter was developed by John Pedersen, who had worked with Browning. Designed as a pocket pistol, the Remington 51 entered the marketplace in 1918. A larger version, designated Remington 53, was offered to the U.S. Army as an alternative to the M1911 but was not put into production. The 53 was in some ways a more efficient design than the M1911, with fewer moving parts and improved accuracy. However, due to the expense of setting up large-scale production it was decided to stick with the Colt design.

## REMINGTON 51
**COUNTRY OF ORIGIN**
United States
**DATE**
1917
**CALIBRE**
8.1mm or 9.6mm (.32in or .38in)
**WEIGHT**
.59kg (1.3lb)
**OVERALL LENGTH**
162mm (6.38in)
**FEED/MAGAZINE**
8- or 7-round magazine
**RANGE**
30m (32.8yds)

## TYPE A MODEL 1902 NAMBU
**COUNTRY OF ORIGIN**
Japan
**DATE**
1902
**CALIBRE**
8mm (.314in)
**WEIGHT**
.9kg (1.98lb)
**OVERALL LENGTH**
230mm (9.06in)
**FEED/MAGAZINE**
8-round magazine
**RANGE**
50m (54.7yds)

The post-war civilian marketplace was not well suited to large-calibre handguns, so Remington concentrated on the .32 calibre 51. Although sales of personal firearms remained strong during the Great Depression, the tough economic climate ensured that the Remington 51 never achieved the sales it perhaps deserved.

### Japanese Handguns

Despite having only recently embraced cartridge firearms, the Japanese Empire decided to adopt a semi-automatic pistol as its military service weapon. This move was possibly motivated by the deficiencies of the Type 26 revolver, but its replacements were equally great disappointments. Designed by Kijiro Nambu, the first of these was the Type A Model 1902, often referred to as the 'Grandpa Nambu'. Built around a weak 8x22mm (.314x.86in) round, the Nambu pistol used an unusual cocking system, with a knob at the rear of the weapon rather than the more common hammer or lever. Despite its curious, somewhat flimsy appearance, it was an accurate and well balanced weapon with a good trigger action. However, these advantages were drowned in a sea of major deficiencies.

The Nambu pistol was predisposed to shoot when it should not and to not shoot when it should. The safety catch was inadequate to prevent the weapon from firing if knocked, while the striker spring was too weak and failed frequently, preventing the weapon from firing even if the feeble magazine springs did not cause a feed malfunction. A new version was produced in 1904, and is now generally known as the 'Papa Nambu'. Most of the modifications built into this weapon were cosmetic and totally failed to remedy its many deficiencies. The 'Baby Nambu' was developed alongside the initial model, but did not enter service until 1909. A smaller version of the 1902 model, it fired an even lighter and weaker 7mm (.27in) cartridge.

Not only were these pistols ineffective in combat, they were overcomplex

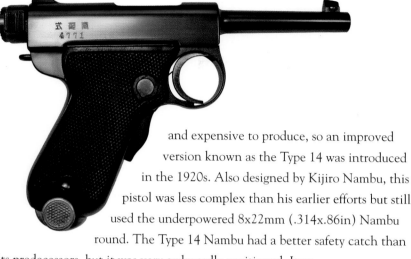

and expensive to produce, so an improved version known as the Type 14 was introduced in the 1920s. Also designed by Kijiro Nambu, this pistol was less complex than his earlier efforts but still used the underpowered 8x22mm (.314x.86in) Nambu round. The Type 14 Nambu had a better safety catch than its predecessors, but it was very awkwardly positioned. It re

tained the same feature whereby the slide locked back when the magazine was empty, but ran forward when it was removed, requiring the slide to be operated when a new magazine was inserted. The magazine release could be over-enthusiastic, causing the magazine to drop out if the weapon was jarred. Some of these deficiencies were remedied by modifications, but the most major of them was not. The tendency of the striker to fail was never fixed beyond providing a space in the holster to carry a spare striker for field repair – assuming the gun's owner survived.

The final incarnation of the Nambu pistol, the Type 94, appeared in the mid-1930s and served with the Japanese military throughout World War II. It was designed to meet the need for a smaller weapon than the

## 1902 'BABY NAMBU'

**COUNTRY OF ORIGIN**
Japan
**DATE**
1902
**CALIBRE**
7mm (.276in)
**WEIGHT**
.65kg (1.43b)
**OVERALL LENGTH**
171mm (6.73in)
**FEED/MAGAZINE**
7-round magazine
**RANGE**
50m (54.7yds)

## TYPE 14 NAMBU

**COUNTRY OF ORIGIN**
Japan
**DATE**
1925
**CALIBRE**
8mm (.314in)
**WEIGHT**
.9kg (1.98lb)
**OVERALL LENGTH**
230mm (9.06in)
**FEED/MAGAZINE**
8-round magazine
**RANGE**
50m (54.7yds)

## TYPE 94 NAMBU

**COUNTRY OF ORIGIN**
Japan
**DATE**
1934
**CALIBRE**
8mm (.314in)
**WEIGHT**
.58kg (1.28lb)
**OVERALL LENGTH**
181mm (7.125in)
**FEED/MAGAZINE**
6-round magazine
**RANGE**
50m (54.7yds)

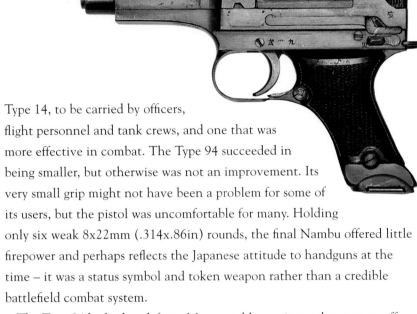

RIGHT: **The Italian Army included large numbers of highly efficient mountain troops trained to operate in extremely difficult terrain. Much of the issued equipment lagged behind personnel in effectiveness, however.**

Type 14, to be carried by officers, flight personnel and tank crews, and one that was more effective in combat. The Type 94 succeeded in being smaller, but otherwise was not an improvement. Its very small grip might not have been a problem for some of its users, but the pistol was uncomfortable for many. Holding only six weak 8x22mm (.314x.86in) rounds, the final Nambu offered little firepower and perhaps reflects the Japanese attitude to handguns at the time – it was a status symbol and token weapon rather than a credible battlefield combat system.

The Type 94 had other defects. Most notable was its tendency to go off if knocked or even – according to many credible sources – if the exposed sear was pressed or squeezed while handling. All this was compounded by being fiendishly difficult to take apart for cleaning, leading to a tendency to neglect the weapon in the field. As a result the Type 94 Nambu is sometimes regarded as a shining example of how bad a handgun can be and still end up being issued in vast numbers.

## GLISENTI MODELO 1910

**COUNTRY OF ORIGIN**
Italy
**DATE**
1910
**CALIBRE**
9mm (.35in)
**WEIGHT**
.82kg (1.8lb)
**OVERALL LENGTH**
210mm (8.25in)
**FEED/MAGAZINE**
7-round magazine
**RANGE**
20m (21.9yds)

## Italian Handguns

Another less than effective weapon of the era was the Glisenti Modelo 1910.
Vaguely similar in appearance to the Nambu family, the Modelo 1910 was
nothing like so awful but still suffered from serious defects. It was developed
from the preceding 1906 model, whose 7.65x22mm (.3x.86in) round was
considered inadequate by the Italian Army when it was offered for trials. The
resulting Modelo 1910 was chambered for 9x19mm (.35x.74in) ammunition
but was structurally too weak to handle 9mm Luger ammunition without
a serious risk of bursting, so the 9x19mm Glisenti round was created. This
resulted in a weapon built to handle the chamber pressures of 7.65mm
ammunition but able to chamber full-powered 9mm Luger rounds if the user
made a mistake.

The Glisenti round itself was underpowered, meaning that even
rechambered the new Italian service pistol lacked the stopping power of its
contemporaries. It did have an instinctive point, however, and was liked by
some users. Others resisted its introduction and kept their Bodeo revolvers,
and even though an upgraded design was put forward in 1912 this proved
little better. The Modelo 1910's unusual features included the lack of the
usual external cocking device, with trigger action used to cock the weapon
instead. Although still officially in service as late as World War II, the
Glisenti pistol was eclipsed by the much better weapons offered by Beretta.

The Beretta Model 1915 was the first handgun produced by the firm,

## BERETTA MODEL 1915

**COUNTRY OF ORIGIN**
Italy
**DATE**
1915
**CALIBRE**
7.65mm or 9mm (.301in or
.35in)
**WEIGHT**
.68kg (1.5lb)
**OVERALL LENGTH**
216mm (8.5in)
**FEED/MAGAZINE**
7-round magazine
**RANGE**
30m (32.8yds)

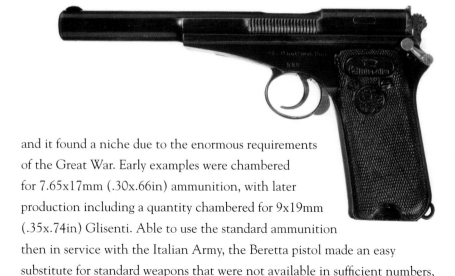

and it found a niche due to the enormous requirements of the Great War. Early examples were chambered for 7.65x17mm (.30x.66in) ammunition, with later production including a quantity chambered for 9x19mm (.35x.74in) Glisenti. Able to use the standard ammunition then in service with the Italian Army, the Beretta pistol made an easy substitute for standard weapons that were not available in sufficient numbers, and thus got itself into the hands of a great many Italian service personnel.

The Beretta 1915 emerged from the Great War with a reputation as being better than the Glisenti pistols and Bodeo revolvers it had competed with, and gradually came to outnumber both in service. It was not, however, declared the official Italian sidearm although its successor, the Model 1934, was.

## Spanish Handguns

The Spanish military was one of the first to embrace semi-automatic sidearms, but this was not necessarily a benefit in the longer term. The Bergman-Bayard pistols taken into service were first-generation weapons and were soon surpassed by new designs. The cartridge they fired, now known in Spain as 9mm (.35in) Largo, proved satisfactory but a better weapon to fire it was obviously needed. This was designed by the Count of Campo-Giro and named after him. It went into Spanish Army service as the Pistola Campo-Giro de 9mm Modelo 1912 and was followed the next year by an updated version. Moving the magazine to the grip rather than in front of the trigger guard as with the Bergmann-Bayard allowed a longer barrel and thus a higher muzzle velocity, getting better performance from the already well respected 9mm Largo ammunition.

Further updates followed, and although the Spanish military had decided to seek a new service weapon by 1920, the Campo-Giro pistol came back out of storage during the Spanish Civil War of the 1930s. In the interim it was a strong influence on the Astra pistols that came later. Meanwhile, the Spanish handgun industry benefited from unusual patent laws that

### CAMPO-GIRO
**COUNTRY OF ORIGIN**
Spain
**DATE**
1912
**CALIBRE**
9mm Largo (.35in)
**WEIGHT**
1kg (2.2lb)
**OVERALL LENGTH**
239mm (9.4in)
**FEED/MAGAZINE**
8-round magazine
**RANGE**
50m (54.7yds)

allowed blatant copying of any device that was not actually manufactured under patent in Spain. This permitted versions of the Browning 1903, along with other handguns, to be manufactured by small gunsmithing companies without permission. One such weapon was the 'Ruby' pistol, which was offered to the French Army in 1914. The French military decided to order

## UNCETA VICTORIA ('RUBY' TYPE PISTOL)

**COUNTRY OF ORIGIN**
Spain
**DATE**
1911
**CALIBRE**
7.65mm (.301in)
**WEIGHT**
.57kg (1.25lb)
**OVERALL LENGTH**
146mm (5.75in)
**FEED/MAGAZINE**
7-round magazine
**RANGE**
30m (32.8yds)

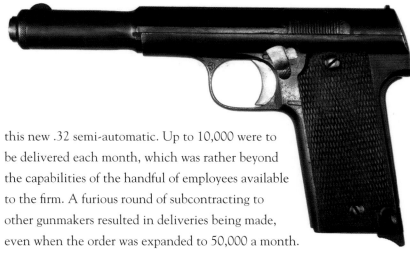

## ASTRA 400
**COUNTRY OF ORIGIN**
Spain
**DATE**
1921
**CALIBRE**
9mm Largo (.35in)
**WEIGHT**
1.14kg (2.51lb)
**OVERALL LENGTH**
225mm (8.86in)
**FEED/MAGAZINE**
8-round magazine
**RANGE**
50m (54.7yds)

this new .32 semi-automatic. Up to 10,000 were to be delivered each month, which was rather beyond the capabilities of the handful of employees available to the firm. A furious round of subcontracting to other gunmakers resulted in deliveries being made, even when the order was expanded to 50,000 a month.

With so many small manufacturers producing the same weapon, variation was inevitable. Thus although the pistols delivered met the same general specifications of .32 calibre and a nine-round magazine, details and even designations varied considerably. Dozens of brand names were used for what was essentially the same pistol, with perhaps up to a million actually made. Production continued into the 1920s for markets beyond the French (and later Italian) militaries. These many different but basically similar weapons are collectively known as Ruby or Eibar pistols, after the city where manufacture began.

The firm Esperanza y Unceta started out in Eibar but in 1913 relocated to Guernica. One of its early products was the Victoria pistol, which was developed from the Browning 1903 rather than being an outright copy.

LEFT: The sudden and rapid expansion of national armies that took place during the Great War created a requirement for enormous quantities of weaponry. At times quality was sacrificed for the sake of sufficient numbers.

## ASTRA 600/43
**COUNTRY OF ORIGIN**
Spain
**DATE**
1943
**CALIBRE**
9mm Parabellum (.35in)
**WEIGHT**
1.08kg (2.38lb)
**OVERALL LENGTH**
205mm (8.07in)
**FEED/MAGAZINE**
8-round magazine
**RANGE**
50m (54.7yds)

A slightly modified version was taken into French service as part of the acquisition programme for Ruby-type pistols, which it was considered by the French Army to be. The firm provided large numbers of these pistols to the French Army under a range of model numbers and designations. One of those was Astra, later chosen as the new name for the company. This first Astra was a Ruby type, but in the early 1920s the firm began offering new designs that were influenced by the Campo-Giro pistol.

The latter required replacement in Spanish service, so the Astra Model 300 and 400 were put forward. The 400 was the primary combat model, with the 300 as a slightly smaller variant. The original calibre was 9mm (.35in) Largo, the current Spanish service round, but later pistols were chambered for 9mm Luger and quantities were supplied in other calibres including .32 ACP, 9mm Glisenti and .380, depending on the wishes of the client. The Astra 400 remained in production until 1941 and was a considerable export success.

## Unsuccessful Projects

Although semi-automatic pistols of modern appearance were beginning to appear, there were also numerous experimental weapons emerging, some of which were more successful than others. In 1901, Rudolf Frommer produced a stripper-clip-loaded pistol available in a variety of chamberings. Using a long-recoil system, this weapon was not a success and was the basis for a 1906 model that similarly failed to achieve much in the marketplace. The 1906 pistol was notable mainly for the fact that it was modified from

**FROMMER
MODEL 1910**
COUNTRY OF ORIGIN
Austro-Hungary
DATE
1910
CALIBRE
7.65mm (.301in)
WEIGHT
.59kg (1.3lb)
OVERALL LENGTH
184mm (7.25in)
FEED/MAGAZINE
7-round magazine
RANGE
20m (21.9yds)

a 10-round internal magazine to take an eight-round detachable box, from which the rather more successful P'08 magazine was developed.

After producing two pistols that failed trials with various military users, Frommer's 1910 pistol was adopted by the Hungarian police. It did not find much favour elsewhere. Frommer's next offering, his 1912 model or Frommer Stop pistol, was of more conventional appearance and was adopted by the Hungarian military. It unnecessarily clung to a long-recoil system that was simply not necessary for its .32 or .380 chambering, and was consequently very expensive to manufacture.

Broadly similar in appearance to early Frommer models, the Webley and Scott self-loading pistol family began with a 1904 model firing .455 revolver

**BELOW: Members of the Royal Ulster Constabulary on the range with Webley revolvers. Heavy, powerful handguns required a great deal of training to enable the user to shoot accurately, which was essential in a law enforcement context.**

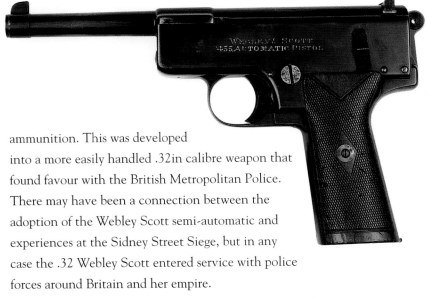

## WEBLEY & SCOTT MK1 NAVY

**COUNTRY OF ORIGIN**
United Kingdom
**DATE**
1912
**CALIBRE**
11.55mm (.455in)
**WEIGHT**
.68kg (1.5lb)
**OVERALL LENGTH**
216mm (8.5in)
**FEED/MAGAZINE**
6-round magazine
**RANGE**
20m (21.9yds)

ammunition. This was developed into a more easily handled .32in calibre weapon that found favour with the British Metropolitan Police. There may have been a connection between the adoption of the Webley Scott semi-automatic and experiences at the Sidney Street Siege, but in any case the .32 Webley Scott entered service with police forces around Britain and her empire.

A series of variants followed, chambered for a range of ammunition culminating in a high-powered .38 round. This was developed into the extremely powerful 1912 model, which fired a custom .455 round that was not compatible with Webley revolvers. The Webley Scott was issued to some artillery personnel and the Royal Flying Corps, and a naval variant was also manufactured. However, excessive recoil and generally awkward shape of the weapon prevented the big Webley Scott from becoming a major success. Smaller-calibre versions were manufactured long after the definitive .455 self-loading pistol had passed away.

### The Classic Semi-automatic Pistol

How far and how fast semi-automatic pistol design developed – despite various failed projects – can be seen from the Colt M1911 pistol. This weapon had its origins in the U.S. military decision to move back to a heavy-calibre handgun after experimenting with lighter rounds. John Moses Browning designed the M1911 around a cartridge of his own design, a 230-grain .45 calibre round. The new cartridge delivered what the U.S. military was wanting from it, providing excellent stopping power without excessive recoil or massive chamber pressures that would require a bulky, heavily constructed weapon to withstand these forces. Although the ballistic performance was impressive, the round's chamber pressure was manageable, enabling Browning to design a weapon around his proven short-recoil system.

The M1911 was not a particularly complex weapon; its mechanism

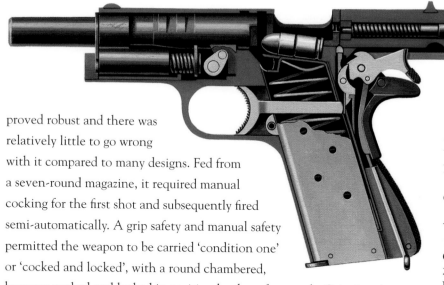

proved robust and there was relatively little to go wrong with it compared to many designs. Fed from a seven-round magazine, it required manual cocking for the first shot and subsequently fired semi-automatically. A grip safety and manual safety permitted the weapon to be carried 'condition one' or 'cocked and locked', with a round chambered, hammer cocked and locked in position by the safety catch. Gripping the pistol in the hand and disengaging the safety with a small movement readied the M1911 for instant action.

It could alternatively be carried with the chamber empty and brought into action by working the slide to chamber a round and cock the hammer. In many cases the manual safety was left off, relying on an empty chamber and the grip safety to avoid accidents. This drill was taught to personnel for whom there was little time for training, as it allowed reasonably safe use of a firearm by less-than-confident individuals. Association with some notable figures in the firearms and security world has created a misapprehension that this is the best way to use a semi-automatic pistol, but in fact this drill was an expedient and nothing more. Most U.S. personnel who received the Colt M1911 during and after the Great War were properly trained in its use, and found it eminently suitable for its purpose. Although only carrying one more round than a revolver, the M1911 was much faster to reload and offered excellent stopping power. As a result, it remained the standard U.S. service pistol into the 1980s.

Along the way, many variants and developed versions began to appear. In the 1920s the M1911A1 was introduced, which incorporated lessons learned in World War I. Most of the changes were cosmetic or ergonomic, such as a larger grip safety spur that reduced the chance of 'hammer bite'. A wider ejection port improved tolerance for difficult field conditions.

Just as the Parabellum '08 was the weapon that established the 9x19mm

## COLT M1911
**COUNTRY OF ORIGIN**
United States
**DATE**
1911
**CALIBRE**
11.43mm (.45in)
**WEIGHT**
1.1kg (2.425lb)
**OVERALL LENGTH**
216mm (8.5in)
**FEED/MAGAZINE**
7-round magazine
**RANGE**
50m (54.7yds)

(.35x.74in) Luger round, so the contemporary M1911 was the gun that established the new .45 ACP round. The two have been in competition ever since, and some might claim that the 9mm eventually won out when the U.S. military went over to 9mm pistols in the 1980s. However, many of those with a choice about their sidearm calibre – notably Special Forces units – continue to favour the .45, and there are still plenty of people that insist that there are basically two types of handgun in the world – guns that shoot .45, and guns that aren't worth having.

Be that as it may, there was one other fundamental difference between the M1911 and the Parabellum 1908. The P'08 was very much an early semi-automatic, incorporating a mechanism that has not since been used. The M1911, on the other hand, was the first truly modern semi-automatic. It has remained in production for a century and been copied many times. Modernized variants have appeared over the years, but there are few weapons that have ever been viable a century after their introduction, and the M1911 is one of them.

## The Rise of the Modern Revolver

Semi-automatic pistols did not, of course, edge out revolvers – not in 1910 and never since. This was not simply due to reactionaries refusing to give up their outdated wheel-guns; revolvers have certain advantages in the right circumstances. Most obviously, revolvers are very simple to use. For poorly trained personnel or for anyone grabbing a handgun off the nightstand at 3a.m., simplicity is of great importance. A revolver is reassuringly solid and simple, with an air of dependability. More importantly perhaps, it is as mistake proof as a weapon can be. A quick glance in the cylinder tells the user that his weapon is loaded and ready to go. Reloading is slower than a semi-automatic but it is very simple, as is the operation of most revolvers. With no manual safety devices to operate, a revolver will shoot when the user wants it to even if he or she is scared half to death and unable to carry out complex fine-motor movements.

That is not to say that the revolver is the tool of ignorance – far from it. However, the weapon's simplicity is an advantage under difficult circumstances and its robust construction makes it suitable for tough conditions. Thus military and law enforcement users in many nations retained the revolver as a service weapon long after inexpensive but reliable semi-automatics offering greater firepower became available.

LEFT: US forces moved back to large-calibre handguns after finding that their .38 handguns often failed to stop highly aggressive warriors armed with hand weapons. The .45 M1911 did not suffer from this problem.

## COLT POLICE POSITIVE

**COUNTRY OF ORIGIN**
United States
**DATE**
1907
**CALIBRE**
5.6mm (.22in)
**WEIGHT**
.68kg (1.5lb)
**OVERALL LENGTH**
260mm (10.25in)
**FEED/MAGAZINE**
6-shot revolver
**RANGE**
20m (21.9yds)

From 1905, Colt revolvers featured their 'positive safety' device, which allowed safe carry with all chambers loaded.

Colt revolvers of that era proclaimed their possession of the new device with names like Pocket Positive and Police Positive. These were typically small-calibre revolvers, chambered for .32 or even .22 ammunition, with some variants using .38 Special. The thinking behind this choice of small-calibre weapons for law enforcement use is open to some debate. It has been suggested that Theodore Roosevelt was influential in the choice while serving as police commissioner in New York City. Standards of police marksmanship were at the time rather poor, so a low-recoil weapon may have seemed like a good choice to avoid making matters any worse.

**RIGHT:** Roosevelt's decision to issue small-calibre weapons to New York Police Department may have been based on the idea that it is easier to control a small-calibre weapon than a more potent one. The modern approach gives officers an effective weapon and the training to use it properly.

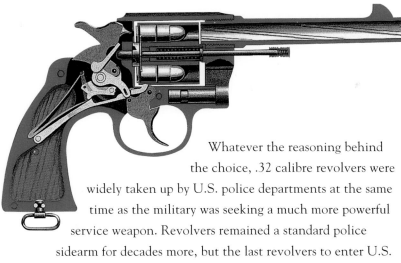

Whatever the reasoning behind the choice, .32 calibre revolvers were widely taken up by U.S. police departments at the same time as the military was seeking a much more powerful service weapon. Revolvers remained a standard police sidearm for decades more, but the last revolvers to enter U.S. Army service were the Colt New Service and the .45 Army Model that was developed from it. The New Service revolver had been in production since 1898, and was chambered for a variety of ammunition. The .45 variant entered U.S. military service in 1909, and was soon updated to create the M1917 New Army Model. This weapon was capable of firing .45 ACP cartridges intended for the M1911, although it needed a pair of half-moon clips in the cylinder to hold the rimless .45 cartridges in place. A modified version allowed the half-moon clips to be dispensed with, although ejection was a distinctly manual process as the lack of rim meant that the ejector did not engage them. Poking cartridges out manually was not an efficient process, but this was the price of being able to share ammunition with the M1911.

The M1917 was the last revolver to be taken into service with the U.S. Army, and was only an interim measure until enough M1911 semi-

## COLT NEW SERVICE
**COUNTRY OF ORIGIN**
United States
**DATE**
1909
**CALIBRE**
11.43mm (.45in)
**WEIGHT**
1.3kg (2.9lb)
**OVERALL LENGTH**
260mm (10.25in)
**FEED/MAGAZINE**
6-shot revolver
**RANGE**
20m (21.9yds)

## COLT ARMY MODEL M1917
**COUNTRY OF ORIGIN**
United States
**DATE**
1917
**CALIBRE**
11.43mm (.45in)
**WEIGHT**
1.13kg (2.5lb)
**OVERALL LENGTH**
273mm (10.75in)
**FEED/MAGAZINE**
6-shot revolver
**RANGE**
20m (21.9yds)

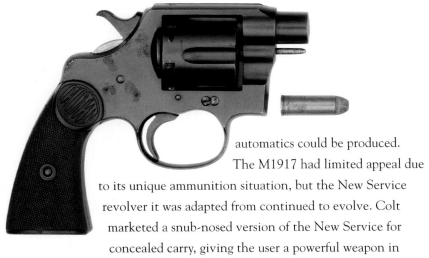

## COLT NEW SERVICE (SNUB-NOSED)
**COUNTRY OF ORIGIN**
United States
**DATE**
1909
**CALIBRE**
11.43mm (.45in)
**WEIGHT**
1kg (2.2lb)
**OVERALL LENGTH**
180mm (7in)
**FEED/MAGAZINE**
6-shot revolver
**RANGE**
10m (10.9yds)

## COLT DETECTIVE SPECIAL
**COUNTRY OF ORIGIN**
United States
**DATE**
1927
**CALIBRE**
9.6mm (.38in)
**WEIGHT**
.6kg (1.3lb)
**OVERALL LENGTH**
171mm (6.7in)
**FEED/MAGAZINE**
6-shot revolver
**RANGE**
30m (32.8yds)

automatics could be produced. The M1917 had limited appeal due to its unique ammunition situation, but the New Service revolver it was adapted from continued to evolve. Colt marketed a snub-nosed version of the New Service for concealed carry, giving the user a powerful weapon in a small package that could easily be carried in a pocket. The downside of 'snub' revolvers of this sort is reduced effective range and accuracy, along with altered balance and an increase in both recoil and muzzle flash. None of these is a serious problem when a snub handgun is used for its intended purpose of close-range self-defence; the smallest snub-nosed revolver offers adequate accuracy at the point-blank ranges where most self-defence shooting occurs. Taking a snub-nosed weapon to the range and expecting tight groups is more of a challenge, however, but the trade-off is probably worth it. Indeed, some authorities believe that a very short barrel makes the bore of a handgun look much larger to someone facing it, and this can be a powerful deterrent.

One of the most widely known snub-nosed revolvers was the Colt Detective Special, which was essentially a Police Positive revolver with a very short 50.8mm (2in) barrel. It was easier to conceal than a larger gun – although the bulky cylinder of a revolver always impairs concealability.

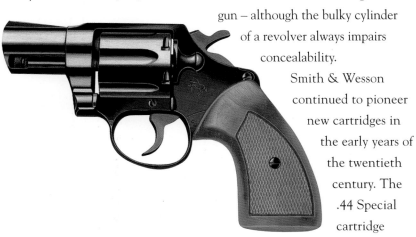

Smith & Wesson continued to pioneer new cartridges in the early years of the twentieth century. The .44 Special cartridge

PROTECT YOUR FAMILY

A
sense
of security
pervades the
home which
shelters a
SMITH & WESSON
Revolver.

SMITH & WESSON,
15 Stockbridge Street,    Springfield, Mass.
Catalogue for a stamp.

LEFT: Although the language of advertising might have evolved, the underlying message has not – 'How would you feel in these people's position? Get one of our guns and the fear will go away…'

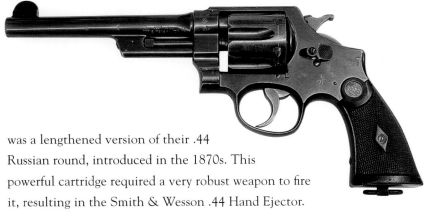

## SMITH & WESSON .44 TRIPLE LOCK

COUNTRY OF ORIGIN
United States
DATE
1908
CALIBRE
11.17mm (.44in)
WEIGHT
1.08kg (2.4lb)
OVERALL LENGTH
298mm (11.75in)
FEED/MAGAZINE
6-shot revolver
RANGE
30m (32.8yds)

## SMITH & WESSON M1917 HAND EJECTOR

COUNTRY OF ORIGIN
United States
DATE
1917
CALIBRE
11.43mm (.45in)
WEIGHT
1.08kg (2.4lb)
OVERALL LENGTH
298mm (11.75in)
FEED/MAGAZINE
6-shot revolver
RANGE
20m (21.9yds)

was a lengthened version of their .44 Russian round, introduced in the 1870s. This powerful cartridge required a very robust weapon to fire it, resulting in the Smith & Wesson .44 Hand Ejector. The new revolver's name was derived from the fact that since it had a side-swinging cylinder, it did not automatically eject cartridges in the manner of a top-break revolver. Instead the user had to push the ejector rod manually. Sometimes referred to as the 'First Model New Century', the .44 Hand Ejector was also known as .44 Triple Lock since the cylinder had three rather than the usual two locking lugs. This was deemed unnecessary for later models. The second variant also lost its ejector shroud, which returned for the third model of the design. An extremely highly regarded handgun, the .44 Hand Ejector was not only one of the best revolver designs ever to go to market, but it also served as a vehicle for the new .44 Special cartridge, which was in turn later developed into the .44 Magnum round.

A variant of the .44 Hand Ejector was converted to fire .45 ACP ammunition, much like the Colt M1917. Indeed, this weapon was perhaps confusingly also designated M1917. The main difference between the two was that the Smith & Wesson model did not need half-moon clips, although ejection required the same manual poking-out process as the

Colt. In the 1920s a rimmed version of the .45 ACP round emerged, allowing revolver extractors to engage the spent cartridge and eject it more efficiently.

The main drawback of the revolver as compared to a semi-automatic pistol is of course loading speed. Inserting cartridges one by one is a relatively slow process, and various mechanical means have been tried to speed it up. Methods range from full-moon and half-moon clips that can be inserted directly into the cylinder, through stripper clips intended to hold ammunition ready and reduce fumbling in a pouch or pocket, to speed strips that align two rounds at a time with the chambers. The quickest means to reload a revolver is the speedloader, which inserts six rounds simultaneously into the cylinder by pressing a plunger. The first speedloader design was patented in 1879, with various developments appearing over time. The basic principle has remained the same, although today there are many different types of speedloader on the market. Although some practice is required before it can be used efficiently, it does cut down loading time and helps the revolver remain a viable personal weapon.

Although semi-automatic pistols offer the same reliability and more ammunition capacity as well as quicker reloading, the revolver continues to offer strong competition in terms of simplicity and reliability. The latter is not just a mechanical issue – an individual's faith in their weapon and their own ability to operate it is an important factor in combat or deterrence, and one of the intangible factors offered by a good revolver is an air of rugged dependability.

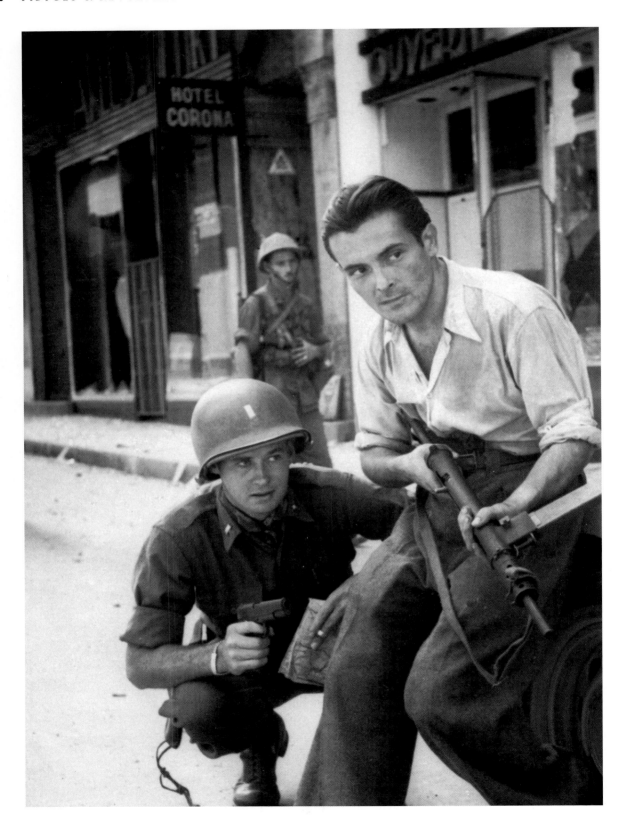

# The World War II Era

The end of World War I did not, of course, bring about sudden peace and worldwide harmony. Other battles continued, and the troubles of Prohibition and the Great Depression resulted in a great deal of low-level conflict. International trade ports in cities like Shanghai were among the most lawless places on the planet, requiring a robust approach to law enforcement that at times resembled urban warfare. Many of the weapons used during this era were, not surprisingly, a legacy of the Great War.

LEFT: The M1911 semi-automatic pistol features in so many war movies and images of US forces from most of the 20th century that it has achieved sort of in-plain-sight invisibility; its absence is sometimes more remarkable than its presence.

New designs were being produced, and vast numbers of weapons manufactured, right up until the end of the war. This left the market flooded with weaponry that was often available at low prices to anyone willing to pay for it. Even though contracts were cancelled and projects curtailed, the world's militaries found themselves with huge amounts of equipment and a vastly reduced need for it. Some of this equipment was put to other uses – bombers were

**STAR MODEL B**
COUNTRY OF ORIGIN
Spain
DATE
1924
CALIBRE
9mm Parabellum (.35in)
WEIGHT
1.1kg (2.4lb)
OVERALL LENGTH
215mm (8.46in)
FEED/MAGAZINE
9-round magazine
RANGE
30m (32.8yds)

converted to pioneering long-range record-setting aircraft, and warships could often be sold on to smaller navies or retasked as experimental vessels – but in the years after the Great War there was a glut of 'legacy' military equipment, and in the economic climate of the time it made more sense to continue using this than to commission new designs. The result was a tough marketplace for weaponry of all kinds, with new designs having to offer something special in order to compete with cheap legacy equipment. In time, block obsolescence would make it necessary to urgently replace huge amounts of equipment, and the increasing likelihood of a new war in Europe made rearmament a priority, but breaking into the market in the 1920s and early 1930s was difficult at best.

RIGHT: Although the Japanese military issued handguns to officers and some other personnel, they were not regarded as viable combat weapons. Given the extremely poor guns available, this was probably just as well.

Some weapon designs benefited from having settled into their niche towards the end of World War I. The U.S. Army was quite happy with its new service pistol, and other than some slight modifications all that was necessary was to continue production at a modest rate. Other militaries, content with war-production weapons for many years, were forced to bring their small arms up to date in a hurry as a new world war loomed. Others needed large quantities of weaponry to rearm after greatly reducing the size of their armed forces. Thus the 1930s saw a renewal of forward momentum in handgun design, and the setting up of new companies to produce sufficient weaponry. Law enforcement and private use had remained a constant, of course, but in the 1930s there were conflicts all over the world, and improved guns were in large-scale demand once again.

## World War Commences

With civil war in China still ongoing and one erupting in Spain, tensions mounted with a Japanese invasion of Manchuria and later much of South east Asia. Then came World War II, a conflict in which the bolt-action rifle was finally eclipsed by semi-automatic and fully automatic infantry weapons. Many of the latter were submachine guns chambered for existing pistol rounds, and demand for military handguns exploded. In the previous war, handguns were a sidearm for officers and an expedient in trench assaults. Specialist personnel such as airmen and tank crews were a tiny minority compared to the vast infantry forces fielded by all nations. World War II, however, involved much greater numbers of aircrew and vehicle crews, who needed a weapon in case of emergencies. A rifle or carbine was too bulky, so large numbers of handguns were required to arm these personnel. Production could not keep pace with demand, especially since other weapons were more urgently needed.

The war also had a covert element that had not existed in the previous conflict, with agents and resistance fighters finding handguns a useful, concealable weapon system. Thus alongside an overdue scramble to rearm mainstream forces with more effective handguns there was also a need for specialist weapons.

The end of World War II did not produce the same conditions as the first. Mistrust among the Allies resulted in what amounted to an armed standoff that kept large numbers of troops under arms and required huge amounts of weaponry. New conflicts began almost as soon as the dust had

ABOVE: **The Spanish Civil War drew in volunteers from all walks of life, often armed with whatever they could lay their hands on. Astra pistols saw service with many different factions, on both sides of the war.**

settled from the last, and while at first these were fought with World War II legacy weapons, development continued and a new generation of equipment gradually appeared. By the early 1960s, semi-automatic battle rifles and fully automatic assault rifles were the standard infantry arm, and the revolver was almost entirely gone as a military sidearm. It remained popular for personal defence, security and law enforcement applications, however, but the semi-automatic pistol was gaining popularity in that sector too.

### Spanish Semi-automatics

The Spanish firm Bonifacio Echeverria SA introduced the Star Model A, B, P and variants upon them in the 1920s. Derived from the Colt M1911, the Star Model A was chambered for the 9mm (.35in) Largo round then in current Spanish service, and was aimed at the domestic market. The Model B was chambered for 9mm Luger and intended for export. One of the buyers of this weapon was the rearming military of Germany,

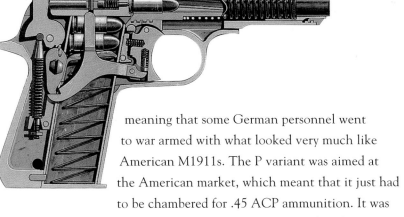

meaning that some German personnel went to war armed with what looked very much like American M1911s. The P variant was aimed at the American market, which meant that it just had to be chambered for .45 ACP ammunition. It was successful in the marketplace, not least because it followed in the footsteps of the very well proven M1911 and its various copies, and remained in production for many years. The Star Model P differed from the M1911 in various ways, notably its lack of a grip safety. Later models more closely resembled the M1911.

In the mid-1930s, an experimental assault pistol was produced under the designation Star PD. Even with extended magazines for more ammunition capacity and an attachable holster/stock, this weapon was as unsuccessful as other weapons of the type, and quickly faded away. The designation PD was later used for a compact .45 pistol, which is an entirely different weapon.

Meanwhile, Astra were also making handguns aimed at the export market. The Astra 600 was manufactured in the later years of World War II for use by the German armed forces. Chambered for 9mm (.35in) Luger, it was heavy and recoiled in a manner that some users found uncomfortable but provided good accuracy and reliability. Relatively few of the pistols ordered were actually delivered before the war's end, with the remainder going to the open market or various users – including the German police – after the war.

Another export handgun was the Model 900, which was a copy of the Mauser C96. It saw action in the Spanish Civil War but a large proportion of those made were exported to China. Others went to Germany and various Latin American clients, with sales to the Middle East in the 1950s. Several variants were produced, including an assault pistol version. This was given model numbers from 901 to 904, designating changes to magazine size and type and, in the case of the 904 variant, calibre. The 901 to 903 models were chambered for 7.63x25mm (.30x.98in) ammunition, with fixed 10- and 20-round magazines in the case of the 901 and 902 respectively. Fully

**ASTRA FALCON**
**COUNTRY OF ORIGIN**
Spain
**DATE**
1956
**CALIBRE**
9mm Short (.35in)
**WEIGHT**
.646kg (1.4lb)
**OVERALL LENGTH**
164mm (6.4in)
**FEED/MAGAZINE**
7-round magazine
**RANGE**
30m (32.8yds)

automatic fire would empty this weapon almost instantly, and stripped-clip reloading was just too slow so the 903 version gained a detachable magazine.

The main flaw with all these weapons was that, even though the recoil of 7.63mm ammunition was fairly low, automatic fire resulted in virtually uncontrollable muzzle climb. The Model 904 attempted to remedy this by reducing rate of fire, but this was at best a partial success. The standard 904 model was chambered for 7.63mm but a 9mm Largo variant, designated 904E, was also marketed.

## BROWNING HI-POWER

**COUNTRY OF ORIGIN**
Belgium/United States
**DATE**
1935
**CALIBRE**
9mm Parabellum (.35in)
**WEIGHT**
.99kg (2.19lb)
**OVERALL LENGTH**
197mm (7.75in)
**FEED/MAGAZINE**
13-round magazine
**RANGE**
30m (32.8yds)

### Browning's Other Classic

Early semi-automatic pistols either carried little more ammunition than a revolver or else had large, bulky magazines. In the early 1920s the French Army decided it wanted the best of both worlds – a large-capacity handgun in a compact package. They naturally also wanted the weapon to have enough stopping power to be an effective combat weapon. The task of reconciling these requirements fell to John Moses Browning, who was commissioned by FN Herstal to produce a handgun to meet the French Army's stipulations. He could not produce a developed version of the M191 as Colt now had the patents for that weapon; the new handgun would have to be designed from scratch.

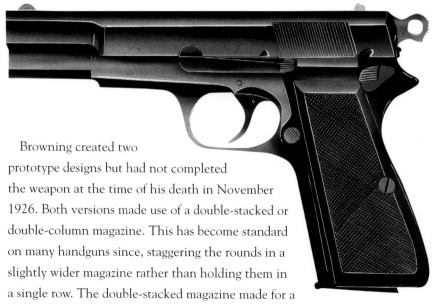

Browning created two
prototype designs but had not completed
the weapon at the time of his death in November
1926. Both versions made use of a double-stacked or
double-column magazine. This has become standard
on many handguns since, staggering the rounds in a
slightly wider magazine rather than holding them in
a single row. The double-stacked magazine made for a
wider handgrip, but not excessively so, especially as the 9x19mm (.35x.74in)
ammunition selected was of fairly modest dimensions. The new pistol was
finished after Browning's death and incorporated some features of his 1911
design for Colt, as the patents on that had expired. The resulting weapon
held 13 rounds, which is where the name 'Hi-Power' or 'Grande Puissance'
comes from – the term refers to firepower rather than the striking power of
any particular round.

Ironically, the French Army did not adopt the Browning Hi-Power, but
the Belgian Army took it into service as the Browning HP-35 (or GP-45).
Other armies followed suit, including the British. At the outbreak of World
War II, the FN plant in Belgium was overrun by Axis forces, which needed
pistols as badly as every other force of the era. Thus many HP-35s went into
Axis service, while the Allies continued to produce them in Canada.

The HP-35 was not available in sufficient numbers to completely replace
older weapons, including Webley and Enfield revolvers, in service during
the war. Older weapons were phased out afterwards, leaving the 9mm
(.35in) Browning (in its guise as the L9A1) as the standard British service
pistol. The HP-35 enjoyed massive export success, achieving sales to many
nations worldwide. Variants appeared over time, with the weapon gaining
an ambidextrous safety and other, shorter-lived modifications. Some
weapons built during and just before the war have a slotted grip to allow
a holster/stock to be fitted. This modification, intended to allow a pistol
to be used as a carbine, faded into obscurity after the conflict. Variants

## L9A1
**COUNTRY OF ORIGIN**
Belgium/United States (UK
armed forces)
**DATE**
1962
**CALIBRE**
9mm Parabellum (.35in)
**WEIGHT**
.88kg (1.9lb)
**OVERALL LENGTH**
196mm (7.71in)
**FEED/MAGAZINE**
13-round magazine
**RANGE**
40m (43.7yds)

chambered for 10.16mm (.4in) calibre ammunition, and featuring double-action triggers, have been marketed but the single-action, 9mm calibre HP-35 remains highly popular today. It has been phased out of service in many military forces, although some retain it, but HP-35s (and copies of it) are still manufactured.

### Smaller Calibre Semi-automatics

Having called for a high-capacity semi-automatic pistol with a level of stopping power that required a fairly large cartridge, the French Army then decided to adopt the 7.65x22mm (.3x.86in) calibre Model 1935 semi-automatic handgun. Despite its designation, the new pistol did not go into production until 1936. A modified version appeared in 1938, mainly to simplify and speed up production. The new French service weapon carried only eight rounds in its magazine – rather fewer than the original specification had called for – and its 7.65mm ammunition was underpowered. Despite this, the Modele 1935 served satisfactorily until the 1950s.

In the meantime, Walther produced a small-calibre double-action pistol designated PP. Most of these pistols were chambered for 7.65x17mm (.32 ACP), with smaller numbers in 9x17mm (.380 ACP) and a few examples in either .22 or .25 calibre. The PP and its smaller cousin (designated PPK) featured a double-action trigger to enable the weapon to be brought instantly into action. Among the intended users were plain-clothes police officers who needed a small, concealable handgun. The PP and PPK were used by German military and police personnel before and during World War II, and afterwards the weapon was widely exported. This resulted in

## WALTHER PPK
**COUNTRY OF ORIGIN**
Germany
**DATE**
1929
**CALIBRE**
9mm Short (.38in) or 7.65mm
(.301 in) or 6.35mm (.25in)
or .5.6mm (.22in)
**WEIGHT**
.59kg (1.3lb)
**OVERALL LENGTH**
148mm (5.8in)
**FEED/MAGAZINE**
7-round magazine
**RANGE**
30m (32.8yds)

the hybrid PPK/S model that was created to comply with U.S. import laws. Since the PPK was just too small to be permitted for import under 'sporting purpose' laws, using a PP frame with the PPK's smaller slide and barrel brought them within legal limits.

Having established a reputation for producing reliable, effective handguns during World War I and immediately afterward, Beretta was finally rewarded with the adoption of their Modelo 1934 handgun as the standard Italian Army sidearm. Although not a small-calibre handgun in the sense of a 7.65mm (.301in) weapon, the Modelo 1934 fired a 9mm Short (.380in ACP) cartridge that was underpowered for a military handgun. Despite this drawback, the Modelo 1934 gave good service with the Italian Army and quantities were also used by German and Romanian forces. A variant

ABOVE: Although firing an underpowered 9x17mm short cartridge, the Beretta Modelo 1934 was a fine handgun that gave good service with the Italian armed forces. It remained in production until the early 1990s.

## CZ-38
**COUNTRY OF ORIGIN**
Czechoslovakia
**DATE**
1938
**CALIBRE**
9mm Browning Short (.38in)
**WEIGHT**
.909kg (2lb)
**OVERALL LENGTH**
198mm (7.8in)
**FEED/MAGAZINE**
8-round magazine
**RANGE**
30m (32.8yds)

## TOKAREV TT30
**COUNTRY OF ORIGIN**
Soviet Union
**DATE**
1930
**CALIBRE**
7.62mm (.3in)
**WEIGHT**
.83kg (1.83lb)
**OVERALL LENGTH**
194mm (7.6in)
**FEED/MAGAZINE**
8-round magazine
**RANGE**
30m (32.8yds)

chambered for .32 ACP (7.65x17mm) was used by aircrews and designated the Modelo 1935. These weapons remained in service into the 1950s and were produced for three decades after that.

Another 9mm Short (.380in ACP) weapon introduced in the 1930s was the Czech CZ-38. This was developed from the earlier Vz22 and Vz24 weapons that were actually designed to shoot 9mm Luger ammunition but were put into production using the 9mm Short cartridge that was at the time the standard Czech Army pistol round. Designed for a more potent cartridge, the Vz22 and Vz24 pistols were unreliable and overcomplex, with breech-locking features that were unnecessary for the lighter round. As a result they tended to be unreliable but remained in service until the German invasion, after which production went to the German Army. The CZ-38, intended to rectify the earlier weapons' deficiencies, was in fact even more flawed.

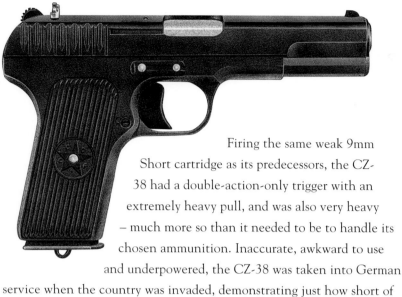

Firing the same weak 9mm Short cartridge as its predecessors, the CZ-38 had a double-action-only trigger with an extremely heavy pull, and was also very heavy – much more so than it needed to be to handle its chosen ammunition. Inaccurate, awkward to use and underpowered, the CZ-38 was taken into German service when the country was invaded, demonstrating just how short of pistols the Axis military was at the time.

The Russian military never viewed handguns as serious combat systems, and was content to field weapons that could serve as a status symbol for officers or a means of enforcing discipline. Even so, by the late 1920s the Nagant revolver was showing its age and a modern replacement seemed to be in order. A design by Fedor Tokarev was accepted for service in 1930. Trials over the next few years resulted in some modifications and the appearance of the Tula-Tokarev TT33 as the standard Red Army sidearm. The pistol was chambered for 7.63mm (.3in) ammunition, largely due to the influence of the Mauser C96 that was a popular private purchase by Russian officers. Although not the most powerful cartridge, the Russian Army felt that 7.63mm (.3in) was adequate for its purpose.

The Tokarev was an extremely robust weapon, tolerant of the dirty, cold conditions that the Red Army operated in much of the time. It was, however, uncomfortable to hold and distinctly lacking in safety devices. With a single-action-only trigger and no grip or manual safety, the Tokarev could not be safely carried with a round chambered; standard practice was to make the weapon ready by working the slide to chamber a round and cock the weapon only if shooting was imminent. Although not a great combat weapon, the Tokarev pistol was sufficiently reliable to do its job under almost any conditions, and was fielded in vast numbers by the Red Army. Examples were also widely sold overseas, notably to China and Eastern Europe. It was phased out of military use in the 1960s.

## TULA-TOKAREV TT33

**COUNTRY OF ORIGIN**
Soviet Union
**DATE**
1933
**CALIBRE**
7.63mm (.3in)
**WEIGHT**
.83kg (1.83lb)
**OVERALL LENGTH**
194mm (7.6in)
**FEED/MAGAZINE**
8-round magazine
**RANGE**
30m (32.8yds)

RIGHT: Although officially superseded by the Walther P38, the Parabellum '08 (or Luger) remained in service with German forces throughout World War II. It became a popular souvenir for Allied troops who could find or buy one.

## 9mm Semi-automatics

After World War II, a fairly sharp divide appeared between the calibres favoured by NATO nations and those used by the Soviet Union and her allies. Attempts at standardization resulted in some calibres more or less disappearing while others became common only in the civilian marketplace.

Among the most common, at least in the West, was the 9mm (.35in) Luger that was adopted as a standard NATO ammunition type and also became a dominant cartridge in the non-military marketplace. This situation arose in part from the pre-war weapons marketplace, where designs were studied by competitors or sold to clients that would at some time in the future be enemies. Despite the variety of other cartridges that were available, most European wartime handguns were chambered for 9mm Luger. This made it possible for one side to scavenge ammunition from the other, and in some cases even weapon components were common to both sides. The British Sten sub-machinegun used the same magazine as the German MP38, and was in turn copied for late-war emergency production to provide weapons for the Volkssturm militia.

The prevalence of certain calibres – including 9mm (.35in) and .45 ACP – made it virtually certain that these would become the standard

**ABOVE:** The Tokarev pistol became as much a symbol of Soviet forces as the Luger was for the German military, not least through staged propaganda pictures like this one.

## WALTHER P38

**COUNTRY OF ORIGIN**

Germany

**DATE**

1938

**CALIBRE**

9mm Parabellum (.35in)

**WEIGHT**

.96kg (2.11lb)

**OVERALL LENGTH**

213mm (8.38in)

**FEED/MAGAZINE**

8-round magazine

**RANGE**

30m (32.8yds)

ammunition of the post-war years. The rise to dominance of these calibres was gradual evolution but it was World War II that provided the filtering process that finally determined which would emerge into the post-war world and which would fade into obscurity. Firmly wedded to the idea of a 9x19mm (.35x.74in) calibre service pistol, the German military sought a replacement for the Parabellum '08 during the 1930s. The new weapon was to offer the same accuracy and overall good performance as the P'08 but simpler and cheaper to construct. Walther put forward a design to meet these criteria, which after some modification was accepted for service as the P38.

The original Heerpistole ('Army Pistol') had a concealed hammer, but the production model adopted by the German military featured one that was partially exposed to allow for manual cocking. The accepted model went into production in 1938 and was not available in sufficient numbers to re-equip the German military before the outbreak of war, or even before its end.

## WALTHER P1/P4

**COUNTRY OF ORIGIN**

West Germany

**DATE**

1957

**CALIBRE**

9mm Parabellum (.35in)

**WEIGHT**

.84kg (1.9lb) or .77kg (1.7lb)

**OVERALL LENGTH**

216mm (8.5in) or 197mm (7.8in)

**FEED/MAGAZINE**

8-round magazine

**RANGE**

50m (54.7yds)

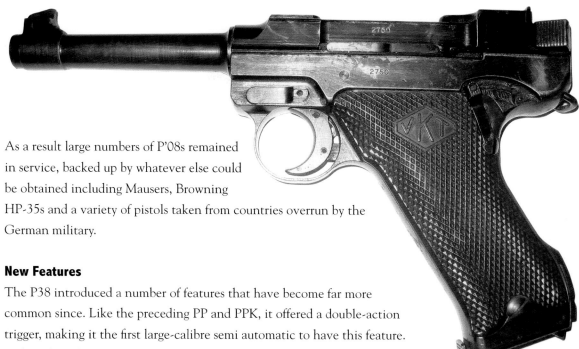

As a result large numbers of P'08s remained in service, backed up by whatever else could be obtained including Mausers, Browning HP-35s and a variety of pistols taken from countries overrun by the German military.

## New Features

The P38 introduced a number of features that have become far more common since. Like the preceding PP and PPK, it offered a double-action trigger, making it the first large-calibre semi automatic to have this feature. A decocking lever allowed the user to lower the hammer after chambering the first round, giving a choice between manually cocking the weapon upon deploying it or firing the first shot double action and subsequent ones single action like any other semi-automatic weapon. Production continued after World War II, mostly in French factories, and it was reintroduced as a police and military sidearm for West German forces. Most post-war P38 pistols were made with an aluminium frame, with those intended for police and army use designated P1 and civilian models still using the P38 identifier. New requirements for German police service, introduced in the 1970s, resulted in a P4 model. Variants, including a very short concealed-carry version, were also fielded.

The Finnish Lahti L-35, although superficially similar to the P'08, was a wholly different design created in Finland. Given the cold conditions of its country of origin, it is not surprising that the weapon's design included a bolt accelerator to improve function in Arctic conditions. The L-35 was adopted for the Finnish Army and served into the 1980s. It was also manufactured in a slightly modified form in Sweden. This Swedish model was designated M/40, and it used a simplified design that omitted the bolt accelerator. The M/40 served in the Swedish Army until the 1980s, but towards the end of its career weapons began to show dangerous weakening and were quickly retired.

## LAHTI L-35
**COUNTRY OF ORIGIN**
Finland
**DATE**
1935
**CALIBRE**
9mm Parabellum (.35in)
**WEIGHT**
1.2kg (2.6lb)
**OVERALL LENGTH**
65in
**FEED/MAGAZINE**
8-round magazine
**RANGE**
50m (54.7yds)

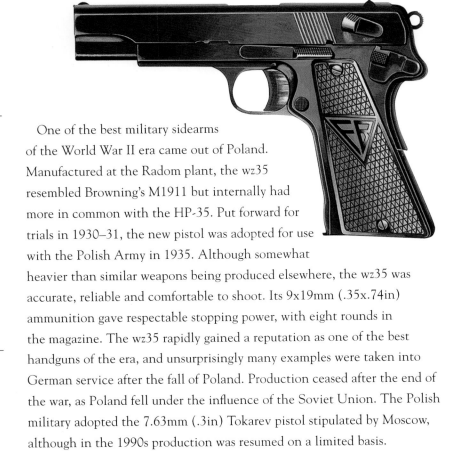

## RADOM WZ35

**COUNTRY OF ORIGIN**
Poland
**DATE**
1935
**CALIBRE**
9mm Parabellum (.35in)
**WEIGHT**
1.022kg (2.25lb)
**OVERALL LENGTH**
197mm (7.76in)
**FEED/MAGAZINE**
8-round magazine
**RANGE**
30m (32.8yds)

One of the best military sidearms of the World War II era came out of Poland. Manufactured at the Radom plant, the wz35 resembled Browning's M1911 but internally had more in common with the HP-35. Put forward for trials in 1930–31, the new pistol was adopted for use with the Polish Army in 1935. Although somewhat heavier than similar weapons being produced elsewhere, the wz35 was accurate, reliable and comfortable to shoot. Its 9x19mm (.35x.74in) ammunition gave respectable stopping power, with eight rounds in the magazine. The wz35 rapidly gained a reputation as one of the best handguns of the era, and unsurprisingly many examples were taken into German service after the fall of Poland. Production ceased after the end of the war, as Poland fell under the influence of the Soviet Union. The Polish military adopted the 7.63mm (.3in) Tokarev pistol stipulated by Moscow, although in the 1990s production was resumed on a limited basis.

### Pistols for Covert Operations

Most handguns were reasonably well suited to covert operations and all but the most bulky could be concealed fairly easily. Small-calibre pistols might not be ideal for combat operations but they could be used for emergency self-defence or to assassinate enemy personnel, and they did have the advantage of better concealability. For the secret agent working behind enemy lines, not being discovered was the only viable defence – no amount of weaponry would prevent disaster if the local garrison came after them all at once. Operatives were not there to fight the enemy – their role was to observe and report, and to liaise with local resistance fighters. Thus they were often provided with a handgun 'just in case'; somehow parachuting an agent into enemy-held Europe with a handgun was more palatable than sending him in completely unarmed. His gun might provide an alternative to capture and torture, and it might just possibly get him out of trouble – at least temporarily.

A handgun could also be used to obtain a better weapon, usually by surprising an enemy soldier and delivering one or more quick shots before any response could be made. A handgun might be traded up in this manner for a more effective submachine gun or rifle, and again for this role any gun would do. The Allies, seeking to cause as much mayhem and distraction in occupied Europe as possible, came up with the idea of airdropping extremely cheap handguns into Europe for use by resistance fighters. The result was the Liberator pistol, an unbelievably crude but workable smoothbore single-shot weapon that could be used for a surprise attack but which was no good at all in a firefight.

The Liberator fired .45 ACP ammunition, but was loaded with a single round by a cumbersome manual process. There was no ejection system; once fired, the spent case had to be poked out of the weapon with a stick. Spare ammunition was held inside the grip, on the off-chance that a resistance fighter got the chance to re-use the weapon. The pistol was designed to be as cheap as possible to make, and was dropped rather randomly into occupied Europe. It mattered little if a consignment of Liberators fell into enemy hands, as the enemy was scarcely gaining in combat power. But the availability of a borderline effective assassination weapon might enable resistance groups to eliminate some enemy personnel and perhaps even obtain some proper weaponry. There is no evidence to suggest that much use was made of the Liberator, but in the dark days of World War II it offered a chance to strike at the enemy for very little outlay.

Rather more sophisticated and specialized was the Welrod pistol, a custom-designed assassination weapon for use by covert agents. The Welrod was chambered for .32 ACP (7.65mm) or 9mm (.35in) ammunition and held eight or six rounds in its magazine. Operation was manual, with each round chambered by pulling back a knob on the rear of the weapon, and the handgrip had to be removed to reload the internal

**LIBERATOR M1942**
**COUNTRY OF ORIGIN**
United States
**DATE**
1942
**CALIBRE**
11.43mm (.45in)
**WEIGHT**
.454kg (1lb)
**OVERALL LENGTH**
141mm (5.55in)
**FEED/MAGAZINE**
Single shot
**RANGE**
8m (8.7yds)

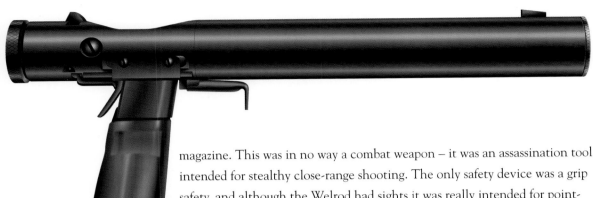

## WELROD

**COUNTRY OF ORIGIN**
United Kingdom
**DATE**
1940
**CALIBRE**
7.65mm (.301in)
**WEIGHT**
1.09kg (2.4lb)
**OVERALL LENGTH**
310mm (12in)
**FEED/MAGAZINE**
8-round magazine
**RANGE**
20m (21.9yds)

magazine. This was in no way a combat weapon – it was an assassination tool intended for stealthy close-range shooting. The only safety device was a grip safety, and although the Welrod had sights it was really intended for point-blank assassination.

Similar in concept was the 'Glove Gun', which was essentially a device to fire a pistol cartridge mounted on the back of a glove. It was triggered by a bar extending forward from the glove, allowing an assassination to be carried out by poking the target with a hand and then moving quickly away. Weapons of this sort do not need to follow the conventional rules of firearm design as they are specialized for a single purpose – to deliver a bullet at point-blank range against an unsuspecting target.

### Post-war Revolvers

The semi-automatic pistol was the official sidearm of most combatant nations in World War II. It was prevalent to the point where figures like General George S. Patton, who carried revolvers as his personal weapons, have come to be considered somewhat quirky. However, the revolver did play a significant part in the conflict, not least because there were simply not enough semi-automatic pistols available. In some nations replacement had not yet been completed; in others, revolvers were brought out of storage to equip the greatly expanded forces being fielded.

After the war, most sales of revolvers were private or to law enforcement agencies; military contracts were very rare. However, there were exceptions. In the 1950s, the bomber crews of Strategic Air Command required a sidearm in case of emergencies. As their aircraft were intended to make very long flights to their targets – halfway around the world, and hopefully back home again – the weight that could be allocated to crew equipment was strictly limited. The solution was the Colt Aircrewman, an aluminium-framed version of Colt's Detective Special revolver chambered for .38 Special. Large numbers were issued, but soon it became apparent that the aluminium frame was not up to the stresses of firing the ammunition. As reports of cracked

frames and cylinders increased, the decision was made to implement a low-powered .38 round, but this did not entirely solve the problem. Eventually the Aircrewman was withdrawn from service and the vast majority of weapons were destroyed. Some Aircrewman revolvers did survive, often in the hands of personnel who had left the service before the recall, but today they are rare.

ABOVE: During Prohibition, semi-automatic pistols became popular with law enforcement personnel who were able to choose their own weapons.

RIGHT: Although semi-automatic pistols were available, revolvers were the standard sidearm for British and Canadian troops throughout World War II.

Smith & Wesson also supplied weapons to Strategic Air Command in the form of an aluminium-framed revolver of their own. Designated M13, it was derived from the S&W Model 12 revolver. The M13 suffered the same problems as its Colt competitor, and military examples went the same way. A civilian variant was marketed, initially as the Military & Police Airweight, then as the Model 12 Airweight. A move from aluminium to steel cylinders occurred after the first year of issue, and aluminium models may not be safe to shoot even with fairly low-powered ammunition. The Smith & Wesson Model 12, like many similar small revolvers, was a popular concealed-carry pistol or backup weapon for police officers. Other revolvers in this category include the Smith & Wesson Model 36. This was the first of the 'J'-frame revolvers marketed by Smith & Wesson, and remains in production today.

Smith & Wesson use a system of letter-coding revolver frames, with

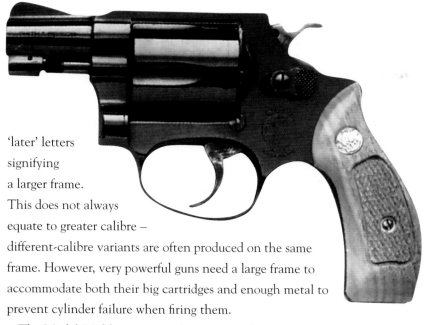

'later' letters
signifying
a larger frame.
This does not always
equate to greater calibre –
different-calibre variants are often produced on the same
frame. However, very powerful guns need a large frame to
accommodate both their big cartridges and enough metal to
prevent cylinder failure when firing them.

The Model 36, like many similar weapons, has seen numerous variants
on its small-frame, five-shot theme. It was initially marketed as the 'Chief's
Special', and was sufficiently popular that the name is sometimes misapplied
to other weapons of the type. Chambered for .38 Special, the Model 36
remains a popular backup or concealed-carry gun.

While the majority of revolvers carry six rounds in the cylinder, not
all revolvers are sixguns. Many small weapons carry five, reducing the
width of the cylinder and therefore the overall bulk and weight of the

## SMITH & WESSON 'CHIEF'S SPECIAL'

**COUNTRY OF ORIGIN**
United States
**DATE**
1950
**CALIBRE**
9.65mm (.38in)
**WEIGHT**
.553kg (1.2lb)
**OVERALL LENGTH**
176mm (6.94in)
**FEED/MAGAZINE**
5-shot revolver
**RANGE**
23m (25.2yds)

## SMITH & WESSON CENTENNIAL

**COUNTRY OF ORIGIN**
United States
**DATE**
1952
**CALIBRE**
9.6mm (.38in) (.38 Special or
.357 Magnum)
**WEIGHT**
.59kg (1.5lb)
**OVERALL LENGTH**
160.3mm (6.94in)
**FEED/MAGAZINE**
5-shot revolver
**RANGE**
30m (32.8yds)

weapon. Another small five-shot 'J'-frame revolver is the Smith & Wesson Centennial, a double-action-only revolver with a concealed hammer. Available in a variety of calibres and numerous named and numbered variants, the Centennial can be chambered for anything from .22 Long Rifle to .357 Magnum ammunition.

Some small-calibre revolvers are built on a relatively large frame. The Colt Trooper, aimed at the law enforcement marketplace, was chambered for .38 Special but a .22 variant was also available. The latter lacked the stopping power that a police weapon requires and was largely intended for training purposes, or for private shooters who wanted a large 'plinking' gun. The .22 Trooper was inefficient, in that its cylinder had room for six .38 rounds and enough metal to fire them safely. When chambered for .22 Long Rifle that meant that there was a lot of wasted bulk and weight. It did make the Trooper suitable for adaptation into a budget .357 Magnum weapon, which in turn led to the cheaper Colt Lawman.

This process of evolution has resulted in numerous models and variants, not always with any discernible logic. Firearms manufacturers are in business like anyone else, and a good name can boost sales. Thus it may make sense to an outside observer to create a logical, codified system of model names and numbers, but sometimes the reputation of an earlier model is seen as a sufficiently important marketing tool to merit transferring to a new weapon – even if it causes the neat model/calibre/variant system to break down.

## Post-war Semi-automatic Pistols

One problem facing the militaries of the world immediately after World War II was rationalization of their equipment. Wartime expedience had resulted in a range of makes, models and calibres being shoved into large-scale production to meet a desperate need. As the dust settled and the shape of the post-war world became apparent, decisions had to be made about the future of small-arms issue in many countries. In some cases, the choice was dictated by economic factors. In others, international politics played a part. As the world began to polarize into superpower alliances, the weapons available to nations sometimes came with unacceptable strings attached.

World War II ended – and the Cold War began – with the Soviet Union in control of most of Eastern Europe. Weapons adopted by the Soviet armed forces became the standard weaponry of Russia's allies – not all of them voluntary. Seeking a new pistol to replace the Tokarev in service with these

**LEFT:** Nikolai Makarov's pistol was in Soviet service for four decades. He was made a Hero of Soviet Labour, among other honours, for his contribution to Russian weapons technology,

## P-64
**COUNTRY OF ORIGIN**
Poland
**DATE**
1965
**CALIBRE**
9mm Makarov (.35in)
**WEIGHT**
.62kg (1.36lb)
**OVERALL LENGTH**
160mm (6.3in)
**FEED/MAGAZINE**
6-round magazine
**RANGE**
40m (43.7yds)

nations, the Soviet Union eventually selected a design created by Nikolai Makarov. The Makarov pistol was influenced by the German PP and PPK, but was built around a new cartridge, officially of 9x18mm (.35x.70in) dimensions. In fact the rounds were not only shorter than 9x19mm (9mm Luger) but also a little wider, so there was no compatibility with Western ammunition. The new design offered reasonable stopping power and was cheap to manufacture. Given the numbers required this was of great importance.

The Makarov served for many years with police and military forces, and remains on issue in many countries although it has been replaced in Russian service. Despite being inaccurate it is small and easy to conceal, and at the

## STETCHKIN

**COUNTRY OF ORIGIN**
Soviet Union
**DATE**
1948
**CALIBRE**
9mm Makarov (.35in)
**WEIGHT**
1.03kg (2.27lb)
**OVERALL LENGTH**
225mm (8.86in)
**FEED/MAGAZINE**
20-round magazine
**RANGE**
20m (21.9yds)

sort of ranges where a concealed weapon tends to come into play accuracy is not a major consideration. The pistol was updated in the 1990s, creating a version known as Makarov PMM. In the meantime original Makarovs were exported and copied worldwide, with the most numerous copies being the Type 59 pistol used by the Chinese armed forces. The Polish P-64 pistol, built around the same round and visually similar to the Makarov, was also influenced by the Walther PPK.

The Polish P-83 Wanad pistol, which followed the P-64 into service, also has a distinctly 'East European' look about it, which is hardly surprising. Produced for the Polish military and police, it was designed around 9x18mm (.35x.70in) Makarov cartridge, but is available in a range of small-calibre chamberings including .38) ACP and .32 ACP. Like many militaries, especially in Europe since the end of the Cold War, the Polish Army has moved to 9x19mm (.35x.74in) as a standard pistol round. Among the replacements for the P-83 is the more 'Western'-looking WIST-94 pistol that is chambered for 9x19mm. It has little resemblance to previous Polish service pistols, which suggests that the Makarov is no longer as influential in Eastern Europe as it previously was.

Hungarian gun designers created the PA-63 pistol by a process of evolution following on from the Walther PPK, and then rechambered their weapon for the Russian Makarov cartridge. Although a very similar weapon capable of firing the same ammunition, the 'Hungarian Makarov' is not a Makarov at all. Variants chambered for .380 ACP and .32 are available but are not common.

The Stetchkin assault pistol was developed as a personal defence weapon for vehicle crews and artillery personnel, and unusually for its era was provided with a detachable stock. Capable of fully automatic fire, the Stetchkin was originally chambered for the 7.62x25mm (.3x.98in) round used in the Tokarev pistol, and was then modified to use 9x18mm (.35x.7in)

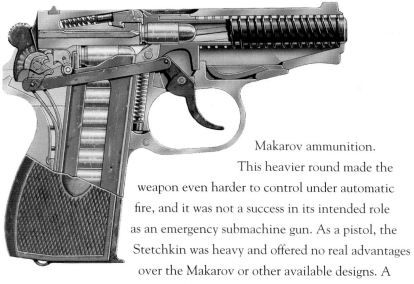

Makarov ammunition. This heavier round made the weapon even harder to control under automatic fire, and it was not a success in its intended role as an emergency submachine gun. As a pistol, the Stetchkin was heavy and offered no real advantages over the Makarov or other available designs. A suppressed version, with a wire stock, was retained in service and may still be in the arsenal of Special Forces units.

Even as the Tokarev pistol was being phased out of Soviet service, attempts were made to sell the design overseas. One example was the 'Tokagypt', developed for sale to the Egyptian armed forces. The Tokagypt was produced in Hungary and chambered for 9x19mm (.35x.74in) ammunition. The Egyptian military eventually rejected it, although the police took it into service. The rest of the manufacturing run went to the general market. The Tokagypt was edged out in favour of a licence-built version of the

## MAKAROV
**COUNTRY OF ORIGIN**
Soviet Union
**DATE**
1951
**CALIBRE**
9mm Makarov (.35in)
**WEIGHT**
.66kg (1.46lb)
**OVERALL LENGTH**
160mm (6.3in)
**FEED/MAGAZINE**
6-round magazine
**RANGE**
40m (43.7yds)

## TOKAGYPT 58
**COUNTRY OF ORIGIN**
Egypt/Hungary
**DATE**
1958
**CALIBRE**
9mm Parabellum (.35in)
**WEIGHT**
.91kg (2.01lb)
**OVERALL LENGTH**
194mm (7.65in)
**FEED/MAGAZINE**
7-round magazine
**RANGE:**
30m (32.8yds)

## BERETTA M1934
**COUNTRY OF ORIGIN**
Italy
**DATE**
1934
**CALIBRE**
9mm Short (.35in)
**WEIGHT**
.65kg (1.4lb)
**OVERALL LENGTH**
152mm (6in)
**FEED/MAGAZINE**
9-round magazine
**RANGE**
30m (32.8yds)

Beretta M1951,
known as the Helwan
in Egyptian service. The
M1951 was created to replace the earlier
Beretta M1934 in Italian military service, and
hopefully to generate sales on the international
military market. A fully automatic version
was produced and went into service with some
police, Special Forces and VIP-protection
units. However, with a very high rate of
fire and a relatively small magazine capacity
the effectiveness of this weapon was limited. Variants of the standard semi-
automatic M1951 chambered for other cartridges (notably 7.65x22mm) were
marketed worldwide.

By 1950, the French military was in
need of a new service pistol. French
procurement was complicated
by the fact that production was
interrupted by occupation during most
of World War II, and then significant
quantities of sometimes mismatched
equipment were handed over as
war reparations. Rationalizing
the equipment of the French
armed forces was a project that
took some time. Eventually,
a developed version of the Modele 1935

## BERETTA M1951
**COUNTRY OF ORIGIN**
Italy
**DATE**
1951
**CALIBRE**
9mm Parabellum (.35in)
**WEIGHT**
.87kg (1.92lb)
**OVERALL LENGTH**
203mm (8in)
**FEED/MAGAZINE**
8-round magazine
**RANGE**
50m (54.7yds)

pistol was settled upon. Visually fairly typical of the era, the MAS 1950
was a conventional 9x19mm (.35x.74in) semi-automatic pistol that proved
adequate for police and military service. Although not especially accurate it
was robust and reliable, and served through the 1950s to the 1970s.

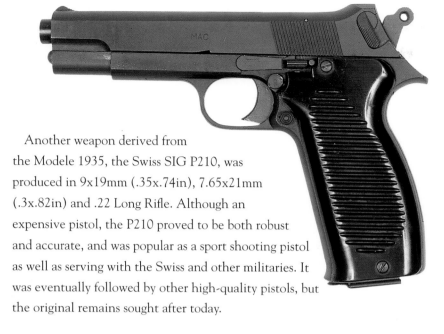

Another weapon derived from the Modele 1935, the Swiss SIG P210, was produced in 9x19mm (.35x.74in), 7.65x21mm (.3x.82in) and .22 Long Rifle. Although an expensive pistol, the P210 proved to be both robust and accurate, and was popular as a sport shooting pistol as well as serving with the Swiss and other militaries. It was eventually followed by other high-quality pistols, but the original remains sought after today.

## Magnum Revolvers

The quest for greater handgun stopping power led to manufacturers – notably Smith & Wesson – experimenting with more powerful ammunition. The result was often a longer cartridge, holding more propellant, mated to an existing calibre of bullet. The .357 Magnum round is one example. The word Magnum means 'big', although whether this referred to a longer cartridge or a more powerful round – or both – is open to opinion. The new

### MAS 1950
COUNTRY OF ORIGIN
France
DATE
1950
CALIBRE
9mm Parabellum (.35in)
WEIGHT
.0.86kg (1.8lb)
OVERALL LENGTH
195mm (7.7in)
FEED/MAGAZINE
9-round magazine
RANGE
50m (54.7yds)

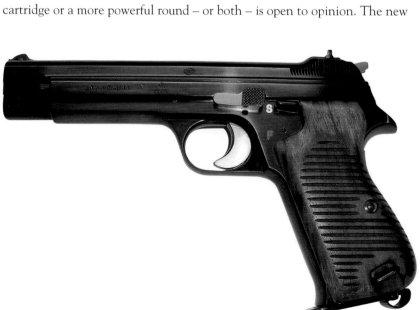

### SIG P210
COUNTRY OF ORIGIN
Switzerland
DATE
1949
CALIBRE
9mm Parabellum (.35in)
WEIGHT
.0.9kg (1.98lb)
OVERALL LENGTH
215mm (8.5in)
FEED/MAGAZINE
8-round magazine
RANGE
30m (32.8yds)

RIGHT: The Magnum-calibre revolver is often thought of as a fairly recent invention, but it has been around for many years. This example was used in an armed robbery in 1938.

round was developed from .38 Special, which due to the vagaries of naming conventions actually has the same bullet diameter. Weapon calibres are sometimes measured from the inside of the bore, sometimes from the depth of the rifling grooves and occasionally the diameter of the bullet itself. To make matters even more potentially confusing, there is some tolerance – but not usually very much – in the diameter of bullet that can be accommodated by a weapon of a given calibre.

Since the .357 Magnum cartridge is slightly longer than a .38 Special, a weapon chambered for .357in Magnum will accept and fire .38 Special. More importantly, it will do so without any danger of bursting since it is built to withstand a higher chamber pressure. The opposite might not be true for a .38 weapon; built on a lighter frame, with less metal in the chamber walls, a .38 handgun might not survive the greater chamber pressures of .357 Magnum. However, since the cartridge is too long to fit in the cylinder, potentially dangerous errors are impossible.

In 1935 Smith & Wesson introduced a revolver built to fire the new Magnum round, creating a very potent handgun in a package only a little heavier than a solidly made .38. With a variety of barrel lengths on offer the new model was at least somewhat adaptable to different roles, although it remained a chunky and heavy weapon. Initially available only in small numbers, the new .357 revolver eventually became a mainstream market success under the designation M27.

Most of the revolvers used in World War II were left over from earlier procurement, and although the M27 did see some service it was not one of the main weapons issued to combat troops. Law enforcement and private users were much more interested in the new generation of big-calibre revolvers, and it was taken into service with police departments and federal agencies in the USA. As a rule, law enforcement agencies have tended to favour powerful handguns over smaller calibres. A lone officer or federal agent might be confronted with multiple assailants and needs to be confident of a 'one-shot stop'. Ironically, having a gun that would indeed bring proceedings to a rapid close often meant not having to fire at all. A gun that commanded respect – and the officer's obvious confidence in it – could be a very powerful deterrent.

The M27 remained in production for many years, and is today available as the M627. Modern Smith & Wesson product designations are a code that identifies the weapon's characteristics to those that understand it. In this case it is simple – '6' indicates a stainless steel frame revolver and '27' refers to the weapon's lineage, which comes down from the classic M27. After World

## COLT PYTHON
**COUNTRY OF ORIGIN**
United States
**DATE**
1955
**CALIBRE**
9.1mm (.357in)
**WEIGHT**
1.08–1.2kg (2.37–2.62lb)
**OVERALL LENGTH**
235mm (9.25in)
**FEED/MAGAZINE**
6-shot revolver
**RANGE**
50m (54.7yds)

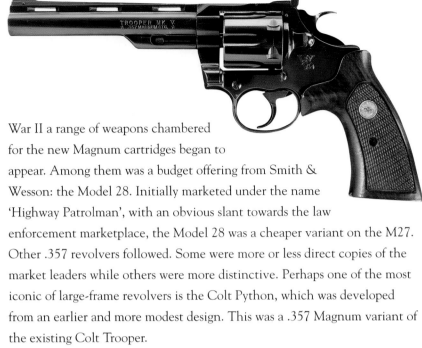

## COLT TROOPER MK V
**COUNTRY OF ORIGIN**
United States
**DATE**
1953
**CALIBRE**
9.1mm (.357in)
**WEIGHT**
1.2kg (2.62lb)
**OVERALL LENGTH**
260mm (10.24in)
**FEED/MAGAZINE**
6-shot revolver
**RANGE**
50m (54.7yds)

War II a range of weapons chambered for the new Magnum cartridges began to appear. Among them was a budget offering from Smith & Wesson: the Model 28. Initially marketed under the name 'Highway Patrolman', with an obvious slant towards the law enforcement marketplace, the Model 28 was a cheaper variant on the M27. Other .357 revolvers followed. Some were more or less direct copies of the market leaders while others were more distinctive. Perhaps one of the most iconic of large-frame revolvers is the Colt Python, which was developed from an earlier and more modest design. This was a .357 Magnum variant of the existing Colt Trooper.

The Colt Model 357 was not an immediate success, but after some work it grew into the Python. With its distinctive (and sometimes copied) ventilated top rib and full-length barrel underlug, the Python has a solid and business-like look about it that appeals to many users. Although an expensive weapon, the Python became popular with those seeking a quality handgun, and remains so to this day. Production was discontinued in the early 2000s. In the meantime, numerous variants appeared including the Colt Anaconda, which was aimed at the high-end sports shooting and hunting markets.

Law enforcement agencies generally liked the new .357 Magnum

## COLT ANACONDA
**COUNTRY OF ORIGIN**
United States
**DATE**
1990
**CALIBRE**
11.4mm (.45in)
**WEIGHT**
1.5kg (3.3lb)
**OVERALL LENGTH**
280mm (11in)
**FEED/MAGAZINE**
6-shot revolver
**RANGE**
45m (49.2yds)

revolvers that became increasingly available from the 1950s onwards. Smith & Wesson created a version of their Model 10 revolver chambered for .357 Magnum specifically to meet law enforcement needs, naming it Model 13. This can be slightly confusing, but the robust and effective .357 Magnum Model 13 is quite a different beast to the excessively flimsy aluminium-framed M13. Smith & Wesson also pioneered the development of the .44 Special cartridge, which grew from their .44 Russian round. This in turn was developed into the extremely powerful .44 Magnum cartridge, which requires a very heavy-framed handgun to handle its huge chamber pressure. Although .44 Magnum weapons are of necessity heavy, which helps soak up some recoil, they produce very significant recoil that many users find difficult to control.

The .44 Magnum weapons did not make a large entry into the law enforcement marketplace, although a few police departments considered them to have potential. The ability of the round to crack a vehicle engine block and thus stop a suspect's car or truck might be useful, but was not in most cases considered to make it worth toting such a heavy weapon around.

The Model 29 revolver from Smith & Wesson established the .44 Magnum round in the marketplace, with sales increasing enormously after Clint Eastwood's *Dirty Harry* movies began to appear. Although the claim that the .44 was the world's most powerful handgun was not strictly true, it was at the

BELOW: The *Dirty Harry* movies helped popularize the .44 Magnum revolver even though it was not, quite, 'the most powerful handgun in the world'. Very few police departments adopted the .44 revolver; most considered it overpowered.

## SMITH & WESSON M29

**COUNTRY OF ORIGIN**
United States
**DATE**
1955
**CALIBRE**
11.17mm (.44in)
**WEIGHT**
1.27kg (2.8lbs) (6in barrel)
**OVERALL LENGTH**
Varies depending on barrel
length
**FEED/MAGAZINE**
6-shot revolver
**RANGE**
50m (54.7yds)

time the most potent handgun available on the open market. As with many long-lived designs, the M29 was updated, with the stainless steel-framed 629 appearing in the late 1970s.

Sturm, Ruger & Company entered the Magnum revolver marketplace in 1955 with the Ruger Blackhawk. This was derived from an earlier small-calibre revolver, the Single Six, which had been introduced to cater to a renewed interest in 'classic Western'-style revolvers fuelled by Hollywood Westerns. As the name suggests the Single Six was a single-action revolver built along classic 'gunfighter-era' lines, including the lack of a transfer bar safety device. It could thus only be carried safely with one chamber empty, like the classic guns it was designed to re-create.

The Blackhawk also lacked a transfer bar when it was introduced, but in the early 1970s a new version (the New Model Blackhawk) was introduced that did have one, and retrofitting was offered to owners of existing weapons.

## RUGER BLACKHAWK

**COUNTRY OF ORIGIN**
United States
**DATE**
1955
**CALIBRE**
9.1mm (.357in)
**WEIGHT**
1.36kg (2.99lb)
**OVERALL LENGTH**
314mm (12.38in) (6in barrel)
**FEED/MAGAZINE**
6-shot revolver
**RANGE**
50m (54.7yds)

In the meantime, a .44 Magnum version of the Blackhawk was marketed, and later variants appeared including the Super Blackhawk. This model was slightly redesigned to make it more comfortable to shoot with a .44 Magnum, and can be fitted with a rail for a telescopic sight. The pistol was designed to appeal to aficionados of Westerns, and closely resembled the Colt Single Action Army. However, as updated models moved further from the weapon's roots a new variant, named Vaquero, was marketed to cater to the increasing Cowboy Action Shooting market. The Vaquero returned to the Blackhawk's more traditional roots, although not so much as the Old Army model, a cap-and-ball revolver intended for re-creationists.

## Propulsion and Ammunition Feed

While some manufacturers were building 'retro' weapons to appeal to a market segment, others were creating new cartridges in the hope of granting increased capabilities to conventional weapons. However, the basic design concept of bullet, cartridge case, propellant and primer had been established for many years, as had the method used to accelerate the bullet on its way.

All conventional firearms use the creation of a great deal of hot gas as their means of propulsion. As the propellant burns it creates this gas, which is trapped in the firing chamber. Pressure increases enormously and the gas seeks a means of escape. The only way out is to push the bullet

BELOW: Revolvers are prone to muzzle flip as their axis of recoil (which lies along the line of the barrel and firing chamber) is high above the user's hand. Short-barrelled weapons with little weight at the front end accentuate this tendency.

down the barrel – in every other direction there is solid metal. So the projectile is accelerated forwards, and – in a semi-automatic weapon – the slide is driven back to work the action. Once the bullet leaves the barrel, gas can expand out from the muzzle and no longer drives it forward. Thus a longer barrel normally results in higher muzzle velocity from the same cartridge, as the bullet has gas pressure behind it for longer. But in all cases, once the round is clear of the muzzle it is no longer accelerating. In fact, it immediately begins to decelerate due to friction from the air it passes through.

### Gyrojet

The Gyrojet pistol was part of a project intended to create small arms that fired small rockets rather than inert projectiles. Stabilized by spin imparted by angled jets, the Gyrojet rocket would continue accelerating after leaving the weapon, becoming more rather than less lethal as it travelled down range. Since the Gyrojet launched its ammunition as a single piece, it needed no ejection system to get rid of a spent cartridge case. Nor did it need to be heavy, with thick firing chamber and barrel walls to resist huge chamber pressures. This made for a lighter and simpler weapon. On the face of it, the Gyrojet concept seemed promising. In practice, however, it did not live up to expectations. Its rocket-propelled rounds left the muzzle with far less velocity than a standard pistol bullet, giving little stopping power at close range. Once up to speed, ballistic performance was far better but accuracy dropped

### GYROJET
**COUNTRY OF ORIGIN**
United States
**DATE**
1965
**CALIBRE**
12.95mm (.51in)
**WEIGHT**
.4kg (.88lbs)
**OVERALL LENGTH**
2760mm (10.88in)
**FEED/MAGAZINE**
6-round internal magazine
**RANGE**
50m (54.7yds)

off very rapidly. The end result was a pistol that was outperformed by the conventional weapons it was intended to make obsolete.

One interesting feature of the Gyrojet was its loading method, with rounds fed into the internal magazine through an open loading port atop the weapon. This style of loading had fallen out of favour years earlier, and compared very poorly with the speed of a conventional magazine change. Thus, despite experiments with underwater weapons and a range of applications from handgun to rifle size, the Gyrojet weapon system was not a success.

While the Gyrojet used an archaic feed system, the 'tround' invented by David Dardick went in the opposite direction. The Dardick concept was for an open-frame revolver, whose cylinder rotated past a loading point. There, a tround was loaded into it from the side, and continued around the cylinder's rotation until it reached the firing point. Surrounded on two sides by the cylinder and one by the frame of the weapon, the tround was then fired. The cylinder acted partially as a transfer system from feed device to firing point, and partly as a firing chamber, creating a sort of magazine-fed revolver weapon. Trounds could be custom manufactured or they could simply be a conventional cartridge encased in a triangular holder.

Some Dardick weapons were manufactured, and had the advantage of being able to take different calibres of ammunition with only a barrel swap; no alteration to chamber, cylinder, feed device was necessary. Despite being an innovative idea, the Dardick principle did not catch on.

BELOW: The Dardick concept was innovative and certainly workable, but other than as a futuristic curiosity the concept had little market appeal. No similar weapon has yet appeared, and it is unlikely that one ever will.

THIS GUN
{ Fires Triangular Cartridges!
Is a 20-Shot Revolver!
Can Be Loaded While Firing!
Comes With Two Barrel Sizes!
Can Be Converted To a Rifle! }

THE revolutionary new Dardick open chamber revolver is as versatile as a six-armed monkey. It comes with two different sized barrels, converts from a pistol to a rifle, fires 20 triangular cartridges, ejects fired cases and can be loaded while firing. The double-action, semi-automatic gun uses the special .38 or .22 Dardick cartridge or, with a simple adapter, any standard ammunition. Open chamber ejection makes it possible to build lighter and faster firing weapons that are more reliable at less cost than standard guns. •

.38 DARDICK SPECIAL comes with an extra .22 barrel, 20 rounds of ammunition and a clip. As yet, no retail price has been announced for this unique gun.

80

# The Cold War & the Modern Era

**Many of the weapons in use today have their roots in military systems developed for the Cold War, or trace their lineage back even further to the early part of the century. By the late 1960s, at the height of the Cold War, handgun design was a mature science in terms of features and mechanical processes, but there was always room for experimentation and improvement.**

New materials, notably plastics, alloys and polymers, became available and were soon incorporated into weapon designs. This did lead to groundless fears that 'plastic pistols' could be sneaked through airport security without setting off metal detectors. Even if these plastic guns could somehow be made to withstand firing chamber pressures without shattering, nobody has yet managed to make a cartridge entirely out of non-metal materials. The new generation of handguns does make extensive use of polymers for the outer surfaces and

LEFT: One way to bring the best accuracy out of a handgun is a tight stance with good ground contact and the weapon firmly gripped in both hands, which in turn are supported by the firer's knee.

## WALTHER P99
**COUNTRY OF ORIGIN**
Germany
**DATE**
1996
**CALIBRE**
10.16mm (.4in) or 9mm Parabellum (.35in)
**WEIGHT**
.65kg (1.44lb) or .63kg (1.38lb)
**OVERALL LENGTH**
184mm (7.2in) or 180mm (7.1in)
**FEED/MAGAZINE**
12-round magazine or 15-round magazine
**RANGE**
60m (65.6yds)

grips, but inside are to be found the traditional steel barrel and mechanical workings. What the new materials offer is a combination of strength and lightness, and of course resistance to corrosion – but not Hollywood-style 'stealth' that can evade detection equipment.

Weapon design is not a matter of using a new technology because it is available, or adding a feature because it has become possible. Every additional link, spring, button or switch on a handgun is a potential failure point and an opportunity for user error. A feature is only worth adding if it can be added reliably and used effectively by the weapon's intended operator. This is one reason why there is still a very strong market for simple revolvers. Many people want a gun that they can pick up and shoot, with no switches,

BELOW: Revolvers are 'simple but sure' weapons with an air of rugged reliability, and high quality is available at a reasonable price. They remain a popular choice for users primarily concerned with personal security and home defence.

buttons, catches, flashing lights or laser-aiming gizmos to fiddle with. Those that have the training, or the time to play around on the range, may find that a more complex weapon serves their needs better... but many top-end users also cite simplicity as being of paramount importance.

The features that will appeal to a particular market segment is not a matter of guesswork – not entirely anyway. Military weapons for mass issue tend to be simple, robust and cost effective; target shooters want accuracy and will pay for it. A 'plinker' or fun gun needs to be comfortable and not too expensive to shoot. Hunters may need accuracy at a range that most people would not consider shooting at, and they may also need to bring down animals that are much bigger and tougher than humans. All these factors, and more, are built into the handgun design process. Weapons for elite military or law enforcement personnel may be tailored to very specific requirements, and users will consider quality and top-end performance to be worth paying for. On the other hand, trying to convince the general shooting public that it is worth paying 30 per cent extra for a particular weapon rather than a competing design, because it has some additional features that they will probably never use, is more of a challenge.

## Brand Reputation

Some manufacturers have an edge in the marketplace as a result of reputation and brand recognition. Even then, this is just a slight advantage – the user will decide if a weapon is worth paying for based on how well it fits what he perceives as his needs, plus a few other factors such as how much it will impress other shooters if he is inclined to care about such things. For the collector, the situation is even more complex. Some weapons are expensive simply because they are rare, or because someone famous once allegedly owned one. Fashions change, and portrayal in a movie – or, increasingly, a video game – can push up the price of an otherwise largely ignored and obscure weapon.

There are rules about what shooters will pay for, and how much they will pay in the 'user' marketplace. For collectors the only real hard-and-fast rule is how much the weapon is worth to the individual in question. Whether to shoot or to display in a cabinet, a non-'working' gun – one that is not intended to put food on the table or to be used for personal defence – is worth whatever the prospective owner feels like paying for it. If the price tag is higher than that then no matter what 'the market' may say, it's not worth the price.

## Updated Classics

There is an unfortunate trend among certain kinds of firearm enthusiast to glance once at a weapon spotted in a movie, on television or 'for real' and rattle off a list of statistics detailing its make, model, calibre and variant designation. Someone who seems to be able to identify any handgun by the merest glimpse in this manner, and is absolutely sure he is right, is probably not. The reasons for this vary. Sometimes it is self-delusion, sometimes a desire to seem knowledgeable by presenting very precise information at the drop of a hat and sometimes it is lack of knowledge. If the only .45 semi-automatic an observer knows about is the M1911A1, then anything that looks vaguely like it will be identified as such.

In the author's experience, this may impress uninformed passers-by but will quickly identify the speaker to knowledgeable people as – at best – something of a poseur rather than a real expert. It can be wearying to be around such people, especially when those who know about firearms have got as far as 'looks like one of the many M1911 derivatives, probably a .45' and are suddenly informed of the weapon's supposed make, model and variant – always, always with excruciating precision – followed by every technical detail of its capabilities. The fact is, most semi-automatic handguns look broadly similar and some are difficult to tell apart without reading the model number. Even then, there are many variants, clones, copies and derivatives that can confuse the situation. It is worth refraining from holding forth about a weapon until you are sure exactly what it is and how it has been modified. That said, some handguns are extremely distinctive and can be identified at a glance. Many of these are unusual designs and may be part of a family of weapons that have retained the same general appearance while evolving through the years.

The Colt M1911 is very much the quintessential combat-calibre semi-automatic pistol. In the years immediately after World War II, the U.S. military decided that a lighter version, for issue to officers, was desirable. Various weapons were put forward, and Colt's offering was a 9x19mm (.35x.74in) version of the M1911. The calibre was specified by the U.S. military, but a variant in .45 ACP was also created for the open market. This weapon was, not surprisingly given its intended recipients, named the Colt Commander. It was Colt's first 9mm weapon. The Commander has been updated since, with a lightweight aluminium-frame version named Lightweight Commander appearing in 1970, followed by a steel-framed

variant of the new model (designated Combat Commander) soon after. The Commander is still in production, mating an alloy frame and modern ergonomic features to the traditional weapon's mechanism and overall feel.

## Walther's Distinctive Design

Many semi-automatics look fairly generic, at least until closely examined. Others, however, are easier to identify. The Walther P38, introduced just before World War II, was a very distinctive handgun that proved eminently satisfactory during its war service. There are few handguns that look much like a P38, making it one of the more distinctive weapons on the market. The fact that it is also a high-quality handgun makes it attractive as a practical or mostly practical weapon for the user with an eye for something a little different to the mainstream. Production of the P38 was interrupted by Germany's defeat and subsequent partition, with the main production centre lying in East Germany. With the Soviet Union imposing its own

**ABOVE:** For a close-quarters situation, especially where doors must be opened and other tasks require a free hand, a handgun with good stopping power may be a better choice than a longarm. .45 calibre weapons, often derived from the classic M1911, remain a popular choice although preferences vary.

ABOVE: The Walther
P38 not only inspired
post-war derivatives,
but it convinced the US
authorities that a double-
action semi-automatic
pistol was not only feasible,
but desirable.

standards on gun manufacture within its sphere of influence, the Walther
was not built in East Germany, while production in West Germany
required a new factory and was not resumed until 1957.

The post-war version of the P38 was designated P1 and became the official
service sidearm of the West German police and military. It was made lighter
by the use of aluminium components, but was essentially the same weapon
as the P38. The shorter P4 version was adopted for concealed carry and
some special operations units. Another highly distinctive semi-automatic is
the Walther P5. Its appearance is closely similar to the PP and PPK pistols,
although its mechanism is designed to meet the extremely high safety
standards of the German police. Multiple safety devices are intended to
ensure that there is little chance of an accidental discharge.

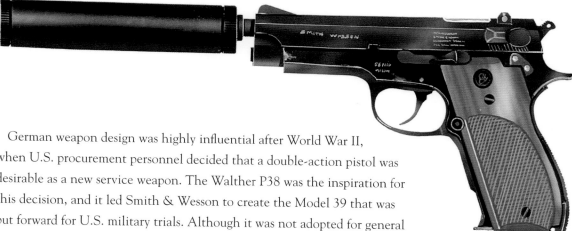

German weapon design was highly influential after World War II, when U.S. procurement personnel decided that a double-action pistol was desirable as a new service weapon. The Walther P38 was the inspiration for this decision, and it led Smith & Wesson to create the Model 39 that was put forward for U.S. military trials. Although it was not adopted for general issue, the Model 39 was sufficiently impressive that police departments took an interest. This made it one of the first semi-automatic pistols to be adopted for general issue to police personnel, and paved the way for the later Model 59 with a larger magazine capacity. In the interim, some Model 39 pistols were taken into U.S. service for use by special-operations units deployed to Vietnam. The standard Model 39 was used alongside a modified version designated Mk22 Mod 0. This was a specialist weapon, with a slide lock and raised sights to allow it to be more easily aimed when fitted with a suppressor. The slide lock prevented the action from cycling when the weapon was fired, effectively turning the pistol into a single-shot weapon but reducing mechanical noise.

The Mk22 Mod 0 pistol was used to eliminate guard dogs without alerting enemy personnel, and gained the nickname 'Hush Puppy' as a result. The

## S&W MODEL 39 HUSH PUPPY

**COUNTRY OF ORIGIN**
United States
**DATE**
1967
**CALIBRE**
9mm Parabellum (.35in)
**WEIGHT**
.96kg (2.1lb)
**OVERALL LENGTH**
323mm (12.7mm)
**FEED/MAGAZINE**
8-round magazine
**RANGE**
30m (32.8yds)

## SOCOM MK 23 MOD 0

**COUNTRY OF ORIGIN**
United States
**DATE**
1996
**CALIBRE**
11.43mm (.45in)
**WEIGHT**
1.1kg (2.4lb)
**OVERALL LENGTH**
245mm (9.6in)
**FEED/MAGAZINE**
12-round magazine
**RANGE**
25m (27.3yds)

modern SOCOM Mk23 Mod 0 serves a similar purpose. Developed for Special Operations Command, it is a .45 ACP pistol designed to have a suppressor quickly attached or removed, for use by Special Forces troops.

As well as the suppressed version, the Model 39 was developed into a custom weapon, allegedly for covert operations, known as the ASP. The ASP pistol was designed for concealed carry and a rapid deployment when needed, with a minimum of projections to snag on clothing. Its magazine had clear Lexan walls to allow remaining ammunition to be checked at a glance. The ASP's trigger guard was shaped to create a rest for the first finger of the weak hand, a feature that is today quite common but was at the time innovative. The Model 39, in the meantime, was developed through several incarnations. The Model 59, a bigger version with a larger magazine capacity, attracted some interest from military buyers but ultimately was not adopted in large numbers. It was, however, a success on the commercial market. The Model 59's two-digit identifier indicates that it is one of Smith & Wesson's 'first generation' semi-automatics. It was followed by a second-generation version designated Model 459 (second-generation pistols have three-digit identifiers) and eventually by the family of third-generation pistols with four-digit identifiers.

Families of weapons, with variants branching off and new generations appearing, are common with many classic designs. The Browning Hi-Power family can be difficult to tell apart at a glance. Earlier Brownings look (not coincidentally) a lot like Colt's M1911, and many other pistols follow

## SMITH & WESSON 459

**COUNTRY OF ORIGIN**
United States
**DATE**
1980
**CALIBRE**
9mm Parabellum (.35in)
**WEIGHT**
.73kg (1.6lb)
**OVERALL LENGTH**
175mm (6.89in)
**FEED/MAGAZINE**
14-round magazine
**RANGE**
40m (43.7yds)

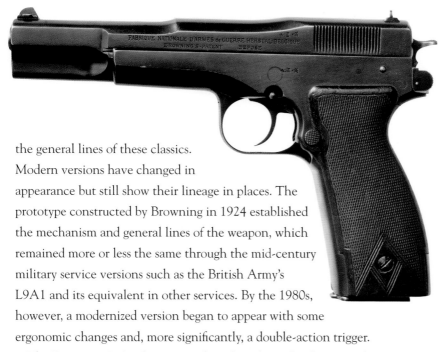

the general lines of these classics. Modern versions have changed in appearance but still show their lineage in places. The prototype constructed by Browning in 1924 established the mechanism and general lines of the weapon, which remained more or less the same through the mid-century military service versions such as the British Army's L9A1 and its equivalent in other services. By the 1980s, however, a modernized version began to appear with some ergonomic changes and, more significantly, a double-action trigger.

The Browning DA substitutes a decocking lever for the manual safety of previous weapons, allowing the hammer to be lowered onto a loaded chamber. The first shot is then fired doubleaction, with subsequent shots delivered in the conventional semi-automatic manner. The weapon can be made safe halfway through a magazine by decocking it, in much the same manner as putting the safety back on after firing a few shots. The Browning BDM took this a stage further by fitting a dual-mode trigger. This can operate in the manner of the BDA, or it can be adjusted with a turn of a screwdriver to double-action-only operation.

### FN GP PROTOTYPE
**COUNTRY OF ORIGIN**
Belgium/United States
**DATE**
1924
**CALIBRE**
9mm Parabellum (.35in)
**WEIGHT**
1kg (2.19lb)
**OVERALL LENGTH**
197mm (7.8in)
**FEED/MAGAZINE**
13-round magazine
**RANGE**
40m (43.7yds)

### BROWNING DOUBLE ACTION
**COUNTRY OF ORIGIN**
United States
**DATE**
1983
**CALIBRE**
9mm Parabellum (.35in)
**WEIGHT**
.99kg (2.19lb)
**OVERALL LENGTH**
200mm (7.87in)
**FEED/MAGAZINE**
14-round magazine
**RANGE**
50m (54.7yds)

## SIG-SAUER P220
**COUNTRY OF ORIGIN**
Switzerland/West Germany
**DATE**
1975
**CALIBRE**
9mm Parabellum (.35in)
**WEIGHT**
.8kg (1.7lb)
**OVERALL LENGTH**
198mm (7.79in)
**FEED/MAGAZINE**
7- or 9 -or 10-round magazine
**RANGE**
30m (32.8yds)

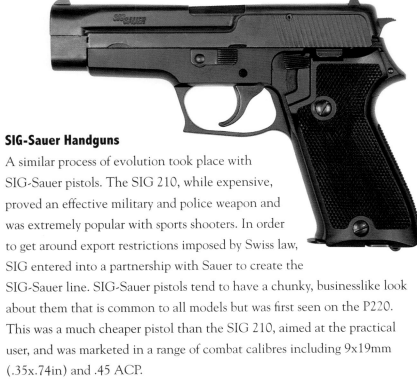

**BELOW: US Coast Guard
personnel undergoing
handgun training. The
SIG-Sauer P226 is a
popular choice of sidearm
for law enforcement
agencies and military
forces, offering accuracy
and reliability in a variety
of calibres.**

### SIG-Sauer Handguns

A similar process of evolution took place with
SIG-Sauer pistols. The SIG 210, while expensive,
proved an effective military and police weapon and
was extremely popular with sports shooters. In order
to get around export restrictions imposed by Swiss law,
SIG entered into a partnership with Sauer to create the
SIG-Sauer line. SIG-Sauer pistols tend to have a chunky, businesslike look
about them that is common to all models but was first seen on the P220.
This was a much cheaper pistol than the SIG 210, aimed at the practical
user, and was marketed in a range of combat calibres including 9x19mm
(.35x.74in) and .45 ACP.

Variants of the P220 were aimed at different users; the P225 was intended
for law enforcement use, and thus had additional safety systems to comply

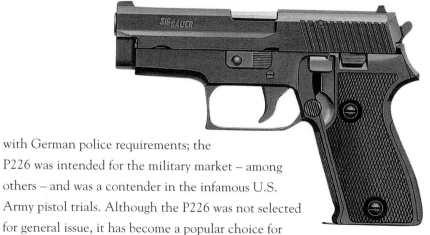

with German police requirements; the P226 was intended for the military market – among others – and was a contender in the infamous U.S. Army pistol trials. Although the P226 was not selected for general issue, it has become a popular choice for special operations and elite forces worldwide. The P245 model was created because many shooters – especially in the U.S. – will only accept a handgun capable of firing .45 ammunition. Compact semi-automatics of this sort are popular as concealed carry or backup guns, trading ammunition capacity for potent short-range firepower.

SIG-Sauer's P230 resembles the Walther PPK, and has a similar role as a concealable small-calibre handgun. It has a minimum of external projections and no manual safety. Instead it features a decocking lever and internal safety devices to prevent firing unless cocked by the double-action trigger. In short, this means that the P230 will only go off when the trigger is pulled. This is an entirely acceptable level of safety for many users, whereas others like a manual safety that prevents firing even if the trigger is pulled. The

## SIG-SAUER P225
**COUNTRY OF ORIGIN**
Switzerland/West Germany
**DATE**
1978
**CALIBRE**
9mm Parabellum (.35in)
**WEIGHT**
.74kg (1.63lb)
**OVERALL LENGTH**
180mm (7.08in)
**FEED/MAGAZINE**
8-round magazine
**RANGE**
40m (43.7yds)

## SIG-SAUER P230
**COUNTRY OF ORIGIN**
Switzerland/West Germany
**DATE**
1977
**CALIBRE**
8.128mm (.32in) or 9.65mm (.380in) or 9mm Police (.35in)
**WEIGHT**
.50kg (1.1)
**OVERALL LENGTH**
168mm (6.61in)
**FEED/MAGAZINE**
8- or 7-round magazine
**RANGE**
30m (32.8yds)

P220 and P230 series both spawned a range of variants, each designated by a different last digit but generally very similar in appearance to the standard model. For example, the P229 is chambered for .40 S&W ammunition and the P228 for 9x19mm (.35x.74in), but the calibre might not be apparent at first glance. The P232 uses new materials in its construction but is otherwise similar to the 232.

### Innovative New Pistols

Heckler & Koch are more famous for rifles and submachine guns than handguns, and have introduced some highly innovative designs over the years. Their first pistol design followed in that tradition, being more like four possible pistols delivered as a kit. With an aluminium frame and steel slide, the HK4 could be configured with different barrels (all supplied) to shoot four different small-calibre rounds. In keeping with the general German concern for safety, the HK4 was fitted with a safety device that took the firing pin out of alignment with the hammer unless the trigger was pulled, making an accidental discharge due to dropping or knocking the weapon very unlikely.

H&K continued to innovate with their pistol line, creating the world's first polymer-framed pistol in 1970. This weapon, the VP-70, was designed to use semi-automatic or burst fire and to take a detachable stock. It was accompanied by the visually similar but more conventional P9. This came

## HECKLER & KOCH P7
**COUNTRY OF ORIGIN**
West Germany
**DATE**
1976
**CALIBRE**
9mm Parabellum (.35in)
**WEIGHT**
.8kg (1.7lb)
**OVERALL LENGTH**
171mm (6.73in)
**FEED/MAGAZINE**
13-round magazine
**RANGE**
40m (43.7yds)

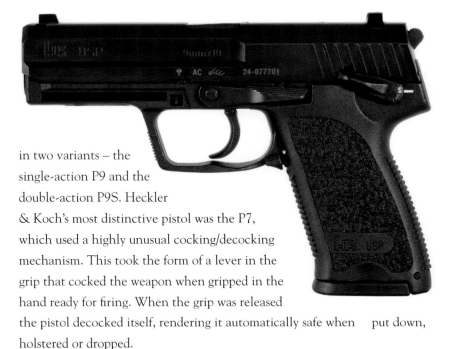

in two variants – the single-action P9 and the double-action P9S. Heckler & Koch's most distinctive pistol was the P7, which used a highly unusual cocking/decocking mechanism. This took the form of a lever in the grip that cocked the weapon when gripped in the hand ready for firing. When the grip was released the pistol decocked itself, rendering it automatically safe when    put down, holstered or dropped.

At the end of the 1980s, Heckler & Koch began work on a new family of handguns that resulted in their USP, a 'universal' pistol that can be configured in a variety of ways to suit different users. The USP was originally designed to shoot .40 S&W ammunition but 9x19mm (.35x.74in) and .45 versions are also available. Once a calibre is decided upon there are nine standard variants, each with different combinations of safety devices and trigger mechanisms. Many of these USP variants have been given a brand name of their own, or modified to create a slightly different weapon for a specific user. Thus the P8 pistol used by the German armed forces is essentially a USP altered to a fit a specific requirement. Variants are designated by number but also have names indicating their general strengths, such as 'tactical' or 'sport'. There are also match-shooting and compact versions of the USP.

H&K also markets the P30 for the police and security market. Like many modern semi-automatics it is designed for ambidextrous operation, with slide and magazine releases on both sides, and is available in different calibres. A Picatinny rail is also fitted, allowing the use of accessories such as tactical flashlights on a standard fitting. Weapon accessories of this sort are nothing new, but the military sector has in recent years begun to use standardized accessory rails, and this practice is now filtering into the non-military handgun market.

## HECKLER & KOCH USP
**COUNTRY OF ORIGIN**
Germany
**DATE**
1990
**CALIBRE**
11.43mm  (.45in) or 10.16mm (.4in) or 9mm Parabellum (.35in)
**WEIGHT**
.748kg (1.65lb)
**OVERALL LENGTH**
219mm (8.64in)
**FEED/MAGAZINE**
8- to 15-round magazine, depending on configuration and calibre
**RANGE**
30m (32.8yds)

ABOVE: The Glock 17 has become a standard sidearm in military forces worldwide. Its high capacity was quite remarkable at the time of its introduction, but has since been matched by other weapons.

## Glock Design Innovations

The Glock range of handguns has become a household name, and the company has produced some of the most widely used weapons in the law enforcement marketplace. Yet Glock only started manufacturing firearms in 1980 – the transition from newcomer to industry standard was largely due to innovation. The range is, like many others, designated by numbers. In the case of the Glock range these start with 17, a reference to the number of rounds in the original weapon's magazine. By using a relatively wide double-stacked magazine, Glock managed to produce a weapon with twice the firepower of many existing combat pistols.

Sometimes inaccurately referred to as a 'Glock Nine', in reference presumably to its calibre, the Glock 17 was not the first pistol to use a polymer frame but it was the first to be a major commercial success. It also introduced a polygonal rifling system inspired by the Whitworth black

powder rifle used by some 1860s era sharpshooters. The Glock 17 was quickly adopted by the Austrian armed forces, with other military and law enforcement users soon following. This move may have raised a few eyebrows, as some police departments that had clung to their revolvers ceased their cries of 'if you can't do it with six, you can't do it' and tooled up with something that carried three times as many rounds.

The Glock 17's safety system is based around the idea that the weapon must be safe if dropped, banged or generally mishandled but if the user pulls the trigger then presumably he wants the weapon to discharge. A trigger safety prevents the weapon firing unless the trigger is properly activated, while the drop safety ensures that only proper trigger pressure will activate it. A third safety device physically blocks the firing pin from making contact with the chambered round until removed by trigger action. Thus the Glock range was made proof against most forms of misfortune, other than human error. The lack of an external manual safety did lead to a phenomenon that became known as 'Glock Leg' as users occasionally pulled the trigger while drawing or holstering the weapon, resulting in accidental discharge into the thigh or lower limb. This was very much a human error rather than

## GLOCK 17
**COUNTRY OF ORIGIN**
Austria
**DATE**
1982
**CALIBRE**
9mm Parabellum (.35in)
**WEIGHT**
.65kg (1.43lb)
**OVERALL LENGTH**
188mm (7.5in)
**FEED/MAGAZINE**
17-round magazine
**RANGE**
30m (32.8yds)

## GLOCK 18
**COUNTRY OF ORIGIN**
Austria
**DATE**
1986
**CALIBRE**
9mm Parabellum (.35in)
**WEIGHT**
.75kg (1.65lb)
**OVERALL LENGTH**
210mm (8.25in)
**FEED/MAGAZINE**
19-round magazine
**RANGE**
50m (54.68yds)

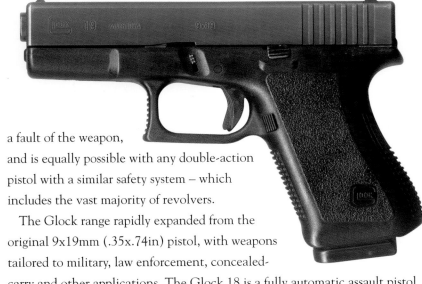

## GLOCK 19

COUNTRY OF ORIGIN
Austria
DATE
1988
CALIBRE
9mm Parabellum (.35in)
WEIGHT
.6kg (1.31lb)
OVERALL LENGTH
174mm (6.85in)
FEED/MAGAZINE
15-round magazine
RANGE
50m (54.68yds)

a fault of the weapon,
and is equally possible with any double-action
pistol with a similar safety system – which
includes the vast majority of revolvers.

The Glock range rapidly expanded from the
original 9x19mm (.35x.74in) pistol, with weapons
tailored to military, law enforcement, concealed-
carry and other applications. The Glock 18 is a fully automatic assault pistol
variant of the 17, and can take standard 17-round magazines or an extended
33-round magazine. The Glock 19 was created as a compact version for
concealed carry or for those that wanted a smaller weapon, but still crammed
in 15 rounds. There has always been a strong market for what used to be
called pocket pistols or purse guns, either as backup weapons or for carry
when something larger is either undesirable or too bulky. Glock moved
into this market with the Glock 26, which required some redesign work to
accommodate its mechanism in a small package.

Although the Glock range started out in 9x19mm (.35x.74in), it soon
became apparent that there was a market for variants chambered in other

## GLOCK 20

COUNTRY OF ORIGIN
Austria
DATE
1990
CALIBRE
9mm Parabellum (.35in)
WEIGHT
.79kg (1.73lb)
OVERALL LENGTH
193mm (7.59in)
FEED/MAGAZINE
15-round magazine
RANGE
50m (54.68yds)

calibres. These include the traditional .45 ACP as well as relatively new cartridges such as the .40 S&W round. There is also a strong market for small-calibre compact guns, and Glock also make specialist weapons designed to shoot Simunitions, a training round that allows shooters to engage in realistic combat training.

In the early 1990s, Steyr introduced a small submachine gun designated TMP (Tactical Machine Pistol) to the market. At the time the Personal Defence Weapon concept was becoming increasingly popular, with militaries worldwide seeking to obtain small, high-firepower weapons for personnel unable to carry a rifle or full-size submachinegun. The TMP was modified into a semi-automatic weapon, designated SPP (Special Purpose Pistol) and its foregrip was replaced with an accessory rail, creating a bulky semi-automatic weapon that shares most of its components with the submachinegun variant. Although rather large for a handgun, the SPP does have the capability to take large-capacity magazines.

## GLOCK 26
**COUNTRY OF ORIGIN**
Austria
**DATE**
1995
**CALIBRE**
9mm Parabellum (.35in)
**WEIGHT**
.6kg (1.34lb)
**OVERALL LENGTH**
193mm (7.59in)
**FEED/MAGAZINE**
15-round magazine
**RANGE**
50m (54.68yds)

## STEYR SPP
**COUNTRY OF ORIGIN**
Austria
**DATE**
1994
**CALIBRE**
9mm Parabellum (.35in)
**WEIGHT**
1.3kg (2.9lb)
**OVERALL LENGTH**
322mm (12.6in)
**FEED/MAGAZINE**
15- or 30-round magazine
**RANGE**
100m (109.36yds)

ABOVE: The TEC-9
gained an unfortunate
reputation in the USA due
to a perceived connection
with criminals who
converted the weapon
back to fully automatic
operation. Several of
its characteristics were
specifically named in the
controversial Assault
Weapons Ban legislation.

Another handgun that started out as a submachinegun is the Intratec
TEC-9, a 9x19mm (.35x.74in) weapon designed in Sweden. After failing
to penetrate the military light automatic weapon market, the TEC-9
was modified to semi-automatic operation and marketed as a handgun.
However, it proved easy to convert back to fully automatic operation and
became associated with criminal activity. Despite efforts to create a version
that was harder to convert, the TEC-9 was banned as part of the U.S.
Assault Weapons Ban, resulting in a version designated AB-10 (standing
for 10-round magazine, After Ban). Although the Assault Weapons Ban
has since been repealed, the TEC-9 and its variants are illegal for civilian
ownership in some areas as they have many features associated with military
weapons such as large magazine capacity, barrel shrouds and a magazine
positioned in front of the trigger assembly.

The CALICO M950 is the handgun version of an innovative system
that can be configured as a carbine or handgun. Chambered for 9x19mm
(.35x.74in) ammunition, the M950 is fed from 50- or 100-round helical

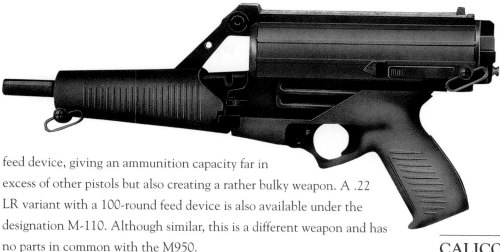

feed device, giving an ammunition capacity far in excess of other pistols but also creating a rather bulky weapon. A .22 LR variant with a 100-round feed device is also available under the designation M-110. Although similar, this is a different weapon and has no parts in common with the M950.

### European Combat Handguns

Some weapons are designed for military users, while others end up being taken into service because they are available as a need arises. The French MAB PA-15 pistol was one of the latter. It was bought as an interim measure as production of the Modèle 1950 came to an end. The PA-15 was primarily issued to marines and military police, whom it served well enough. For more specialist purposes, however, the French military turned to a revolver. The Manhurin MR73, normally chambered for .357 Magnum ammunition, was adopted for service with the Gendarmerie and specialist police units such as hostage-rescue and counter-terrorist formations. Manufactured to an extremely high standard, the MR73 offered capabilities beyond what the typical police officer would probably need, but which might be required by elite units in a difficult situation. One unusual feature is the ability to convert the MR73 to fire 9x19mm (.35x.74in) ammunition by swapping the cylinder.

The company manufacturing these weapons, Manhurin, started out as a machinery fabrication business but moved into firearms production after World War II, making Walther P38s under licenCe. All revolvers were tested for accuracy before leaving the factory, and were test-fired with extremely high-powered ammunition. This ensured that they would handle the innumerable rounds of 'normal' .357 Magnum ammunition that special police units require personnel to fire in practice.

The P38, alongside the Browning GP-35, remained in service with the Austrian military until the 1970s, by which time replacement was

### CALICO M950
**COUNTRY OF ORIGIN**
United States
**DATE**
1990
**CALIBRE**
9mm Parabellum (.35in)
**WEIGHT**
1kg (2.2lb)
**OVERALL LENGTH**
365mm (14.3in)
**FEED/MAGAZINE**
50- or 100-round magazine
**RANGE**
60m (65.61yds)

## STEYR GB

**COUNTRY OF ORIGIN**
Austria
**DATE**
1981
**CALIBRE**
9mm Parabellum (.35in)
**WEIGHT**
.854kg (1.9lb)
**OVERALL LENGTH**
216mm (8.5in)
**FEED/MAGAZINE**
18-round magazine
**RANGE**
40m (43.74yds)

overdue. The search for a suitable handgun resulted in Steyr-Daimler-Puch producing what became the Steyr GB. This weapon used some of the propellant gases from the barrel to slow down the blowback action of the slide and give time for the projectile to leave the muzzle. The Steyr GB featured a double-action trigger with decocking lever and proved accurate. It should have been a commercial success, but bad timing meant it did not do as well as expected. Unsuccessful in the U.S. Army pistol trials, the GB was denied success at home by the emergence of the Glock 17 into the marketplace. The Glock was taken into Austrian service and the Steyr GB could achieve only modest private sales rather than the hoped-for large-scale military contracts.

The weapon that edged out the Steyr GB in the U.S. Army trials was the Beretta 92, which re-established Beretta as one of the big players in modern handgun design. Having established a solid reputation for workmanlike combat handguns in the World War I era, Beretta became somewhat lost in the wilderness during the 1940s. The company's return to the mainstream was largely due to a move away from the weak 9mm (.35in) Glisenti round used only by Italian weapons.

The Beretta Modello 1951 suffered from a number of defects when it was first designed, notably a lack of what today would be termed user-friendliness as well as accuracy. A redesigned version, doing away with experimental alloy construction in favour of tough and proven steel, appeared in 1957, and was further improved into the 1980s. New models began to appear, some in small calibres such as .32 ACP and .380. Among them was the Series 81, or Cheetah, which was offered in calibres from .22i LR up to .380. Weapons of this sort were successful in the compact handgun marketplace and helped Beretta return to previous success.

Meanwhile, development of the Model 1951 resulted in a new 9mm semi-automatic designated Model 92. Ironically, the new weapon featured a light alloy frame, a concept dropped from the 1951 original it had been developed from. Advancing technology now made it possible to use lighter materials, and reduced weight was traded for increased magazine capacity. The Model 92 went through a series of upgrades, creating the 92S that was aimed at the law enforcement marketplace. The 92SB, a further upgrade made with the military in mind, crossed the Atlantic to take part in the U.S. military pistol trials being held to find a replacement for the venerable M1911A1. The Beretta design eventually won out and was taken into U.S. service as the M9.

Development of the Model 92 continued, resulting in the creation of an assault pistol version designated Beretta 93R. The R stands for 'raffica', or 'burst', and the 93R is designed to fire bursts at a very high cyclic rate. To assist controllability a folding foregrip is fitted, and a wire stock can also be used. The 93R can use the standard Beretta 92 15-round magazine or a 20-round extension magazine. However, the effectiveness of a burst-fire handgun is open to some debate. In theory, if the rate of fire is very high then the weapon will not move much off target during the burst, and a skilled user will be able to put down withering firepower – at least for a short time.

Guns of this sort have some applications as personal defence weapons for military personnel such as pilots or snipers who cannot carry much weight but might possibly need heavy firepower, and as weapons for bodyguards protecting VIPs from armed attack. Some consider the option of automatic fire to be a useful capability; others feel it is a gimmick at best and a liability at worst. Rather than spraying more bullets, Beretta's Model 96 went with a heavier cartridge to increase its combat effectiveness. Aimed at the law

## BERETTA 92
**COUNTRY OF ORIGIN**
Italy
**DATE**
1976
**CALIBRE**
9mm Parabellum (.35in)
**WEIGHT**
.97kg (2.125lb)
**OVERALL LENGTH**
211mm (8.3in)
**FEED/MAGAZINE**
15-round magazine
**RANGE**
50m (54.68yds)

enforcement marketplace, it is chambered for the increasingly popular .40 S&W round. This cartridge is in the same general class as 9x19mm (.35x.74in) but is widely considered to have better stopping power and ballistic performance without creating heavy recoil.

### Czechoslovakian Weapons

Czechoslovakia fell under the influence of the Soviet Union after World War II, with the result that Czech weapons of the Cold War era tended to follow Russian practice. The CZ 52 has a clear visual similarity to the Makarov. It was originally envisaged as a 9x19mm (.35x.74in) weapon, but pressure to conform with the rest of the Soviet-dominated bloc resulted in a redesign to use 7.62x25mm (.3x.98in) ammunition. It is now possible to obtain 9mm (.35in) barrels to facilitate conversion. The CZ 52 was notable for very significant felt recoil. This was not least due to its high bore-axis, which is a common feature of early double-action semi-automatics. The redesign from 9mm to 7.62mm included a conversion back to conventional single-action operation, making the high barrel position unnecessary. However, it was retained, and with the axis of recoil energy very high above the user's hands, the muzzle tends to flip up more than on a weapon with a lower axis.

The CZ 52 was phased out of Czech military service in the early 1980s and replaced with the CZ 82. The new service pistol was designed from the outset to take 9x18mm (9mm) Makarov ammunition. The choice of

## PSM (MILITARY MODEL)
**COUNTRY OF ORIGIN**
Soviet Union
**DATE**
1973
**CALIBRE**
5.45mm (.215in)
**WEIGHT**
.46kg (1.01lb)
**OVERALL LENGTH**
160mm (6.3in)
**FEED/MAGAZINE**
8-round magazine
**RANGE**
40m (47.74yds)

calibre was again as a result of pressure from Russia, whose armed forces had adopted 9mm Makarov as standard. The Czech Army was offered the Russian Makarov but chose to produce their own pistol that, while somewhat more expensive to build, is of better quality than the Makarov and has a greater ammunition capacity. The CZ 82 and its commercial variant, CZ 83, are well known for robust construction although this comes at the price of being somewhat heavy. The CZ 83 is essentially an export version of the CZ 82 and is offered in 9mm Makarov, 9x17mm Browning Short (.38in ACP) and 7.62x17mm Browning (.32in ACP). Both are double-action weapons with an ambidextrous safety.

Much more 'Western' in appearance is the CZ 75, which appeared in the mid-1970s chambered for 9x19mm (.35x.74in). This, along with a design that used fairly standard Browning concepts, ensured that the CZ75 was an attractive export weapon. It has achieved very good overseas sales and has been widely copied or licence built. Various other weapons are based on the CZ 75, notably the Jericho 941 and Norinco NZ-75. The T95 pistol marketed by Tanfoglio is also derived from the CZ 75, and is available in combat and compact models as well as a variety of custom configurations. Available in a wide range of calibres, the T95 has achieved considerable sales success in Europe and the USA as both a working and sporting gun.

The CZ 75 has been adopted by numerous police departments in the USA and other nations, and is widely respected as one of the best handguns of its type. Not surprisingly it has spawned several variants. Among them is the compact CZ 75B and the CZ 75 P-01, a modernized variant used by the Czech police. A fully automatic version of the CZ 75 is also available. One of its more unusual features is the ability to carry a spare magazine in front of the trigger guard where it can serve as a foregrip. There is no alteration to the feed mechanism; the magazine in use is still inserted through the handgrip. Some earlier examples of the automatic version have an extended

## CZ 75
**COUNTRY OF ORIGIN**
Czechoslovakia
**DATE**
1976
**CALIBRE**
9mm Parabellum (.35in)
**WEIGHT**
.98kg (2.16lb)
**OVERALL LENGTH**
203mm (8in)
**FEED/MAGAZINE**
15-round magazine
**RANGE**
40m (47.74yds)

ABOVE: There was a
time when 'inexpensive'
translated to 'probably
very poor indeed' but this
has not necessarily been
the case since the middle
of the twentieth century.
Modern techniques allow
high-quality machining and
large-scale production to go
hand in hand.

barrel with a compensator. This reduces muzzle climb by venting some of
the propellant gases upwards to counter the tendency of the muzzle to flip.
Although it has a separate model number, the CZ 85 is an updated version
of the CZ 75, and is very similar in most ways. The main difference is an
ambidextrous safety, reflecting the recent trend towards ambidextrous
weapon design.

The CZ 75 and CZ 85 pistols are manufactured in the Czech Republic,
taking their designation from the Ceská zbrojovka arms factory. The CZ-99,
on the other hand, is manufactured by Zastava Arms, formerly the Crvena
Zastava factory in Serbia. Very similar to the SIG-Sauer P226, the CZ-99
is aimed at the good-quality-but-inexpensive end of the combat handgun
market, and has been manufactured under licence in other countries. Like
many recent pistols, the CZ-99 is available in 9x19mm (.35x.74in) or .40
S&W calibre. This reflects recent interest in new calibres after several
decades in which the standard ammunition types have remained more or less
unchanged. Standard CZ-99s have no manual safety, but one is available as
an option. A compact variant of the pistol is also marketed.

A developed version of the CZ-99, designated PP-Z, stands as a good
example of modern combat handgun design. Although built around .45
ACP ammunition, it can be easily converted to other calibres. An accessory

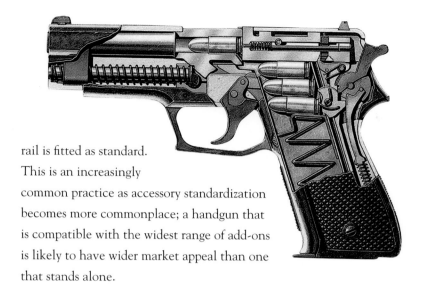

rail is fitted as standard.
This is an increasingly
common practice as accessory standardization
becomes more commonplace; a handgun that
is compatible with the widest range of add-ons
is likely to have wider market appeal than one
that stands alone.

## Modern Revolvers

At first glance it may seem that a revolver is… a revolver. Calibres may vary
but the principle is always the same. This is, however, a false impression.
There does tend to be more visual difference between semi-automatic
designs than revolvers, but many are quite different from one another and a
few have unique characteristics.

The basic principle of the revolver, the thing that makes it what it is, is
the rotating cylinder. This imposes a certain basic shape and a requirement
for internal machinery to rotate the cylinder, lock it in place and operate
the hammer. This lockwork is located in the frame, between the trigger and
the hammer, with a hammer spring running down the inside of the grip. It
is a single integrated mechanism whose composition can vary depending on
whether the weapon is single action, double action or double-action-only.

Many people assume that revolvers always hold six rounds, possibly
because of the term 'sixgun', but although six is a convenient number –
translating to one round per 60 degrees of rotation of the cylinder – other
capacities are quite common. Five-shot revolvers are popular backup guns,
and can be slimmer than a six-shooter in the same calibre, and small-calibre
guns may hold more rounds. Attempts have been made over the years to
create high-capacity revolver-type weapons, but these have not succeeded.
Small-calibre revolvers with two concentric circles of chambers and a
movable firing pin have been attempted but proved both ineffective and
extremely bulky. The 'harmonica gun' concept, which replaced the cylinder

## SIG-SAUER P226
**COUNTRY OF ORIGIN**
Switzerland/West Germany
**DATE**
1981
**CALIBRE**
9mm Parabellum (.35in)
**WEIGHT**
.75kg (1.65lb)
**OVERALL LENGTH**
196mm (7.71in)
**FEED/MAGAZINE**
15-round magazine
**RANGE**
30m (32.8yds)

with a rectangular device resembling a harmonica that moved laterally to present cartridges in turn, proved even less workable.

Thus the revolver attained its basic shape and internal form quite early in its history and has seen only fairly minor changes since. One of those is the fluted cylinder, with sections of the outer surface machined out between the chambers to reduce weight. Doing so ensures that there is sufficient metal between the chamber and the outside world to prevent a disaster, but removes the areas that are not needed. How much of the cylinder's outer surface can be removed depends on the potency of the weapon's chosen cartridge. So long as the fluting does not make the cylinder wall thinner than the direct distance from the outer point of the chamber to the cylinder surface, it will not affect strength. Fluted cylinders have been standard for decades, and a weapon without fluting tends to have an archaic look about it. Of course, in a deliberately 'retro' weapon this is desirable.

The Ruger Single Six revolver appeared in the early 1950s. As the name suggests it was a six-shot single-action weapon. The Single Six was targeted at a particular market area, riding the wave of interest in Westerns that existed at the time. Thus it had a deliberately traditional appearance and

RIGHT: The Ruger Single Six was created to meet a perceived market requirement for a retro-style revolver. The popularity of Western movies ensured that the weapon was well received in the marketplace, though post-1972 models introduced a modern safety device.

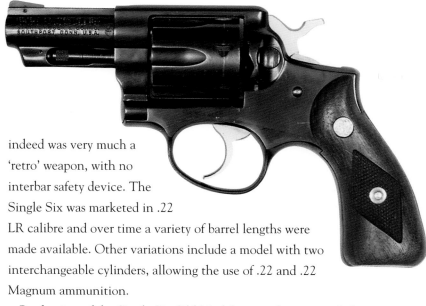

indeed was very much a 'retro' weapon, with no interbar safety device. The Single Six was marketed in .22 LR calibre and over time a variety of barrel lengths were made available. Other variations include a model with two interchangeable cylinders, allowing the use of .22 and .22 Magnum ammunition.

Production of the Single Six Old Model, as it is known, ended in 1972 and a new Single Six was marketed soon afterward. The New Model has a transfer bar and is thus safe to carry with all chambers loaded, and is available in various models including Single Ten with a 10-round capacity cylinder and SingleNine, chambered for nine rounds of .22 Magnum ammunition. Also in the early 1970s, Ruger marketed several versions of a double-action combat revolver, with slight variations defining three models known as Security Six, Police Service Six (or simply Service Six) and Speed Six. These handguns can be considered the epitome of 1970s revolver design, and were taken into service by several law enforcement agencies as well as private users.

## RUGER SINGLE SIX
**COUNTRY OF ORIGIN**
United States
**DATE**
1953
**CALIBRE**
5.58mm (.22in)
**WEIGHT**
.9kg (2lb)
**OVERALL LENGTH**
259mm (10.2in)
**FEED/MAGAZINE**
6-shot revolver
**RANGE**
20m (21.87yds)

## RUGER SECURITY SIX
**COUNTRY OF ORIGIN**
United States
**DATE**
1972
**CALIBRE**
9.1mm (.357in) (.357 Magnum)
**WEIGHT**
.95kg (2.09lb)
**OVERALL LENGTH**
235mm (10.2in)
**FEED/MAGAZINE**
6-shot revolver
**RANGE**
40m (43.74yds)

## RUGER GP100

**COUNTRY OF ORIGIN**
United States
**DATE**
1985
**CALIBRE**
9.1mm (.357in) (.357
Magnum)
**WEIGHT**
1kg (2.2lb)
**OVERALL LENGTH**
240mm (9.5in)
**FEED/MAGAZINE**
6-shot revolver
**RANGE**
50m (54.68yds)

The 'Six' range was initially chambered for .357 Magnum or .38 Special, with a 9x19mm (.35x.74in) variant added to the line later. This version used a specialist ejection system to allow rimless 9mm rounds to be extracted from the cylinder. A .38 ACP version was also made available for export. A stainless-steel version of the 'Six' line, designated GS32-N, was produced for the government and military marketplace, and was followed by stainless-steel versions of all standard models. In the late 1980s the line was replaced by the GP100, which is broadly similar but more resistant to wear from firing .357 Magnum ammunition. As with many such guns, the GP100 is available in a range of barrel lengths and a seven-round version chambered for .327 Federal Magnum ammunition was produced for a time.

Taurus produces a range of revolvers for various applications. The Raging Bull 444 is available for .44 Magnum and .454 Casull ammunition. The latter had just become available at the time when Clint Eastwood as Dirty Harry was proclaiming the .44 Magnum as the most powerful handgun calibre in the world, which technically made him wrong. However, at the time .454 Casull was very uncommon. Today it is available to hunters or sports shooters that want an extremely 'hot' cartridge for their big-frame revolvers. The Raging Bull is available in various barrel lengths, and is complemented by the visually very similar 911 Tracker revolver. This is a nine-shot weapon capable of firing .22 LR or Magnum rounds and producing virtually no felt recoil as it shoots a small cartridge from a big frame. Handguns like this are popular for vermin control or for 'plinkers' who like the feeling of a big gun without the immense recoil and the expense of large-calibre rounds.

Other manufacturers produced effective large-calibre revolvers for the hunting, security and home defence marketplace. Colt marketed the King Cobra, a developed version of the earlier Trooper (which itself was a step

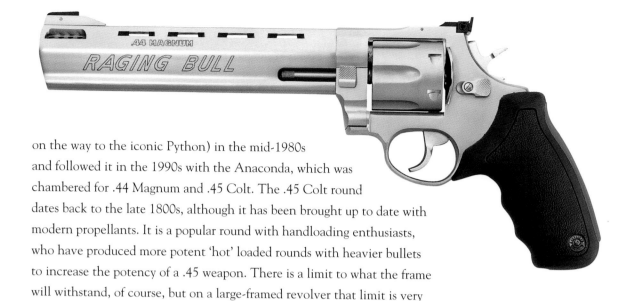

on the way to the iconic Python) in the mid-1980s and followed it in the 1990s with the Anaconda, which was chambered for .44 Magnum and .45 Colt. The .45 Colt round dates back to the late 1800s, although it has been brought up to date with modern propellants. It is a popular round with handloading enthusiasts, who have produced more potent 'hot' loaded rounds with heavier bullets to increase the potency of a .45 weapon. There is a limit to what the frame will withstand, of course, but on a large-framed revolver that limit is very high and it is possible to obtain extremely impressive performance from this calibre weapon.

Unusually, Smith & Wesson's Model 625 revolver is chambered for .45 ammunition. It would seem logical that, given the immense popularity of .45 ammunition with semi-automatic users, a revolver in the same calibre would be attractive. However, although the 625 and its successors such as the Model 325 Night Guard are well liked by some shooters, the 45-calibre revolver has never achieved great popularity. The Model 625 can use

## TAURUS RAGING BULL
**COUNTRY OF ORIGIN**
Brazil
**DATE**
Approximately 2000
**CALIBRE**
11.5mm (.454 in) or 11.17mm (.44in)
**WEIGHT**
1.79kg (3.93in)
**OVERALL LENGTH**
419mm (16.5in)
**FEED/MAGAZINE**
5- or 6-shot revolver
**RANGE**
50m (54.68yds)

**LEFT:** Long-barrelled, high-powered revolvers are too big and heavy to carry around all day for self-defence, but remain popular with competitive shooters. Great skill is required to control such a powerful weapon well enough to shoot accurately.

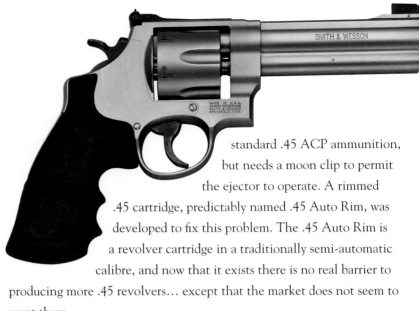

## SMITH & WESSON 625

**COUNTRY OF ORIGIN**
United States
**DATE**
1987
**CALIBRE**
11.43mm (.45in)
**WEIGHT**
1.13kg (2.5lb)
**OVERALL LENGTH**
238mm (9.38in)
**FEED/MAGAZINE**
6-shot revolver
**RANGE**
40m (43.74yds)

standard .45 ACP ammunition, but needs a moon clip to permit the ejector to operate. A rimmed .45 cartridge, predictably named .45 Auto Rim, was developed to fix this problem. The .45 Auto Rim is a revolver cartridge in a traditionally semi-automatic calibre, and now that it exists there is no real barrier to producing more .45 revolvers… except that the market does not seem to want them.

Similarly the Spanish firm Astra, although often associated with semi-automatic pistols, marketed effective and highly conventional double-action revolvers such as the Astra .357 Police model and its predecessors. An experiment with 9x19mm (.35x.74in) chambering was not popular; the division between revolver and semi-automatic cartridges seems to go deeper than just the mechanics of ejecting a rimless semi-automatic round from a revolver.

### Modern Semi-automatics

The modern semi-automatic pistol is a working tool for most users. The almost infinite variety of calibres and features available allow a weapon to be chosen to fit almost any need. One result of this is a great deal of division among shooters about which weapons are better than others for a specific purpose, and which are 'classics' (defined in all manner of ways) that will still be around or at least fondly remembered many decades from now. Smith & Wesson solved the problem of having vast numbers of different models and variants by adopting what is sometimes referred to as their 'telephone number' designation system. For those that understand the code, the capabilities of a weapon are presented in its name. Thus the S&W 1006 is obviously a third-generation weapon (it has a four-digit number) and is chambered for 10x25mm (.39x.98in) ammunition. It has a stainless-steel construction and a double-action trigger. Variants in the 10XX line have

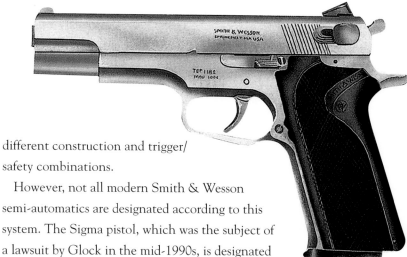

different construction and trigger/
safety combinations.

However, not all modern Smith & Wesson
semi-automatics are designated according to this
system. The Sigma pistol, which was the subject of
a lawsuit by Glock in the mid-1990s, is designated
S&W XX, with the last two digits indicating
calibre. Thus S&W 357 is chambered for a .357 SIG, a round created to
allow semi-automatic pistols to shoot an equivalent cartridge to the popular
.357 Magnum round used in revolvers.

The S&W Military and Police family is another complete range of
handguns, ranging in calibre from .45 ACP to .22 LR. The range includes
full-sized and compact weapons, and some variants with single-stacked
magazines to enhance concealability or suit small-handed users. Other
variants are driven by legal considerations rather than ergonomics or
ballistic performance; in some U.S. states the maximum magazine size

### SMITH & WESSON 1006
**COUNTRY OF ORIGIN**
United States
**DATE**
1989
**CALIBRE**
10mm (.39in)
**WEIGHT**
1.7kg (3.75lb)
**OVERALL LENGTH**
203mm (8in)
**FEED/MAGAZINE**
9- or 10-round magazine
**RANGE**
50m (54.68yds)

### SMITH & WESSON SIGMA
**COUNTRY OF ORIGIN**
United States
**DATE**
1993
**CALIBRE**
10.16mm (.4in)
**WEIGHT**
.74kg (1.63lb)
**OVERALL LENGTH**
197mm (7.75in)
**FEED/MAGAZINE**
15-round magazine
**RANGE**
50m (54.68yds)

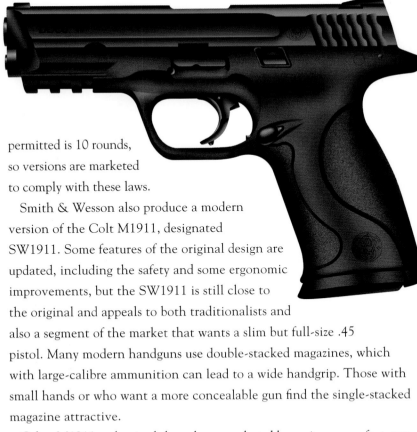

## SMITH & WESSON M&P SERIES

**COUNTRY OF ORIGIN**
United States
**DATE**
2005
**CALIBRE**
9mm Parabellum (.35in),
10.16mm (.40in) S&W,
9.06mm (.357in) Magnum,
11.43mm (.45in), 9.65mm
(.380in), 5.59 mm (.22in)
**WEIGHT**
.68kg (1.5lb)
**OVERALL LENGTH**
190mm (7.5in)
**FEED/MAGAZINE**
Various magazine sizes
**RANGE:**
50m ((54.68yds))

permitted is 10 rounds, so versions are marketed to comply with these laws.

Smith & Wesson also produce a modern version of the Colt M1911, designated SW1911. Some features of the original design are updated, including the safety and some ergonomic improvements, but the SW1911 is still close to the original and appeals to both traditionalists and also a segment of the market that wants a slim but full-size .45 pistol. Many modern handguns use double-stacked magazines, which with large-calibre ammunition can lead to a wide handgrip. Those with small hands or who want a more concealable gun find the single-stacked magazine attractive.

Other M1911-style pistols have been marketed by various manufacturers. Para Ordnance established its niche in the marketplace with a range of modern 1911s, chambered in several calibres besides .45 ACP and using

## STAR PD

**COUNTRY OF ORIGIN**
Spain
**DATE**
1975
**CALIBRE**
11.43mm (.45in)
**WEIGHT**
.71kg (1.56lb)
**OVERALL LENGTH**
180mm (7.1in)
**FEED/MAGAZINE**
6-round magazine
**RANGE**
30m (32.8yds)

SCHWARZENEGGER

THE TERMINATOR

LEFT: The AMT Hardballer gained a marketing advantage in the 1980s when the Terminator asked for a '.45 long slide with laser sighting'. Phased plasma rifles, had they been available at the time, might have enjoyed similar product placement recognition.

double-stacked magazines. Single-action and double-action variants were produced. Likewise, the Spanish firm Star Bonafacio Echeverria produced a popular compact 1911 variant named Model PD, which carried a six-round magazine. Although some examples suffered from a tendency to degrade after a relatively short period of use due to their aluminium construction, the Star PD 45 remains a well respected compact .45. The PD was followed by the .45 calibre Firestar and 30M, a broadly similar 9mm version. This had a lightweight variant designated 30K.

Some 1911 copies are just that – straight copies. In the 1970s, the Brazilian Army took delivery of a new service pistol from Imbel, designated M973. Other than using a nine-round magazine of 9x19mm (.35x.74in)

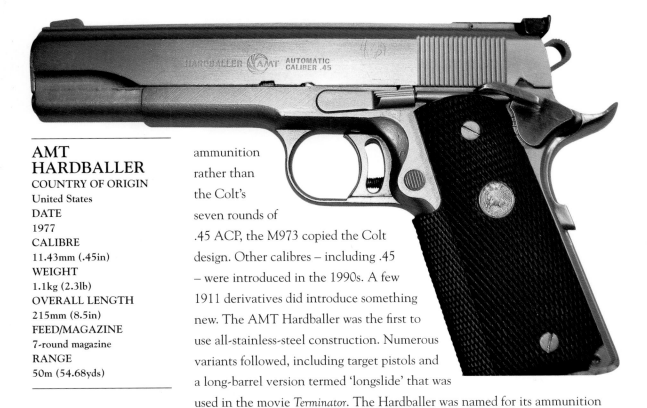

## AMT HARDBALLER

**COUNTRY OF ORIGIN**
United States
**DATE**
1977
**CALIBRE**
11.43mm (.45in)
**WEIGHT**
1.1kg (2.3lb)
**OVERALL LENGTH**
215mm (8.5in)
**FEED/MAGAZINE**
7-round magazine
**RANGE**
50m (54.68yds)

ammunition rather than the Colt's seven rounds of .45 ACP, the M973 copied the Colt design. Other calibres – including .45 – were introduced in the 1990s. A few 1911 derivatives did introduce something new. The AMT Hardballer was the first to use all-stainless-steel construction. Numerous variants followed, including target pistols and a long-barrel version termed 'longslide' that was used in the movie *Terminator*. The Hardballer was named for its ammunition – it requires full metal jacket rounds to feed properly. It is most famous as a .45, but variants in 10mm (.39in) and other chamberings have been marketed.

Colt's own updated 1911 models include the Series 80, with a firing pin block for improved safety and the option of a weapon chambered in 9x19mm (.35x.74in) or .45 ACP. The Double Eagle is also available in .45, although it is normally chambered in 10mm (.39in). Following tradition, there is a mid-sized Officer's model and compact variant named Double Eagle Commander. The Double Eagle is an updated and developed 1911 version, with a double-action trigger and decocking lever, but it reached the marketplace well after other companies had already produced similar weapons.

The FN Five-Seven is anything but traditional, but its concept does date back to one long-forgotten aspect of firearms design – the idea of carrying a longarm and a handgun in the same calibre. This practice fell into disuse after the flintlock era, but was revived for a time in the late nineteenth century. In the Old West it was considered by many to be beneficial to have a rifle or carbine in the same calibre as a revolver, allowing just one calibre of

ammunition to be carried. Since that time, pistol and longarm calibres have been very different, but the Five-Seven pistol was designed to complement the H&K P90 Personal Defence Weapon and uses the same ammunition. This is a 5.7x28mm (.224x1.1in) round that offers similar performance to 9x19mm (.35x.74in) but with better penetration and a flatter trajectory, which assists accuracy. The Five-Seven pistol uses the same advanced polymers in its construction as the P90 carbine.

## Specialist Revolvers

Most, but not all, specialist revolvers are designed for hunting or long-range target shooting competitions. Both may require sighting aids beyond the usual close-range iron sights fitted to a typical combat revolver, and both require accuracy at ranges beyond the distance that the average shooter can hit anything with a handgun. Hunting guns also need to be able to bring down large game effectively and humanely. Many large game animals are

### COLT MK IV SERIES 80
**COUNTRY OF ORIGIN**
United States
**DATE**
1983
**CALIBRE:**
11.43mm (.45in), 9.6mm (.38in) Super, 9.6mm (.380in) ACP
**WEIGHT**
.69kg (1.51lb)
**OVERALL LENGTH**
221mm (8.7in)
**FEED/MAGAZINE**
7-, 8- or 9-round magazine
**RANGE**
50m (54.68yds)

### FN FIVE-SEVEN
**COUNTRY OF ORIGIN**
Belgium
**DATE**
2000
**CALIBRE**
5.7mm (.224in)
**WEIGHT**
.62kg (1.36lb)
**OVERALL LENGTH**
208mm (8.2in)
**FEED/MAGAZINE**
20-round magazine
**RANGE**
50m (54.68yds)

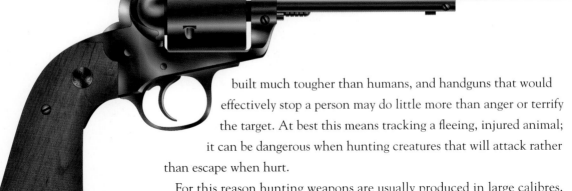

## RUGER BISLEY

**COUNTRY OF ORIGIN**
United States
**DATE**
1984
**CALIBRE**
11.2mm (.44in) Magnum
**WEIGHT**
1.4kg (3.1lb)
**OVERALL LENGTH**
342mm (13.5in)
**FEED/MAGAZINE**
6-shot revolver
**RANGE**
50m (54.68yds)

built much tougher than humans, and handguns that would effectively stop a person may do little more than anger or terrify the target. At best this means tracking a fleeing, injured animal; it can be dangerous when hunting creatures that will attack rather than escape when hurt.

For this reason hunting weapons are usually produced in large calibres, generally with a quite long barrel, and often with a tapped rib to allow a scope to be mounted. Telescopic sights mounted on powerful handguns need to be extremely tough to survive the recoil stresses generated by the weapon, and obviously require suitably robust mountings. Thus hunting guns tend to be impressive pieces of machinery. This is not machismo – it is necessary to get the job done.

There are a few extremely large-calibre revolvers around, some of which were made purely to see what can be done. Others are prestige pieces, but vastly powerful handguns are occasionally carried for self-defence. Not against humans, as they are ridiculously overpowered for this. Instead guns of this sort hark back to the idea of the Howdah Pistol, a handgun designed to allow hunters to defend themselves from whatever they had just tried to shoot (and possibly succeeded in shooting, just not fatally) with their rifle. Overpowered guns of this sort are often custom built, or manufactured in very small numbers around a specialist cartridge or one that has been cut down from a rifle round. Pistols of this kind are not for the inexperienced or the faint-hearted, but they can be an alternative to carrying a heavy rifle all day when in country inhabited by dangerous animals, or offer a life-saving backup to a rifle or shotgun.

Other specialist revolvers are designed to meet a need not covered by mainstream weapons, and may be mass-produced or one-offs. These may be the modern equivalent of the Velo-Dog pistol, an artefact of the times. They are produced to meet the perceived need for a weapon to counter a threat that might actually exist or simply be popularly imagined.

In 1894, Colt produced a highly accurate version of the M1873 Single

Action Army called
the Colt Bisley.
Production ceased in
1915 but the concept of a
'Bisley'-branded target revolver
was resurrected by Ruger in 1984. Ruger's Bisley is a
variant of the Blackhawk, a long-barrelled .44
Magnum weapon with a single-action trigger. Its
styling includes an unfluted cylinder and 1800s style grips,
in keeping with its 'retro' image. Rather more modern in appearance is
Ruger's Redhawk, a double-action revolver originally chambered for a .44
Magnum ammunition. Various calibres are now available, along with a new
version named Super Redhawk. This features a less traditional styling and is
chambered for .44 Magnum as well as other extremely powerful ammunition.

A short-barrelled 'Alaskan' variant is also available. Where the full-length
Super Redhawk can be used as a hunting weapon in its own right, the
Alaskan is intended as a defensive weapon for hunters and others who might
encounter dangerous animals such as bears in the wilderness. One drawback
with shorter-barrelled weapons firing very heavy cartridges is muzzle flip;
another is that large cartridges need a long barrel to burn all the available
propellant before the round leaves the muzzle. However, when faced with an
angry bear a .44 is one of the best choices for self-defence and compromises
to make it easy to carry are probably worth the trade-off.

Taurus produced a lightweight .44 Magnum revolver, Model 444, as
an emergency weapon for hunters or anyone else who might encounter
dangerous animals. A light .44 is unpleasant to fire, and would not be an
ideal choice for someone expecting to do a lot of practice, but weapons of
this type offer a good combination of stopping power and ease of carry in
their intended role. However, not all specialist handguns are hunting or

## RUGER REDHAWK

**COUNTRY OF ORIGIN**
United States
**DATE**
1979
**CALIBRE**
11.17mm (.44in) Magnum
**WEIGHT**
1.5kg (3.37lb)
**OVERALL LENGTH**
241mm (9.5in)
**FEED/MAGAZINE**
6-shot revolver
**RANGE:**
50m (54.68yds)

## KORTH COMBAT MAGNUM

**COUNTRY OF ORIGIN**
West Germany
**DATE**
1965
**CALIBRE**
9.1mm (.357in) Magnum
**WEIGHT**
1.133kg (2.4lb)
**OVERALL LENGTH**
240mm (9.4in)
**FEED/MAGAZINE**
6-shot revolver
**RANGE**
50m (54.68yds)

prestige weapons. The Korth Combat Magnum was always intended as a working handgun, but one that was handmade to extremely high standards. Some were put together in smaller calibres as target pistols but 'working' guns tend to be chambered for .357 Magnum.

Another approach to the self-defence revolver is represented by the Taurus Raging Judge. This is a variant on the Raging Bull .44 revolver, developed to

**RIGHT: The Taurus Raging Judge revolver was developed for close-range self-defence. It is unusual in that it is one of the few handgun-shotguns on the market.**

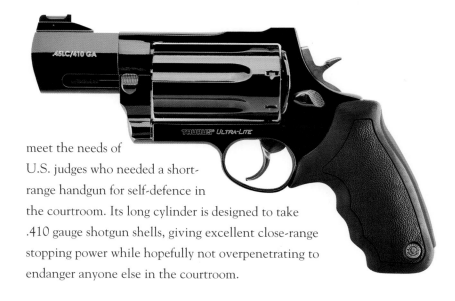

meet the needs of
U.S. judges who needed a short-
range handgun for self-defence in
the courtroom. Its long cylinder is designed to take
.410 gauge shotgun shells, giving excellent close-range
stopping power while hopefully not overpenetrating to
endanger anyone else in the courtroom.

**TAURUS
RAGING JUDGE**
COUNTRY OF ORIGIN
Brazil
DATE
c. 2000
CALIBRE
11.4mm (.45in)/.41 gauge
shotgun
WEIGHT
1.17kg (2.57lb)
OVERALL LENGTH
190mm (7.5in)
FEED/MAGAZINE
5-, 6- or 7-shot revolver
RANGE
20m (21.87yds)

## Compact Handguns

Compact handguns tend to be 'working' guns for the most part, often
carried concealed or as a backup weapon, or sometimes purchased because
their small dimensions make them light and easy to handle for smaller
individuals. Many compacts are scaled-down variants of a standard combat
pistol, usually with a smaller magazine capacity and frame, and a shorter
barrel. This can pose some serious engineering challenges when a full-
sized mechanism must be fitted into a tiny weapon. One solution is to use
smaller-calibre ammunition, accepting reduced potency as a consequence of
smaller size. One advantage of small-calibre guns is that they can be simpler
because the chamber pressures they must deal with are lower. The majority
of combat-calibre semi-automatic pistols use a locking mechanism to hold
the slide and breech in place until the projectile has left the muzzle. The
mechanism is then released to begin cycling the action. A smaller-calibre
weapon does not need a locking mechanism and can operate on a simple
blowback principle, meaning it needs fewer components which in turn
means less weight and space.

   In the early 1970s, as the German police were looking for a new handgun,
the Walther PP Super was introduced. Based in the earlier PP/PPK, the
PP Super was built to fire the 9x18mm (.35x.70in) Police cartridge which
was then under consideration for law enforcement issue. This round
represented the upper end of what a simple blowback-operation compact
pistol could handle, offering the most stopping power a compact pistol

RIGHT: Police weapons are not only subject to stringent safety requirements for the weapon itself, but must also be secured to prevent a holstered weapon being grabbed or dropped during an arrest attempt.

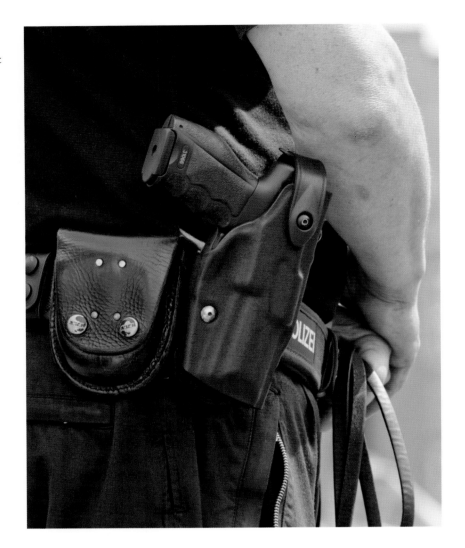

was likely to deliver. It has different dimensions to the 9x18mm Makarov ammunition and is incompatible. After much debate, the German police settled on 9x19mm (.35x.74in) as the standard calibre rather than 9mm Police, and consequently the PP Super fell out of the running as it could not handle the more potent cartridge.

In the late 1950, what is now Zastava Arms began producing a licensed version of the Tokarev TT-33 pistol, chambered for the same 7.62x25mm (.3x.98in) ammunition. This was followed in 1970 by the M70, a compact version chambered either for .38 ACP or .32 ACP. After a period of police and military service, most of these weapon were sold on as replacements became available, entering the civilian and export marketplace.

The other school of thought regarding compact guns is that if it is needed

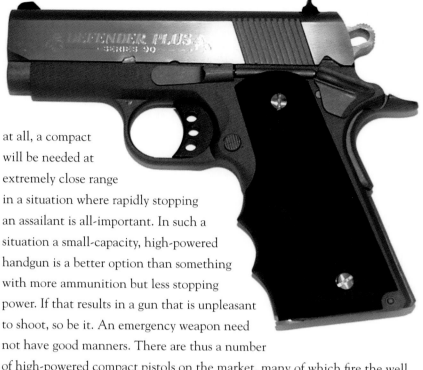

at all, a compact
will be needed at
extremely close range
in a situation where rapidly stopping
an assailant is all-important. In such a
situation a small-capacity, high-powered
handgun is a better option than something
with more ammunition but less stopping
power. If that results in a gun that is unpleasant
to shoot, so be it. An emergency weapon need
not have good manners. There are thus a number
of high-powered compact pistols on the market, many of which fire the well
resected .45 ACP round. Among these is the Colt Defender, an aluminium-
framed compact semi-automatic. The Defender is aimed at the .45 ACP
end of the marketplace, but a 9mm variant (offering one more round in the
magazine) is also available. Essentially a miniaturized and updated version of
the M1911, the Defender follows the philosophy that a compact handgun is
a full-sized weapon crammed into a small space, rather than a lesser cousin.
Thus despite having a small magazine capacity and a short barrel it has
conventional combat handgun sights. A weapon of this sort can substitute
for a full-sized handgun for those that prefer or only have space to carry
something small.

The Detonics Combat Master was the first of a new generation
of compact pistols. Previously, a compact .45 had to be more or less
handbuilt by creating a cut-down version of a full-sized weapon. The
Detonics company took a new approach – creating a compact from the
ground up. The new weapon had to be easy enough to manufacture that
it could compete in the marketplace. The resulting Detonics Combat
Master became very well respected and gained some publicity from TV
shows such as *Miami Vice*. It was, however, very expensive and Detonics
ran into financial trouble despite producing scaled-up versions named

## COLT DEFENDER 1948

**COUNTRY OF ORIGIN**
United States
**DATE**
1948
**CALIBRE**
11.43mm (.45in)
**WEIGHT**
.63kg (1.38lb)
**OVERALL LENGTH**
171mm (6.75in)
**FEED/MAGAZINE**
7-round magazine
**RANGE**
20m (21.87)

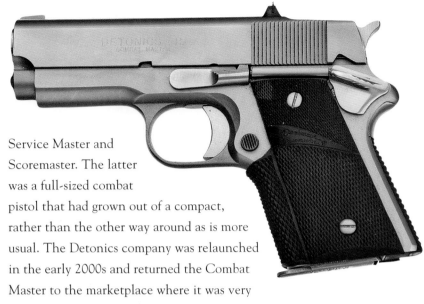

## DETONICS COMBAT MASTER
**COUNTRY OF ORIGIN**
United States
**DATE**
1975
**CALIBRE**
11.43mm (.45in)
**WEIGHT**
.96kg (2.12lb)
**OVERALL LENGTH**
177mm (7in)
**FEED/MAGAZINE**
6-round magazine
**RANGE**
20m (21.87)

Service Master and Scoremaster. The latter was a full-sized combat pistol that had grown out of a compact, rather than the other way around as is more usual. The Detonics company was relaunched in the early 2000s and returned the Combat Master to the marketplace where it was very well received. With a six-round magazine of .45 ACP, plus one in the chamber, a weapon of this sort compares favourably to a five-shot .38 revolver as a backup gun, and takes up about as much room.

The .45 compact niche has attracted numerous companies, including Taurus. The PT145 is a fairly typical small-frame semi-automatic benefiting from modern materials and design concepts. Its polymer frame is lighter than an equivalent steel construction, and the position of the barrel is as low as the weapon's mechanism will allow. This reduces muzzle flip, which

## KEL-TEC PF-9
**COUNTRY OF ORIGIN**
United States
**DATE**
2006
**CALIBRE**
9mm (.35in) Parabellum
**WEIGHT**
.414kg (.91lb)
**OVERALL LENGTH**
149mm (5.85in)
**FEED/MAGAZINE**
7-round magazine
**RANGE**
30m (32.8yds)

can be very pronounced on short-barrelled weapons that have little front-end weight to counteract it.

The Kel-Tec PF-9 was created to be the slimmest and lightest of all the available compact pistols that use a 'combat' calibre. Using a single-stack seven-round magazine of 9x19mm (.35x.74in) ammunition, it is a very small package but there is a limit to how small a 9mm handgun can be made. For maximum concealability, perhaps at the expense of stopping power, weapons like the Smith & Wesson Model 2213 use very small-calibre (5.58mm/.22in LR) ammunition. Tiny pistols of this sort are easy to carry and can serve as a deterrent – any gun is a whole lot better than no gun at all – but their ability to stop an assailant is open to question.

The question of how to cram enough firepower into a very small weapon is a tough one. Rather than creating a compact revolver or semi-automatic, the COP derringer returned to the 'pepperbox' principle. With four barrels, fired in turn by a rotating firing pin, the COP offers limited capacity – four rounds – but it can fire .357 Magnum ammunition. Trigger pull is heavy since this is a double-action weapon, recoil is high and effective range is short. However, none of that really matters in the sort of situation where a gun like this is needed. The pistol is no longer in production, although there is some interest in weapons of a similar type, and rumours that manufacture might at some point resume. The main obstacle to this is the increasing effectiveness of compact semi-automatics and revolvers. Among these is the Ruger LCR (Lightweight Compact Revolver), which is available in .38 or .357 Magnum.

Weapons like the LCR are specifically designed for the concealed-carry market, with a streamlined shape and no external hammer to snag when drawing the weapon. Modern materials allow a relatively light and slim weapon to handle powerful loads, and ergonomic design helps reduce felt recoil. No compact pistol is going to win long-range shooting prizes, but the new generation of compacts can do more than offer point-blank self-defence.

## COP DERRINGER

**COUNTRY OF ORIGIN**
United States
**DATE**
1978
**CALIBRE**
9.1mm (.357in) Magnum
**WEIGHT**
.8kg (1.75lb)
**OVERALL LENGTH**
142mm (5.6in)
**FEED/MAGAZINE**
4 barrels, single shot per barrel
**RANGE**
10m (10.93)

## Large Calibre Semi-automatics

The creation of very powerful Magnum cartridges inevitably led to the development of a semi-automatic pistol to fire them, but this posed many challenges. A revolver cylinder, once aligned with the barrel and firing mechanism, is a very robust construct with few avenues for gas to escape. A semi-automatic pistol, on the other hand, has more components that can fail or be misaligned by large chamber pressures. Thus creating one that could withstand the stresses generated by powerful rounds was problematic.

The first Magnum-calibre semi-automatic pistol was marketed by the Auto Mag company and had the same name. Sometimes described as looking a bit like a 1950s science fiction ray gun, the Auto Mag featured a heavily reinforced barrel and an angled grip. This was literally the only weapon of its kind in the world at the time, and could be switched from .44 Magnum to .357 Magnum calibres by swapping the barrel. The Auto Mag company ran into financial difficulties and production of the pistols was carried on by other companies for a while. The original Auto Mag remained in production from 1970 to 1982, but then became unavailable. A new version, with a slight name change to Automag, appeared in the late 1980s.

## AMT AUTOMAG III
**COUNTRY OF ORIGIN**
United States
**DATE**
1992
**CALIBRE**
7.62mm (.3in) Magnum
**WEIGHT**
1.275kg (2.8lb)
**OVERALL LENGTH**
350mm (13.8in)
**FEED/MAGAZINE**
8-round magazine
**RANGE**
50m (54.68)

The Automag II (and subsequent models III–V) was a much more conventional-appearing handgun than the original Auto Mag. Configured as a long-barrelled, large semi-automatic, models II–V were available in a range of calibres from .22 Winchester Magnum Rimfire to a .50 Action Express. Such a large and extremely powerful handgun was never a serious option for personal defence or combat use, except perhaps in the case of Hollywood action heroes. The Automag range was however attractive to hunters and sporting shooters who liked the feel (or perhaps the machismo) of shooting a really potent weapon. The Automag II–V was in production from the late 1980s to 1996, with various companies subsequently buying the rights to produce one or other model. The Automag II (chambered for 5.58mm/.22in WMR) has returned to

BELOW: **The Desert Eagle is an iconic firearm, but one that is really too big for practical carry. The fact that it could shoot a .50 calibre round was enough to establish its reputation; other calibres are also available but it is the .50 that attracts most attention.**

## DESERT EAGLE

**COUNTRY OF ORIGIN**
United States/Israel
**DATE**
1983
**CALIBRE**
12.7mm (.5in), 11.17mm
(.44in) Magnum, 9.1mm
(.357in) Magnum
**WEIGHT**
2.05kg (4.5lb)
**OVERALL LENGTH**
260m (10.25in)
**FEED/MAGAZINE**
7-, 8-, or 9-round magazine
**RANGE:**
50m (54.68yds)

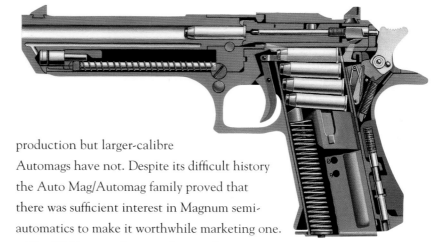

production but larger-calibre
Automags have not. Despite its difficult history
the Auto Mag/Automag family proved that
there was sufficient interest in Magnum semi-
automatics to make it worthwhile marketing one.

The Wildey pistol, somewhat similar to
the Auto Mag in appearance, reached the market in the early 1970s. It
featured in various movies, notably Charles Bronson's *Death Wish* series,
which increased awareness of it. The Wildey pistol was chambered for a
variety of very powerful rounds including .475 Wildey, .45in Wildey and,

from the mid 2000s
onward, the .44 Auto Mag
round. The Wildey is still in production,
and a carbine version is available.

## Desert Eagle

Most famous of the big semi-automatics is the Desert
Eagle. Developed by Magnum Research and Israeli
Military Industries, the Desert Eagle is normally chambered for .50 Action
Express, .44 Magnum and .357 Magnum ammunition. It is designed to be
modified quickly and easily, changing the calibre by swapping the barrel and
bolt assembly. Like other huge semi-automatics, the Desert Eagle is not well
suited to security use, except perhaps as a fairly dramatic deterrent to violence.
Nor is it ideal as a military sidearm. There is a persistent rumour that Israeli
Special Forces use the Desert Eagle, but this seems unlikely as a number of
authorities agree that the Desert Eagle is too big for comfortable carry and too
heavy to be brought on target in a fluid, close-range combat. The Desert Eagle
is well suited to hunting and prestige sports shooting, and some models have
scope fittings as standard.

A visually similar weapon, the Jericho 941, is marketed as the 'Baby Eagle'.
Although developed by the same organizations that created the Desert
Eagle, the Jericho 941 is in fact a completely different weapon derived from
the Czech CZ 75. It uses a .41 Action Express round that was developed for
it. Likewise, the Micro Desert Eagle, a .380 pocket pistol, is related to the
Desert Eagle only by marketing strategy.

The Magnum-calibre semi-automatic is very much a niche market, and
will probably remain so. Most 'practical' users need something a bit easier to
carry and to handle in combat. However, the large semi-automatic is often
considered a prestige firearm and sought out as an additional gun or as part
of a collection. As with any other collector's item, the actual merits of the
weapon matter less than how highly the collector and his peers regard it.

### JERICHO 941
**COUNTRY OF ORIGIN**
Israel
**DATE**
1990
**CALIBRE**
10.41mm (.41in)
**WEIGHT**
1.1kg (2.4lb)
**OVERALL LENGTH**
210mm (8.2in)
**FEED/MAGAZINE**
10-round magazine
**RANGE**
50m (54.68yds)

**LEFT: Gun shows often
have a miscellany of
weapons for sale. Condition
can vary considerably, and
it is always worth having a
new purchase checked over
by a reputable gunsmith if
you do not have the skill to
do it yourself. Some older
guns can be in anything
but safe-to-shoot condition,
even if they look OK.**

# Glossary

**Action** The working mechanism of a firearm, responsible for the main activities of loading, firing and ejecting. Action is also used sometimes in the same way as 'receiver'.

**Bolt** The part of a firearm which usually contains the firing pin or striker and which closes the breech ready for firing.

**Blowback** Operating system in which the bolt is not locked to the breech, thus it is consequently pushed back by breech pressure on firing and cycles the gun.

**Bore** The interior section of a gun's barrel.

**Boxlock** A type of action in a break-open gun where all of the lockwork is contained within a box-like housing. Boxlocks are the most common type of double-barrelled shotgun mechanism, being relatively inexpensive to manufacture and extremely robust.

**Breech** The rear of the gun barrel.

**Breech-block** Another method of closing the breech which generally involves a substantial rectangular block rather than a cylindrical bolt.

**Bullpup** Term for when the receiver of a gun is actually set in the butt behind the trigger group, thus allowing for a full length barrel.

**Carbine** A shortened rifle for specific assault roles.

**Centrefire** A cartridge that has the percussion cap located directly in the centre of the cartridge base.

**Chamber** The section at the end of the barrel which receives and seats the cartridge ready for firing.

**Closed bolt** A mechanical system in which the bolt is closed up to the cartridge before the trigger is pulled. This allows greater stability through reducing the forward motion of parts on firing.

**Compensator** A muzzle attachment which controls the direction of gas expanding from the weapon and thus helps to resist muzzle climb or swing during automatic fire.

**Delayed blowback** A delay mechanically imposed on a blowback system to allow pressures in the breech to drop to safe levels before breech opening.

**Double action** Relates to pistols which can be fired both by cocking the hammer and then pulling the trigger, and by a single long pull on the trigger which performs both cocking and firing actions.

**Ejector** A system for throwing the spent cartridge cases from a gun.

**Extractor** A system for lifting spent cartridge cases out of the chambers, making them easily removed by hand.

**Flechette** An bolt-like projectile which is smaller than the gun's calibre and requires a sabot to fit it to the barrel. Flechette rounds achieve very high velocities.

**Gas operation** Operating system in which a gun is cycled by gas being bled off from the barrel and used against a piston or the bolt to drive the bolt backwards and cycle the gun for the next round.

**GPMG** Abbreviation for General Purpose Machine Gun. A versatile light machine gun intended to perform a range of different roles.

**Guage** The calibre of a shotgun bore. The term relates to the number of lead balls the same diameter as the bore that it takes to make 1lb (0.45kg) in weight.

**LMG** Abbreviation for Light Machine Gun.

**Locking** Describes the various methods by which the bolt or breech block is locked behind the chamber ready for firing.

**Long recoil** A method of recoil operation in which the barrel and bolt recoil for a length greater than that of the entire cartridge, during which extraction and loading are performed.

**Muzzle brake** A muzzle attachment which diverts muzzle blast sideways and thus reduces overall recoil.

**Open bolt** A mechanical system in which the bolt is kept at a distance from the cartridge before the trigger is pulled. This allows for better cooling of the weapon between shots.

**PDW** Abbreviation for Personal Defence Weapon. A compact firearm, smaller than a regular assault rifle but more powerful than a pistol, intended as a defensive weapon for personnel whose duties do not normally include small arms combat.

**Receiver** The body of the weapon which contains the gun's main operating parts.

**Recoil** The rearward force generated by the explosive power of a projectile being fired.

**Recoil operated** Operating system in which the gun is cycled by the recoil-propelled force of both barrel and bolt when the weapon is fired. Both components recoil together for a certain distance before the barrel stops and the bolt continues backwards to perform reloading and rechambering.

**SAW** Abbreviation for Squad Automatic Weapon.

**Self-loading** Operating system in which one pull of the trigger allows the gun to fires and reload in a single action.

**Shaped charge** An anti-armour charge designed to concentrate the effect of an explosive warhead by focusing a cone of superheated gas on a critical point on the target.

**Short recoil** A compressed version of recoil operation in which the barrel and bolt move back less than the length of the cartridge before the bolt detaches and continues backwards to perform reloading and rechambering.

# Index